# Apprenticeship
## *in* Literacy

## Transitions
## Across Reading
## and Writing

LINDA J. DORN
CATHY FRENCH
TAMMY JONES

Stenhouse Publishers
York, Maine

Stenhouse Publishers, 431 York Street, York, Maine 03909
www.stenhouse.com

*Credits*
Page 13: *Nighttime.* Copyright © 1990 by J. Cowley.
Reprinted by permission of the Wright Group.
Page 26: *I Went Walking.* Copyright © 1989 by S.
Williams. Reprinted by permission of Harcourt Brace.
Page 27: *The Music Machine.* Copyright © 1992 by J.
Cowley. Reprinted by permission of the Wright Group.
Page 27: *Pumpkin, Pumpkin.* Copyright © 1986 by J.
Titherington. Reprinted by permission of Greenwillow, a
division of William Morrow & Co., Inc.
Page 27: *The Doorbell Rang.* Copyright © 1986 by P.
Hutchins. Reprinted by permission of Greenwillow, a
division of William Morrow & Co., Inc.
Page 33: *Goodnight, Goodnight.* Copyright © 1989 by B.
Parkes. Reprinted by permission of Rigby.

*Library of Congress Cataloging-in-Publication Data*
Dorn, Linda J.
    Apprenticeship in literacy : transitions across read-
ing and writing / Linda J. Dorn, Cathy French, and
Tammy Jones.
        p.   cm.
    Includes bibliographical references (p.   ) and index.
    ISBN 1-57110-088-1 (alk. paper)
    1. Language arts (Early childhood)—United States.
2. Reading (Early childhood)—United States. 3. English
language—Composition and exercises—Study and
teaching (Early childhood)—United States.
I. French, Cathy.  II. Jones, Tammy (Tammy P.)  III. Title.
LB1139.5.L35D67    1998
372.6—dc21                              98-16570
                                        CIP

Cover design by Richard Hannus, Hannus Design
Associates
Cover photographs by Laura Gatlin and Cathy French

Manufactured in the United States of America on acid-
free paper
03 02 01 00        9 8

*To our children, Harrison, Ariana, Jeff, Tony, Scott, Ruth Anne, and Liz, and our grandchildren, Jessica, Chad, Justin, Ben, and Heather.*

# Contents

# Acknowledgments

In writing this book, we apprenticed ourselves to many people who have supported us with their insights, knowledge, and genuine understanding of teaching and learning.

First, this book would not have been possible without the teachers from whom we learned and who offered us their support, encouragement, and enthusiasm: Carla Soffos, Angela Owen, Sandy Bryant, Lynn Raney, Kelli Ward, Pat Reece, Kim Camp, Harriet Pool, Esther Watson, Carolyn Blome, Judy Reed, Donna Pryzbys, Judy Vest, Suzanne Moss, Betsy Davies, Regina Hamilton, and Lisa Bowden. They studied and shared with us, invited us into their classrooms, juggled their schedules, and prepared to be videotaped and photographed on a moment's notice. Each of them has contributed substantially to our work and has made a real difference in the lives of many children. To them goes our sincere appreciation.

We also owe many thanks to a number of administrators and school districts who are visibly committed to literacy for all children and provided invaluable support in a variety of ways: Esther Crawford, assistant superintendent of instruction, Dianne Crites, principal, and Susie Jackson, principal, North Little Rock School District; Danny Taylor, superintendent, Patsy Fleniken, director of curriculum and instruction, and Georgeanne Peel, principal, Russellville School District; Jerry Guess, superintendent, and Eloise Robinson, principal, Camden-Fairview School District; Phillip Bell, superintendent, Chris Dayer, principal, and Janice Bryant, assistant principal, Mayflower School District. Their knowledge of effective literacy practices and their unwavering belief in the importance of teachers' work have enabled us to stimulate and expand our understanding of teaching and learning interactions whereby all children can acquire their highest literacy potential.

We will always be grateful for the help and support of the early childhood curriculum specialists at the Arkansas Department of Education. Their commitment to their own learning and to the teachers and children in their cooperative regions inspired us to present our ideas. Many thanks to Pat Busbea, Stephanie Copes, Kent Elkins, Linda Haynie, Kay Bonds, Mike Moss, Mary Norris, Ann

Averitt, Annette Rawls, Carol Hulsey, Sandy Bolden, Kathy Heagwood, Connie Choate, Jan Bridges, and Jeannette Cordell.

We also acknowledge Mary Kay McKinney, coordinator of early childhood education and reading, Arkansas Department of Education, for her ability to extend our thinking in diverse ways, her continuous support of teachers and children, and her patience and confidence in our work.

We offer special thanks to Mike Hargis, director of the Arch Ford Education Service Cooperative, and Phillip Young, its assistant director, for their unrelenting support and their extraordinary expertise in helping us stay focused on the importance of high-quality instruction for all children.

We are especially grateful to Representative Robert McGinnis for his legislative efforts in promoting effective literacy practices in Arkansas. His time and energy have helped children all across the state become successful readers and writers.

We owe a heartfelt debt of gratitude to the teacher education staff at the University of Arkansas at Little Rock (UALR) for their deep dedication to teachers and children. Their commitment to share their knowledge through collaborative partnerships with other Arkansas school districts, education service cooperatives, and the department of education has enabled educators statewide to advance their professional growth and renew their understanding of teaching and classroom practice. A special thanks to Debbie Williams, Stephanie Copes, Janita Hoskyn, Margie Burton, and Tammy Gridley for their ongoing support, insights, and willingness to proofread the manuscript.

We also acknowledge Martha Drury and the indispensable editorial assistance of Philippa Stratton, without whose help and guidance this book would not be in your hands now.

We give a very special thanks to our families, who have lovingly stood by with words of encouragement. Linda and Tammy thank their husbands, Jan and Steve, and Cathy thanks her parents, Bob and Virdie Redus. They have always been there supporting us in every aspect of our work.

Finally, there would be no book without the hundreds of young children who have shifted our thinking and caused us to revise our theories about how children think and learn. Beginning with our own children and grandchildren, we acknowledge the many literacy lessons you have taught us.

# Introduction

We decided to write this book for only one reason: we have a story to share with teachers. We have been teachers ourselves for a large part of our lives; it seems as though we have always worked with children. The memories we have accumulated in the classroom have played a vital role in shaping the direction of this book. Other memories are also embedded here, those gained from teaching in the Reading Recovery® program. These experiences have dramatically changed our theories about how young children learn. We believe many of these theories are relevant to our work with *all* children.

The teachers we worked with wanted a theoretically based, easy-to-read book to guide them in implementing a balanced literacy program in kindergarten through third grade. In preparing to write it, the three of us met with several classroom and specialty teachers to observe and discuss their literacy practices. All these teachers had participated in literacy training that focused on an apprenticeship approach to learning. As the three of us did the actual writing, we again met regularly with

these teachers to discuss the work in progress. We all agreed that a major emphasis would be on identifying and articulating the transitions that occur as children become more competent readers and writers. At the same time, we agreed that the teacher's role is to mediate learning through language and appropriate literacy opportunities that enable children to reach their highest potential. Thus our title: *Apprenticeship in Literacy: Transitions Across Reading and Writing.*

In the book, you will meet a number of teachers who daily apply the theories of how children learn. But first we'd like to introduce ourselves, so that you'll know why this book is important to us.

**Linda:** For the past eight years, I have held a university position in Reading Recovery and early literacy. However, that is not what I want to talk about just now. Instead, I want to tell you about my experiences in the classroom. Eight years ago, I was a third-grade teacher in a whole language school for high-risk children. Based on free-lunch criteria, the school had a 99 percent at-risk population. My classroom curriculum consisted of literature circles, writers workshop, and an integrated balance of whole- and small-group instruction. Classroom assessments included informal reading inventories, running records, literacy checklists, writing samples, and portfolios of literacy artifacts that I considered important documentation for showing changes across time. I also worked with two other reading specialists in the school on an intergenerational reading project designed to help parents learn how to read. So it was not unusual to find parents, grandparents, or other family members in the classroom working alongside the children. Because of our whole language approach, the school received attention in the media and at the local university. Almost weekly, visitors came to observe my classroom.

I was a committed and dedicated teacher who sincerely believed in every child's right to literacy. This belief was shared by my colleagues. We displayed a large banner in the school hallway that stated: "We believe every child can learn to read." Yet, regardless of my commitment and hard work, every child in my classroom did *not* become a successful reader and writer by the end of third grade.

My struggling readers were my greatest challenge. They had acquired inappropriate reading habits that were difficult to break. Although these children made gains during the year, they were not able to catch up with their peers. My teacher friends and I discussed the frustrations we felt in ensuring that our lowest-achieving readers reached their highest potential in literacy. We organized teacher support groups, and we studied the theories and effective practices associated with successful literacy programs. We talked about "celebrating the small steps," but we all knew that the small steps were not good enough for the child who had much more to learn, much further to go.

In Arkansas, Reading Recovery was then being discussed as an effective intervention program for struggling readers in first grade. Reading Recovery is based on the premise that intervention is the key to preventing reading failures. These discussions were timely: many classroom teachers besides me weren't able to teach their lowest-ability children to read successfully.

I left the classroom to learn more about Reading Recovery. During my training year, I applied theory to practice as I tutored low-achieving first-grade children in the Reading Recovery program. I saw children who were destined for special education services or long-term remediation programs become self-regulated learners after only twelve to sixteen weeks of intensive tutoring. I remembered the faces of my most troubled third-grade readers and I asked myself, What would they be doing now if they had received Reading Recovery in first grade?

Recently I was invited to talk with a group of Title I reading teachers. I knew several of these teachers from my classroom years; we were part of a larger group of whole language teachers who met regularly to discuss our teaching. As I planned for this meeting, I thought about those days and I reflected on the frustrations we had shared. I thought about my classroom with its very "literate look," the children who were so excited about their learning, and what I would do differently with these children now. As I talked with my colleagues, I shared the insights I had gained from my experiences in Reading Recovery, and I confessed to what I called the "theoretical gap in my classroom teaching."

This book is grounded in the lessons I have learned. The first and probably most important is that we cannot design a program for low-achieving children based on a deficit model of learning. Unfortunately, most Title I programs are geared to remediate a child's weaknesses. This same model has been applied to our classrooms, simply because we, as teachers, are overwhelmed by the great deficits of low-achieving children. However, I now realize that teachers must identify the knowledge, skills, and strategies that children bring to us and create learning opportunities that use these strengths as a means to acquire new knowledge. I also realize the importance of the teacher's instructional language in shaping the children's learning through guided participation. I have new insights about the role of modeling, coaching, and scaffolding children as they work in their learning "zones." And I believe that teachers need to plan instructional interactions that promote the flexible transfer of knowledge and strategies across a wide range of literacy events. Finally, I believe that the goal of instruction is to create self-regulated learners who possess the capacity to guide, monitor, and evaluate their own learning.

During the past eight years, I have worked regularly with Reading Recovery children and have maintained a close relationship with classroom and Title I teachers. I have never forgotten the children from my past. Writing this book is a means of sharing some important principles of learning that I believe make a difference in the literacy development of young learners.

**Tammy:** The title of this book, *Apprenticeship in Literacy: Transitions Across Reading and Writing,* also describes my educational career. I began teaching twelve years ago, in a Title I classroom. I had just graduated from college, with only three credit hours in reading, and I found myself faced with struggling readers in the fourth, fifth, and sixth grades. My teaching position was a new one at the school; there was no reading program or set curriculum in

place. Fortunately, I had a very supportive principal who trusted me to design my own.

One of my first students was a fourteen-year-old nonreader, Tosca, who had never attended school a day in her life. Her family owned a circus; from the time she was born, they traveled internationally, never staying in one place long enough to enroll in school. The challenge of teaching Tosca to read scared me to death.

Reading had been natural for me; I could read the newspaper by the time I was four. I kept asking myself, How did that happen? How did I learn to read? All I could remember was that my mother read me a huge number of books. I distinctly recall her talking about the pictures and tracking the lines of print with her finger. It was a very joyful time for me.

So I began Tosca's reading program by sharing many books with her. Tosca was a very eager student. She quickly learned how to write her name, as well as the early concepts about print. My next step was to teach her the alphabet and at the same time show her a few survival skills related to print. We started in the grocery store, looking closely at and analyzing labels. I tried to help her use the picture of the product along with the printed symbol to decode the words. This worked very well, and Tosca began to make progress. However, although I knew she needed to learn how to read stories, I didn't know where to start. A colleague recommended that I use a particular reading program that evolved around a very controlled and contrived vocabulary. Some of the words were written phonetically to give the reader a hint of the correct sounds to make. Tosca and I began daily lessons. It didn't take long to see the joy of learning disappear from her face. She worked diligently and never questioned my methods. I wanted so badly for Tosca to read her first real book, so that she could experience the joy of interacting with stories. But I began to notice that she could not transfer her learning from her practice book to real books. Again, I was at a complete loss for what to do. I guess you could say that for the rest of the year I just "winged" it with Tosca. I read stories to her every day just as my mother had read to me; we also read out of a basal reader; and we continued the controlled reading program. By the end of the year, Tosca was reading on a second-grade level. Her mother wrote to me thanking me for all my help. She was ecstatic that she could now send Tosca to the grocery store alone. Tosca felt a sense of accomplishment too, because she was now able to follow the directions on a cake-mix box.

But Tosca taught me as much as I taught her. She still needed more literacy learning and so did I. I began the following year looking closely at all kinds of literacy programs. My supportive principal agreed to let me purchase them and try them. I had the same fourth, fifth, and sixth graders in my program. Not one student had learned to read on grade level the previous year, despite my hard work and effort. I taught my heart out and received excellent evaluations from my principal. I was trying everything and every program imaginable in order to teach these children to read on grade level. *Nothing worked!* The children became "lifers": they attended my Title I reading class until they moved into seventh grade and their program stopped. I was very dissatisfied with my program, even though on paper it looked like a successful one. The children were achieving the minimal NCE gain required by the Title I program guidelines. All of the administrators were happy, but I knew things could be better.

I began reading professional books and attending workshops. The presenters seemed to know what they were talking about and their ideas were interesting. I would go back to the classroom and implement these activities. Most of the time, they were cute, fun projects, but when the activity was completed I didn't know what to do next. Something was missing from my teaching.

About this time I began working on my master's degree in reading at a local university, and I ran across research on the Reading Recovery program. According to the research, Reading Recovery enabled low-achieving children to reach grade level in a short span of time: just what I had been searching for! Much to my dismay, Reading Recovery was not available in Arkansas at the time. A year later, Reading Recovery was funded by the Arkansas State Legislature in collaboration with the University of Arkansas at Little Rock. During that first year, I was trained as a Reading Recovery teacher. The following year, I received my training as a Reading Recovery teacher leader. This in-depth training was exactly what I'd dreamed of. As I worked with Reading Recovery children, I was amazed at the progress they made so quickly. My experiences with these children gave me a new understanding of the complexity of the learning process and the role of the teacher in promoting young children's literacy development.

During the past five years, I have made presentations to many Title I teachers in my area. I listen to them describe many of the same problems I experienced years ago. Too many teachers continue to look for the quick fix—the packaged program that promises to cure the problems of our struggling readers. As a result, our reading labs are full of the same children, who return year after year for remediation. My reason for writing this book is to provide reading teachers with a theory-based resource they can use to implement an apprenticeship approach to teaching reading and writing to the children in their classrooms.

**Cathy:** For the past ten years, I have conducted staff development training for teachers as both a reading specialist and an early childhood curriculum specialist at an Arkansas educational service cooperative. I have been a sounding board for teachers who come to the workshops frustrated with their methods and materials for teaching struggling readers. Most are dedicated teachers who truly want to learn how to help the most at-risk child become a successful reader. However, some teachers are looking only for cute ideas and a quick fix.

I worked hard to find the best reading ideas that combined cute with current research, and I presented seminars to hundreds of classroom teachers from this point of view. However, as I began my Reading Recovery teacher leader training, I challenged the usefulness of certain ideas and reading programs for teaching young children how to read. I also began to challenge my ways of training teachers in effective literacy practices. My training in Reading Recovery was a transitional period during which my theories of teaching both children and teachers began to change significantly.

For example, I saw the power of continuous, regular training sessions that used authentic teaching contexts to stimulate discussions about how children learn. (I had previously conducted one-shot, one-day staff development seminars.) Now as I work with classroom and specialty teachers, I use an apprenticeship approach that offers on-the-job opportunities, clear demonstrations, guided participation, and immediate feedback that relates directly to teaching their own children. During class meetings, teachers are given time to analyze transitions in children's reading and writing behavior and encouraged to articulate and reflect on their teaching decisions. In addition to visiting colleagues in their class-

rooms, teachers bring videotapes of specific teaching and learning situations (writing conferences, guided reading groups, shared reading, etc.) currently under discussion.

These interactions with teachers helped me recognize the need for this book. I hope it provides clear demonstrations for guiding reflective discussions about children's learning.

As you read the book, you will also spend considerable time in the classrooms of Carla, a reading teacher, and Angela, a first-grade classroom teacher. They play a very important role, and are wonderful and inspiring professionals, part of a large literacy team committed to ensuring that all first-grade children are successful readers by the end of their first-grade year. Their dedication makes a difference in the lives of children. Their classrooms contain active learners who are always on the cutting edge of development. They truly listen to their students and observe the processes they engage in as they read and write. They continually formulate their theories as they interact with their students and in turn plan their instructional interactions based on these theories.

Carla and Angela learn constantly from the children in their classrooms. Their classrooms are learning communities in which children are accepted no matter where they are on the continuum of reading and writing development. The children are recognized as individuals, and instruction is designed to accommodate their learning zones.

In writing this book, we have tried to sound a theme that we believe illustrates an apprenticeship approach, one that emphasizes changes in both student and teacher learning. From a Vygotskian point of view, language is the tool that shapes this higher-level understanding. The many interactions we include show how teachers use language to help young children acquire new knowledge. We believe that teachers must be able to articulate the changes that occur as children become more competent learners and must be able to provide transitional interactions that keep children working in the zone of proximal development. This is the basis of an apprenticeship approach to literacy.

# The Right to Literacy

W e somewhat hesitantly begin this book by mentioning the difficulties of struggling readers. Classroom teachers want a book of effective practices for working with young children, and we don't want to start on a negative note. However, as teachers, our frustrations originated because of the difficulties we were experiencing with our problem readers.

Research indicates that if children do not become successful readers by the end of third grade, it is very difficult for them to catch up with their peers in later years. Clay (1993) explains that inappropriate reading habits can be a real stumbling block to higher levels of understanding. The probability that a child who is a poor reader in the first grade will remain a poor reader at the end of the fourth grade is 88 percent (Juel 1988). This alarming figure is emphasized in the extensive work of Barr and Parrett (1995), who stress that all children need to learn to read successfully before the end of third grade. The role of the classroom teacher is a critical factor in ensuring the success of struggling readers. In *Unfulfilled Expectations* (1991), Snow and her research team clearly document the relationship between high-quality classroom instruction and the success of at-risk students. Yet we all know that simply immersing children in literacy-rich environments is not enough to offset the difficulties of struggling readers. For children to become successful learners, they need us, as their teachers, to be knowledgeable about the literacy process and to provide them with constructive reading and writing opportunities that guarantee their right to literacy. From what conceptual framework can we do that?

## Sociocognitive Processes in Teaching and Learning

Literacy is no longer regarded as simply a cognitive skill to be learned. Rather, it is viewed as a complex interactive and interpretative process whose development is determined by the social and cultural context (Bruner 1967; Luria 1982; Vygotsky 1978). As adults and children engage in interactive oral discussions about written language, children acquire important tools for the mind (Bodrova and Leong 1996).

During these literate events, the adult as the more knowledgeable person carefully monitors the child's interpretation of the situation and provides timely support that enables the child to achieve the greatest levels of understanding.

According to Vygotsky, cognitive development and social interaction are perceived as complementary processes that work together to promote the child's intellectual growth. So an influential force in the child's learning is the teaching that occurs around the literacy event. From a Vygotskian perspective, mental development, teaching, and learning share reciprocal relationships that cannot be discussed separately. We believe that in order to promote higher-level literacy development in young children, teachers must:

- Carefully observe young children in the process of learning.
- Design instructional interactions that involve children in using their personal knowledge as a foundation for constructing new learning.
- Monitor children's progress in the new situation and be prepared to make spontaneous adjustments in their levels of support to ensure that children continue to learn.
- Use their observations of children's learning to evaluate and plan new instructional interactions that validate old knowledge and activate new learning.

The complementary actions of *validation* and *activation* lead the child to a higher level of cognitive development: (a) the teacher praises (acknowledges) what the child knows and (b) the teacher uses the known information as a bridge to activate new problem-solving. From research on brain theory, we have learned the importance of connecting individual sources

of knowledge to a larger network of information. When we ask young learners to use something they know to learn something new, they make an important discovery—their knowledge can be generalized. This is a lesson that many at-risk readers have not yet learned; instead, they view each learning experience as a new experience. These children need us, as their teachers, to structure literacy events and informative dialogues that emphasize the constructive and generative value of their own learning.

Observation and responsive teaching play critical roles in the literacy development of young children. Wells and Chang-Wells (1992) describe this process as "leading from behind," which implies that teachers must have a good understanding of what children know in order to guide them toward higher levels of development. During shared experiences, the teacher listens carefully to the child and is prepared to make spontaneous adjustments in her contributions that reflect the child's current ability. Language is a powerful tool with which to negotiate and regulate responsibility for completing the task at hand. In the following example, the balance of control shifts between the teacher and the child as they both use language to negotiate an appropriate ending for the story:

> Allen and Janie, his teacher, are completing the writing of a story based on eating M&M candies. Janie asks, "Now what are we going to call this book?" Allen turns to a blank page at the end of the book and remarks, "Hey, we got one more!" Janie responds, "Oh, yeah, we need to put something on that last page." Then, Janie attempts to link Allen's story to a similar story entitled *The Chocolate Cake* (Melser 1990), which has a repeated pattern of "mmmm" on each page. She asks, "What do we say when something tastes really good? Do we say 'mmm'?"

In response, Allen expands on Janie's intentions and initiates his own ending, "We can write 'It's all gone.'" Janie acknowledges Allen's contribution as an appropriate ending for the story as she exclaims, "It's all gone! That's a great way to end your story!" (Dorn 1996, pp. 31–32)

These ideas are supported by the work of Rogoff (1990), who emphasizes the importance of social interaction for stimulating children's cognitive growth through guided participation in structured literacy activities. Rogoff views children as apprentices in learning who acquire a diverse collection of skills and knowledge under the guidance and support of more knowledgeable persons. In the beginning, the adult assumes responsibility for structuring the learning task and guiding the interaction, but as the child acquires higher-level understanding, there is a noticeable transfer of responsibility from the adult to the child.

During socially constructed events, language is used to communicate a useful (i.e., meaningful) message to another person. In an apprenticeship setting, adults model the significance of written language as an important tool for documenting and communicating information. For example, Cathy and her daughter Elizabeth are preparing to cook Thanksgiving dinner. As Cathy prepares the turkey, Elizabeth creates a recipe for cooking it (see Figure 1.1). During this social moment, Elizabeth learns an important lesson about the functional role of written language in planning and organizing information for everyday experiences. These literate opportunities provide young children with a strong foundation for success in reading and writing.

Waterland applies apprenticeship to reading in the primary grades. She describes how the adult has three parts to play in helping the child learn to read:

**Figure 1.1**  Elizabeth's turkey recipe. ("Turn on the oven and heat for 80 degrees. Cook it for 5 minutes. Now you eat it.")

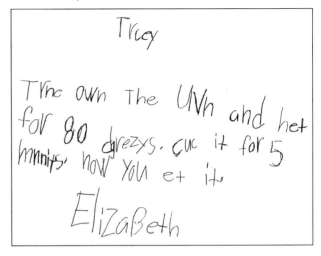

- The adult chooses kinds of text that enable the child to learn about reading.
- The adult reads the parts of the story that the child is unable to read while hesitating at appropriate places to encourage the child to contribute the parts he or she knows.
- The adult ensures that the child will be successful by eliminating any negative or competitive aspects of the situation. (1985, pp. 13–14)

Wood, Bruner, and Ross (1976) use the term *scaffolding* to describe a support system for helping children achieve success on a task that would be too difficult for them to accomplish on their own. In an apprenticeship approach, the teacher and child work together in constructing a meaningful interaction around a common literacy event. The teacher analyzes the child's level of independent functioning on the new task, discovers the child's intentions for solving the task, and supports the child with appropriate comments.

Scaffolding is portrayed in the following example. Mrs. Reed and Nicholas have just finished reading a simple book about moms and their jobs. Mrs. Reed asks Nicholas, "What does your mom do?" Nicholas responds, "She works at Burger King." Then Mrs. Reed asks Nicholas if he would like to write a story about his mom and her job. Nicholas picks up his marker and writes an *m* on his page. The balance of support changes with Nicholas's developing control for accomplishing the writing task:

| Response | Analysis |
|---|---|
| **Mrs. Reed:** That's great that you knew *my* started with *m*. | Provides explicit feedback. |
| Just let me put that *y* on the end of *my*. | Supplies unknown information. |
| Now, what is that word? | Increases word accessibility. |
| **Nicholas:** My. | Accesses word information. |
| **Mrs. Reed:** What is your next word? | Prompts for new action. |
| **Nicholas:** Mom (*Making no attempt to write it*). | |
| **Mrs. Reed:** It starts like *my*. Say *my* and *mom*. What did your mouth do? | Increases letter-sound accessibility. |
| **Nicholas:** *M…m…m…* It didn't open. *M…m…y… m…m…m…o…m…m…* | Accesses sensory information. |
| **Mrs. Reed:** Yes, did you feel your mouth close at the beginning and at the end of *mom*? | Provides informative feedback. |
| **Nicholas:** (*Picks up the marker, writes* m, *skips a space, adds another* m *for* mom, *then hands the marker to Mrs. Reed to add the middle letter.*) | Initiates new action. |

In this short episode, we see how Mrs. Reed uses her observations of Nicholas to guide her levels of support. According to Wood (1980, 1988), the critical part of scaffolding is the adult's ability to determine the child's zone of proximal development, thus providing appropriate instructional strategies that create a shift in the child's level of cognitive functioning.

## Where Is the Zone of Proximal Development?

In our work with classroom teachers, the question most often asked is, How do we help young children—particularly low-achieving children—learn faster? The answer lies in the zone of proximal development. Typically in education we have focused our attention on the child's actual development as indicated by particular assessments. From Vygotsky's perspective, advanced learning does *not* occur at the actual level of development; rather, it occurs in the zone of proximal development, "the distance between the actual developmental level as determined by individual problem-solving and the level of potential development as determined through problem-solving under adult guidance or in collaboration with more capable peers" (Vygotsky 1978, p. 86). Adults work within this zone to support and scaffold a child until he or she can function independently, thus enabling the child to move to a higher level in cognitive functioning. Basically, behavior development occurs on two levels:

1. *Zone of actual development (ZAD).* The child's independent level of performance, what the child knows and can do alone.
2. *Zone of proximal development (ZPD).* The maximum level of development the child can reach with assistance. Varying

degrees of partially assisted performance lie within the ZPD.

Higher levels of understanding occur as a result of assisted performance in the zone of proximal development. What the child was able to accomplish with assistance yesterday becomes the independent level today, moving the child to a higher level of intellectual development.

According to Vygotsky, through adult-assisted performance, "learning awakens a variety of internal developmental processes that are able to operate only when the child is interacting with people in his environment and in cooperation with his peers" (1978, p. 90). In a cognitive apprenticeship approach, a teacher considers the mediating influence of the social situation (i.e., the literacy event) for helping the child develop a conscious awareness of specific knowledge. This theory places an importance on explicit demonstrations and active engagements that are capable of awakening and guiding the child's literacy development to a higher level.

Let's apply this theory of assisted learning to two examples taken from a writing conference between Mrs. Rogers and Allison, a first grader. The first example illustrates how Mrs. Rogers uses language to help Allison construct a story based on a personal experience. In the second example, Mrs. Rogers uses language to direct Allison's attention to problem-solving strategies for helping herself during the actual writing.

Mrs. Rogers observes that Allison is having difficulty starting her story. She sits beside Allison and asks, "Did you do anything special this weekend?" Allison responds, "I went to the zoo." Mrs. Rogers smiles and says, "Well, that sounds like fun. I haven't been to the zoo in a long time. Can you tell me more about it?" As the conversa-tion continues, Allison tells Mrs. Rogers about the monkey, the bear, and the elephant at the zoo. She concludes with a warning that "you can't feed the animals because it will make them sick." After responding enthusiastically to Allison's story, Mrs. Rogers encourages her to rehearse the story for writing: "That is a great story. Let's put it all together, so we can listen to how it will sound to your readers." Mrs. Rogers's final statement has three intentions:

- To provide Allison with a verbal model of the story that Allison can use to monitor her written version.
- To direct Allison's attention to the importance of reflection as a tool for evaluating her own work.
- To emphasize that the reason for writing is to communicate a coherent and meaningful message to a particular audience.

Next Mrs. Rogers uses language to direct Allison to productive strategies for helping herself write the story:

| Teacher/Child Language | Intention of Language |
| --- | --- |
| **Mrs. Rogers:** How would you start to write *went*? | Prompt child to constructive activity. |
| **Allison:** I don't know. | Seek help. |
| **Mrs. Rogers:** Say it slowly and listen to what you can hear. *W—e—n—t*. | Prompt the child to use slow articulation to hear sounds in sequence. |
| **Allison:** *W—e—n—t*. I hear a *t*. | Apply process of slow articulation and analyze final sequence of sound. |
| **Mrs. Rogers:** There is a *t*. Where do you hear it? | Confirm child's knowledge and prompt for further analysis. |
| **Allison:** *W—e—n—t*. At the end. | Use strategy in new problem-solving activity. |

| | |
|---|---|
| **Mrs. Rogers:** Yes, it is at the end. Say it again and listen to the beginning. | Confirm child's knowledge and prompt for further analysis |
| **Allison:** *W—e—n—t.* I hear a *w*. | Analyze beginning sequence. |
| **Mrs. Rogers:** Yes, that's good listening. You heard the *w* at the beginning and the *t* at the end. I'll write the other letters for now. This is the way *went* looks in books. Use your checking finger to see if it looks right. | Provide explicit feedback and direct child's attention to new confirming activity. |
| Now reread your story and think of what comes next. | Prompt for rereading to anticipate text response. |
| **Allison:** I went to… | Reread and anticipate the next word. |
| **Mrs. Rogers:** You can write *to.* | Activate old knowledge for application to a new situation. |
| Now you know some ways to help yourself. Say your words slowly and write what you can hear. Don't forget to reread each time to help you think of the next word in your story. I'll be back in a few minutes and you can show me what you've written. | Prompt child to use strategies for independent problem-solving. |

Mrs. Rogers uses the writing situation as an instructional tool for helping Allison acquire important learning in several areas. Her teaching priorities are revealed in her closing comments:

- Words can be analyzed according to their sequence of sounds.
- Rereading helps a writer predict the next word.

The role of the adult in helping children acquire higher level knowledge cannot be understated. Observant teachers collect important data for making informed decisions that keep children working at the cutting edge of their development (i.e., the zone of proximal development). Because new learning is both generative and recursive, the teacher must adjust his or her support in compliance with how the child is responding to the task at hand.

## Progressing Through the Zone of Proximal Development

As children progress through the zone of proximal development, it is important that teachers value the ups and downs of new learning and are able to provide adjustable support that accommodates this learning. Tharp and Gallimore (1988, pp. 33–39) describe the learner's progression through the ZPD and the role of the adult in guiding the child to a higher level of cognitive activity. It may be helpful to apply this theory to the previous example with Allison and Mrs. Rogers. We will begin with stage 1 (i.e., Allison's present stage) and make predictions for her progression through the ZPD that reflect a movement from teacher-regulated activity to child-regulated activity.

In stage 1 of the ZPD, Allison requires a great deal of support in accomplishing a particular task. The responsibility for regulating her participation in the task rests primarily with the teacher, who is constantly adjusting support to ensure that Allison is successful. For instance, Mrs. Rogers bases her teaching priorities on knowledge of the learning process (the role of phonology in reading and writing development) and her observations of Allison's current abilities (saying words slowly as a way to analyze sounds in words). Wells and Chang-Wells (1992) describe how instructional interactions must be based on the child's current ability and the adult's pedagogical intentions and how the adult must be prepared at any moment to modify the level of instructional support in light of feedback from the child. This suggests that clear models and guided participation are critical elements of a successful interaction that has the potential for supporting new learning. In an apprenticeship setting, Allison will learn how to use teacher-demonstrated models for guiding her own learning to a higher level.

During stage 2, Allison will display the capacity to assist her own learning process. During the previous writing activity, Mrs. Rogers gave Allison an opportunity to learn how to use problem-solving strategies. As Mrs. Rogers left the writing conference, she reminded Allison of two important strategies that she must now use to help herself. At stage 2, external prompts (e.g., teacher's language) are no longer needed because the child provides her own support system through self-directed speech. In the case of analyzing sounds in words, we expect Allison independently to initiate the action of slow articulation and use this strategy for matching sounds to letters. Through repeated practice, Allison's knowledge about letters and sounds will become more automatic.

In stage 3, assistance from the adult or the self is no longer needed, because the behavior has been internalized. At this stage, Allison will be able to write words fluently and flexibly in different places and for varied purposes. The behavior (i.e., analyzing letters and sounds) places no new demands on the brain. The goal of instruction has been reached when Allison becomes a self-regulated learner with the capacity to use her knowledge for monitoring, guiding, and regulating her own learning activity.

During Stage 4, an internalized behavior can be temporarily disrupted by a variety of influences, such as environmental changes, new cognitive demands, or physical trauma. When this occurs, the goal of instruction is to guide the learner back through the ZPD, providing the necessary levels of support to regain automatization. For instance, there may be times when Allison will have to slow down and attend to certain features of print. Also, there may be times when Allison's writing will reflect a regressive behavior in regard to a known sound, and Mrs. Rogers will have to issue a gentle reminder about how to access this information ("Say the word slowly and listen to the middle."). It is important to keep in mind that new learning is somewhat fragile and may be temporarily thrown off track when the brain becomes absorbed with new problem-solving activity. With a little self-help or teacher-help, the learner will regain automatic control of the behavior.

According to Vygotsky, instruction is a major contributor to children's growing consciousness and the regulation of their own cognitive processes. As children engage in literacy conversations with more knowledgeable persons, basic cognitive processes are transformed into higher intellectual functions. Vygotsky describes how each intellectual function must appear two times: first on a social, external plane between two or more people, and next on a personal, internal plane within the child.

This theory is important for education because it emphasizes the interaction between teacher and student as integral to independent problem-solving. Vygotskian theory maintains that children move from other-regulatory (external) to self-regulatory (internal) behavior through interactions with individuals in their environment. The child's ability to organize and monitor his or her own thinking occurs as a result of demonstrations during social exchanges with others. Mediated learning experiences with more literate individuals demonstrate the language needed to guide the child toward regulating his or her own thinking. The end point of teaching is a self-regulated learner who exhibits the potential to use his or her knowledge for varied purposes and in different situations (Diaz et al. 1990; Luria 1973).

## Promoting Conscious Awareness of Literate Knowledge

Children develop a conscious awareness of their own mental functions as they engage in literate activities with their teacher. In her book *Children's Minds,* Donaldson (1978) establishes the link between the growth of consciousness and the growth of the intellect: "If the intellectual powers are to develop, the child must gain a measure of control over his own thinking and he cannot control while he remains unaware of it" (p. 129). Consciousness is constructed through the child's interactions with the world. The more literate person represents the consciousness of the child, thus enabling the child to experience the behavior vicariously (Bruner 1986), but coming to control the behavior as self-awareness leads to internalization.

The research on metalinguistic awareness emphasizes the importance of helping young children acquire a conscious awareness of the structure and function of written language. This awareness does not develop as an isolated skill; instead, it is naturally woven into the literacy process. During interactive events, teachers use explicit language as an important tool to help children acquire higher-level understanding about literacy concepts. For instance:

- Language is used to activate the child's awareness of specific concepts about print (e.g., before the teacher reads one page, she remarks, "I'm going to use my finger to read this page because it helps me match my words.").
- Language is used to promote the child's self-reflective activity (e.g., the teacher invites the child to "show me on this page where you put your nicest space between your words").
- Language is used to provide the child with explicit feedback that acknowledges his use of a particular concept about print (e.g., the child says a word slowly and the teacher remarks, "I like the way you are saying the word slowly. That helps you to hear the sounds, doesn't it?").
- Language is used to help the child develop a more conscious awareness of the importance of a particular concept of print (e.g., after the child writes a capital letter at the beginning of the sentence, the teacher remarks, "How did you know to write a capital letter there?").

In cognitive apprenticeship, the adult guides the child toward a meaningful interaction with her, making adjustments in her support based on constant feedback received from the child. Through these personal communications, the child begins to internalize the actions and the language of the adult and begins to use these tools as internal devices to guide and monitor his own processing behavior. Vygotskian theory proposes that once an externalized activity becomes an internalized function, the structure and the organization of the brain is changed, moving the child to a higher intellectual level (Diaz et al. 1990; Luria 1982; Vygotsky 1978).

## Establishing Organizational Systems for Learning

Using Vygotsky's point of view, we must get the brain organized to learn how to think so that learning can be generalized to new areas. When sensory information becomes integrated in the brain, it triggers a series of coordinated movements that provide personal feedback for each other. For instance, when a child constructs a form (tactile) for the sound he hears (auditory) and checks it with his eyes (visual), the child receives feedback from each sensory system. It is as though the brain is checking each sense against the other and confirming its identity. Slywester (1995) describes it this way: "When objects and events are registered by several senses (e.g., seeing, hearing, and touching), they can be stored in several interrelated memory networks. A memory stored in this way becomes more accessible and powerful than a memory stored in just one sensory area, because each sensory memory checks and extends the others" (p. 14). So there must be a smooth coordination of behavior if the child is to receive the maximum feedback from each sensory category.

Language and action work together to help children develop conscious awareness of their literacy. The following example illustrates how the teacher combines language and physical actions in order to focus the child's perceptual attention on the features of an unknown word from the story. Jeff is having difficulty with the word *here* in his new book. So that Jeff can finish the story with its meaning relatively intact, Mrs. Watson tells him the word. Afterward she turns back to the difficult page and asks Jeff to locate the "problem word." Without hesitation, Jeff locates the word *here*. Mrs. Watson then uses the word *here* to help Jeff learn how to integrate multiple sources of sensory information:

| Teacher Prompt | Sensory Systems | Materials |
|---|---|---|
| Check the word with your finger and see if it looks like *here*. | Visual, tactile. | Magnetic letters. |
| Say the word as you check it. | Auditory, visual, tactile. | Magnetic letters. |
| Write the word and say the word as you write it. | Tactile, visual, auditory. | Paper and pencil. |
| Find the word in your story. | Visual. | Text. |
| Check to see if the word in your story looks like the word you just made. | Visual. | Text, paper, and pencil. |
| Read that page again. | Visual, auditory. | Text. |

In the early stages of development, the word is represented through external, concrete, and manipulative tools that eventually become internalized as mental tools that can exist without external support. For Jeff, the magnetic letters are a temporary tool for learning how to attend to the visual features of an unknown word in his story. This momentary scaffold gives Jeff a perceptual model that can be checked against other sources of information from the text. For example, when the teacher first asks Jeff to locate the word, Jeff is able to do it based on the meaning and structural pattern of the story. The teacher's final prompt brings Jeff back to the story for integration and confirmation of all sources. The teacher's language plays an important role in guiding the child through the perceptual process. The goal of instruction is that Jeff will internalize the external models into an internal model that can be used flexibly to monitor and plan his behavior during various literacy events. The table below illustrates the continuum of teacher/child control in the development of self-regulated activity:

| Teacher-Regulated Behavior (External Tools) | Child-Regulated Behavior (Internal Tools) |
|---|---|
| Clear and concrete demonstrations | Internal manipulations |
| Explicit and redundant speech | Self-directed speech |
| Teacher control | Internal control |

## Developing Self-Regulated Learners

A self-regulated reader is one who uses his knowledge to advance his own learning. Self-regulation is defined as "the child's capacity to plan, guide, and monitor his or her behavior from within and flexibly according to changing circumstances" (Diaz et al. 1990, p. 130). This definition implies a network of strategies working together toward a common goal. During instructional interactions, students acquire strategies for remembering, comparing, searching, checking, and confirming relationships.

In *Becoming Literate,* Clay (1991) describes a reading system that comprises a network of interrelated strategies that work together to ensure the reader will have a meaningful and self-extending experience. The characteristics of a self-extending system include the child's capacity to:

- Monitor reading and writing.
- Search for cues in word sequences, in meaning, in letter sequences.
- Discover new things.
- Cross-check one source of cues with another.
- Repeat to confirm reading or writing.
- Self-correct, assuming the initiative for making cues match or getting words right.
- Solve new words by flexible and varied means.

The important thing here is that no action exists in isolation from another action. These internal processes that the child engages in are interlocking systems that tap into each other, providing feedback and feedforward assistance (Clay 1991) for making the reading process run smoothly and effortlessly. The learner grows intellectually as he uses his existing knowledge to regulate his own learning and guide it to a higher cognitive level.

The diagram in Figure 1.2 illustrates the complexity of self-regulated learning. As illustrated, behavior such as generating, monitoring, confirming, linking, planning, reflecting,

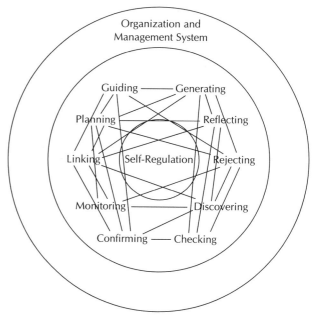

**Figure 1.2** The interrelationship and organization of self-regulatory behavior.

and guiding depends on the reader's ability to activate information beyond the initial response and to use this personal form of feedback for problem-solving in the new situation. These problem-solving actions are organized into a complex system of internal activity that has one goal: to make sense of the incoming information.

Holdaway (1979) describes the importance of establishing self-regulation in the learner. "There is no better system to control the complexities and intricacies of each person's learning than that person's own system operating with genuine motivation and self-determination" (p. 170).

## Teaching for Transfer

At this point, we need to discuss another important concept in self-regulatory learning—the role of teaching for transfer. The definition of self-regulation (see page 10) implies that the learner is engaged in reflective and metacognitive processing. Thus we believe we cannot talk about self-regulatory learning without also discussing its relationship to other interlocking behavior:

- *Teaching for Transfer.* When a teacher teaches for transfer, she must be aware of what the child knows. Therefore, the teacher designs instructional interactions that provide the learner with opportunities to transfer existing skills, strategies, and knowledge to new problem-solving activity across changing and varied situations.
- *Teaching for Strategies.* When a teacher teaches for strategies, she is prompting the child toward processing activity based on the child's existing knowledge and the ability to apply problem-solving strategies while working with unknown information.

- *Applying Processing Behavior.* When a child applies processing behavior, he taps into the brain's storehouse of information, notices relationships, and applies problem-solving strategies in order to construct meaning for the activity at hand.
- *Self-Regulation.* When a child becomes a self-regulated learner, he uses his current skills, strategies, and knowledge at a new level of cognitive activity; that is, he plans and guides new learning and uses existing knowledge for solving new problems in a variety of situations.

Here we see an emphasis on observation and the teacher's role in prompting the child to use existing knowledge to solve new problems. In order for self-regulation to occur, the teacher must be a careful observer of the child's knowledge and must know how to present opportunities that enable the child to transfer this knowledge across changing circumstances. Also, children must have appropriate types of materials that enable them to apply existing skills and knowledge in flexible ways while simultaneously being presented with opportunities to use known information for solving new problems. Furthermore, the teacher must be able to select productive examples that create memorable experiences that the child will use later. Figure 1.3 illustrates the relationship between self-regulation, observation, and materials.

Campione, Shapiro, and Brown (1996) provide the following definition of transfer: "Transfer means understanding; and understanding is indexed by the ability of learners to explain the resources (knowledge and processes) they are acquiring and to make flexible use of them in the service of new and continued learning" (p. 39).

Now the question is, How does transfer happen? In support of Vygotsky's theory, the

**Figure 1.3** Relationship between teaching and learning, observation, and materials.

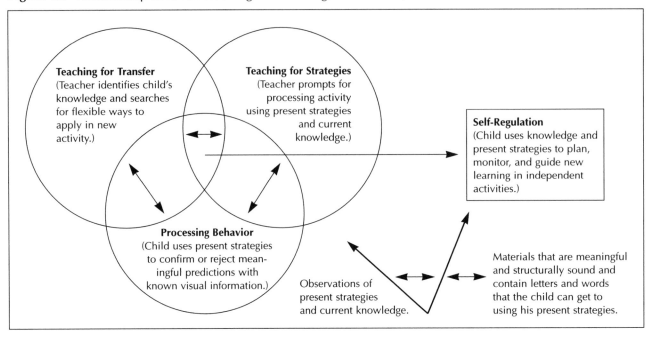

heart of transfer lies with the adult, who must design instructional activities that enable learners to recognize the stability of their knowledge and its potential for working out new problems in different places. Children depend on adults to observe what they know and to select appropriate materials and activities that help them realize that learning is generalizable.

So the role of the teacher is to engage children in instructional interactions that will not only facilitate new learning but will also promote the transfer of acquired knowledge and strategies beyond the initial learning context to new situations and for different purposes (Lupart 1996). Again, we must stress the importance of an observant teacher who knows how to create instructional experiences with generative learning value.

We know from Tharp and Gallimore's recursive cycle that new learning is fragile and can be disrupted by new demands or changes in the environment. For that reason, the adult's

role in scaffolding the child at points of difficulty (that is, in the ZPD) is critical in enabling the child to acquire knowledge that is both stable and flexible. From a Vygotskian point of view, intellectual development occurs when the child recognizes the self-generative value of his own knowledge for guiding and monitoring new learning. Therefore, an important lesson for children is that their knowledge is stable regardless of the changing situations in which it occurs.

In later chapters, we will return to the transfer principle as we describe how the teacher designs opportunities (at both an assisted and independent level) for the child to learn how to manipulate his or her existing knowledge for different purposes and in different contexts. The following areas provide a framework for further discussions:

•  The instructional and interactive dialogues of the teacher and children.

- The structure of the various (but related) literacy events.
- The processing behavior of the children across reading and writing events.

## Processing Behavior Versus Items of Knowledge

The ability to solve a word provides the learner with an important tool for learning new words. Thus the emphasis needs to be placed on the problem-solving rather than on the word. The teacher plays a critical role in shaping children's processing behavior; but in order for this to happen, teachers must understand the skills and strategies that are used by good readers. In addition, teachers must be able to:

- Observe the knowledge, skills, and strategies used by their students when they read and write.
- Use supportive materials that enable their students to practice effective strategies across a range of reading and writing events.
- Use language prompts that direct students' attention to the processing activity rather than to the accuracy of the word.
- Be willing to accept some errors that do not interfere with meaning.

Apprenticeship requires that "the adult accept that the child will make mistakes (in fact, *must* make mistakes) and will need time to sort these out and permission to ignore them if they do not matter" (Waterland 1985, p. 15). Teachers who emphasize accuracy are depriving their students of opportunities to learn how to generalize problem-solving and confirming strategies to new situations.

An emphasis on problem-solving is illustrated in the following example with Stephanie

and her teacher. The previous day, the teacher had introduced a simple little book entitled *Nighttime* (Cowley 1990) to Stephanie. During the introduction, she exposed Stephanie to two new words, *stable* and *sty*. Stephanie used the specialized vocabulary as she related the pictures to these words. It is important to remember that Stephanie is a first-grade student from the city; these particular words had little meaning for her. Stephanie's running record on the following day provides an interesting analysis of the complexity of her problem-solving behavior:

✓   ✓   ✓ ✓   ✓ <u>table</u>
The horse is in the stable
  ✓   ✓ ✓ ✓   ✓ <u>stable</u>
The pig is in the sty.

Examining Stephanie's responses, we can make several assumptions about her processing activity. First, since *stable* was an unfamiliar concept (in spite of her introduction to the word on the previous day), we can understand how Stephanie may have mentally linked this strange new word to a known word that sounded like it. We can also assume that she activated the sound pattern, rather than the visual pattern, in response to the conceptual load of the text. This seems logical since Stephanie is an emergent reader with limited knowledge about visual patterns at this time. However, as Stephanie reads the next line, notice how she attaches the memory trace of *table* to the *st* chunk (which is a known source of visual information from her name) and responds with the word *stable* for *sty*. In the transcript below, the teacher emphasizes the processing activity behind the second error. First, the teacher rereads the line fluently and engages Stephanie in a brief dialogue about the "place where pigs live." Then she says:

**Teacher:** When you were reading that part of your story, you noticed something at the beginning of the word, didn't you? What did you notice?

**Stephanie:** *St.*

**Teacher:** That's right. Do you know another word that starts like that?

**Stephanie:** My name. Stephanie.

**Teacher:** Yes, *Stephanie* and *sty.* They do start the same, don't they? That's good that you were looking at the beginning of the word. That helps you when you're reading, doesn't it. Let's read that page together.

If the teacher had chosen to go to the word *stable* or *sty* and insisted that Stephanie sound out the letters for the sake of the word, the teaching would have focused on accuracy. In contrast, the teacher chose to emphasize two important processing strategies: (a) using first-letter cues and (b) searching for known chunks of visual information. From this perspective, the child acquires a tool that can be used to initiate new problem-solving activity on different texts.

We know that reading is a meaning-making process that is successful when a reader understands the author's intended message. When a story makes sense, the reader receives valuable feedback that confirms everything is proceeding reasonably and coherently. Confirmation feedback regarding meaning preserves the integrity of the story and enables the reader to anticipate the occurrence of new events almost before the next line is read or the page is turned.

If the reader misses the point of the story, the goal of reading (which is understanding) is jeopardized. In an apprenticeship approach, the teacher guides the child to apply checking and confirming strategies that are grounded in meaningful interactions with the text. Therefore, the teacher's role in responding to the child's error is critical in helping the child build effective processing systems that lead to more complex reading activity.

Let's look at an example. Blake is reading a story about a little boy who lost his teddy bear. The pictures illustrate that the boy is searching in several places for the lost bear. Yet when Blake reads the text, he substitutes the word *here* [is the teddy bear] for *where* [is the teddy bear]. Since *here* and *where* are visually similar words, we can assume that Blake's response was influenced by visual information. However, a serious problem arises when Blake does not notice the effect that his substitution has created on the story's development. In the following transcript, the teacher focuses Blake's attention on checking for meaning:

**Teacher:** You said, "Here is the teddy bear." Can you find the teddy bear in the picture?

**Blake:** He's not there.

**Teacher:** No, he's not. So, does it make sense to say "Here is the teddy bear"?

**Blake:** No.

**Teacher:** Well, if the boy is still looking for the teddy bear, what do you think he would say?

**Blake:** Where is the teddy bear?

**Teacher:** Read it and see if you are right.

**Blake** (*Reading*): "Where is the teddy bear?"

The success of children's reading and writing endeavors is largely determined by the adult/child interaction during literacy events. The child is encouraged to be an active participant, with his or her interpretation of the text validated by the acceptance of the adult (Wells and Chang-Wells 1992). As the adult supports the child at his or her present level of understanding, the child is gently pushed into thinking about literacy at a higher level.

## Closing Thoughts

- Prevention of reading problems must begin in the early grades. If children are not reading on grade level by the end of third grade, their chance of success in later years is minimal. One significant characteristic of problem readers is their lack of literacy experiences during their preschool years. Schools must compensate by providing the children with rich literacy classroom programs and supplemental literacy services that focus on early intervention.

- Children acquire higher-level mental functions through social interactions with observant and responsive adults. Therefore, teachers should be trained in how to observe children's processing behavior and how to use this information in responding to children.

- School instruction should be aimed at children's potential level of development (i.e., the zone of proximal development). Teachers should use information about children as a basis for designing instructional situations that allow them to use existing knowledge as a scaffold for new problem-solving activity.

- An apprenticeship approach to literacy emphasizes the role of the adult in supporting children's developing control of literacy knowledge. In this model, the teacher provides clear demonstrations, engages children appropriately, monitors their level of understanding, makes necessary accommodations to ensure they are successful, and withdraws support as they exhibit greater control. A critical factor is the teacher's ability to remove the support in accordance with children's higher levels of understanding.

- In the early years, we must get the brain organized for learning how to learn. Schools must provide children with massive opportunities to make connections, establish relationships, and manipulate their knowledge across a wide range of literacy experiences.

- The goal of teaching is to develop self-regulated learners—children with the capacity to use their knowledge for guiding, monitoring, and planning new cognitive activity. During instructional interactions, teachers give children opportunities to tap into existing knowledge and to apply problem-solving strategies to novel information.

- Teachers structure literacy opportunities that promote the flexible transfer of knowledge, skills, and strategies to different situations. In the process, children learn the stability of knowledge and the power strategies have to be generalized to new areas of learning.

# A Cognitive Apprenticeship
# Approach to Literacy

When we meet with teachers, we use the seven theoretical principles (see Figure 2.1) to guide our discussions of the teaching and learning interactions in an apprenticeship approach. Cognitive apprenticeship implies that children acquire cognitive and metacognitive processes through assisted instruction with a sensitive and knowledgeable adult (Collins et al. 1989). The teacher carefully observes the knowledge and skills of young children and uses language to build bridges that enable children to use what they already know to acquire new and unknown information (Clay and Cazden 1990; Lyons et al. 1993; Rogoff 1990). Thus the teacher focuses on "arranging and structuring children's participation in activities, with dynamic shifts over development in children's responsibilities" (Rogoff 1990, p. 8). In other words, teachers must create transitions in both language and activities to reflect children's higher-level development. To that end, predictable routines and organizational structures that provide the children with expectations and standards for promoting independence are very important.

## The Role of Language in Promoting Literacy

From Vygotsky's point of view, instruction leads development; therefore, the role of teaching is strongly emphasized. We cannot discuss teaching without also examining the language of instruction. During literacy activities, teachers use language as a tool for communicating specific knowledge, skills, and strategies to children. The following chapters include numerous examples of language interactions whereby teachers:

- Use language prompts that stimulate children's problem-solving processes across a wide range of literacy activities (see Figure 2.2).
- Provide immediate feedback that explicitly describes children's behavior, thus reinforcing the desirable response (see Figure 2.3).

In all cases the teacher's language is immediately related to a problem that has arisen from

**Figure 2.1** Seven principles of an apprenticeship approach to literacy.

1. *Observation and Responsive Teaching*
   Teachers observe children's literacy behavior and design instructional experiences based on children's strengths and needs.
2. *Modeling and Coaching*
   Teachers use modeling and coaching techniques with clear demonstrations and explicit language.
3. *Clear and Relevant Language for Problem Solving*
   Teachers use language prompts that enable children to plan and initiate cognitive actions for resolving problems during literacy activities.
4. *Adjustable and Self-Destructing Scaffolds*
   Teachers provide adjustable scaffolds that are removed when they are no longer needed in a particular area.
5. *Structured Routines*
   Teachers provide routine interactions with organizational structures that enable independence.
6. *Assisted and Independent Work*
   Teachers provide balanced opportunities for children to work at assisted and independent levels.
7. *Transfer*
   Teachers teach for the transfer of knowledge, skills, and strategies across shifting circumstances and for varying purposes.

**Figure 2.2** Language prompts for helping children learn how to problem-solve.

**Language to Promote Cue Integration**

- Does that make sense?
- Does that sound right?
- Does that look right?
- Does it look right and sound right to you?

**Language to Promote Self-Monitoring Actions**

- Could it be ____?
- Were you right?
- Try that again.
- What else can you do?
- What did you notice?
- What's wrong?
- Read it again and see if you can figure out what is wrong here.
- What can you do to help yourself there?
- Are you thinking about your story?
- Do you know something about that word that can help you?

**Language to Link Reading and Writing**

- If you were writing that word, how would you start it?
- Say the word ____ slowly. What sounds can you hear?
  Can you find a word on this page that has those letters?

**Figure 2.3** Feedback language for describing appropriate literacy actions.

**Child:** (*The child hesitates when he comes to an unknown word.*)
**Teacher:** I like the way you stopped and checked on that word.
**Child:** (*The child rereads and self-corrects his error.*)
**Teacher:** You went back and fixed that, didn't you? That was good checking.
**Child:** (*The child reads in a fluent and expressive manner.*)
**Teacher:** You read that just like talking. That makes it interesting to listen to.

children's reading and writing and focuses on helping children apply appropriate strategies for resolving the conflict. However, for learning to occur, children must be able to:

- Understand the intent of the teacher's language for communicating a specific message.
- Perform successfully the action for which they are being prompted.

Teachers can monitor their language by asking two simple and important questions:

- Is your language meaningful to the child?
- Is your language relevant to the task at hand?

Using these questions as guides requires teachers to:

- Identify what the child brings to the task.
- Identify what is important for accomplishing the task.

If a child is expected to apply information before he has the necessary background experience (or concept knowledge), the activity will be empty and meaningless. This means that the child must understand the relevance the teacher's language has for helping himself. The teacher is responsible for observing the child for signs of understanding and adjusting her language to ensure that the child will gain meaning from the interaction. Through recurring successful experiences, the child learns the significance of the teacher's prompts for planning and solving problems. The goal of instruction is achieved when the child learns how to plan and initiate appropriate actions for directing his own reading progress.

## Teaching for Common Understanding

Does your language have meaning to the child? Consider a teacher who repeatedly prompts the child to reread a word of text and sound the first letter. If the child consistently engages in this behavior but does not use it to initiate an appropriate response to the word, the child may not understand the relevance of the prompt. For the teacher's language to be meaningful to the child, the child must experi-

ence a productive attempt. It is only through these successful experiences that the true meaning of the teacher's language becomes evident.

This leads us to an important concept in apprenticeship learning: *intersubjectivity* (Rogoff 1990; Wertsch 1984, 1985). Simply put, this means that the teacher and children share a similar understanding of a particular task. Because of their limited experiences, young learners may be confused by the mature language of the teacher. If a mismatch in communication occurs, the teacher must use language to negotiate understanding and reestablish a common link.

For example, during a shared writing experience (Dorn 1996), Mrs. Reed invites George to write a "little" *d*. George misunderstands her intentions and writes a very small capital *D*. Mrs. Reed realizes her language is creating confusion for George and attempts to clarify her meaning. She picks up the marker and writes a lowercase *d* on the page. With a puzzled expression on his face, George examines the size of Mrs. Reed's *d* and comments, "I thought you said make it little." Mrs. Reed then increases her level of support, writes the two forms, and directs George's attention to them. As she explicitly points to the two letters, she says, "You were making a capital *D*, and I was talking about this kind of *d*. That's a lowercase *d*—or a little *d*." Mrs. Reed accepts responsibility for ensuring that George will gain meaning from the shared experience.

When a teacher is working in a child's zone of proximal development (ZPD), the child's definition of a situation will naturally be different from the teacher's definition (see Wertsch 1984), simply because the ZPD is an area in which the child needs our assistance. Because the development of new learning depends on the child's meaningful interpretation of the situation, the teacher must keep in mind that the child is faced with two challenges (Phillips and Smith 1997):

- To find meaning in the teacher's words.
- To make an appropriate response to the teacher's words in a context that the child does not yet understand.

## Language Principles That Support Problem Solving

Rogoff (1990) characterizes apprenticeship learning as shared problem solving between an active learner and a more skilled partner. She identifies the following features of guided participation: "the importance of routine activities, tacit as well as explicit communication, supportive structuring of novices' efforts, and transfer of responsibility for handling skills to novices" (p. 39). This can be brought about through modeling, coaching, scaffolding, articulating, and reflecting (Collins et al. 1989).

### Modeling

In modeling the teacher demonstrates a literacy task, and the children observe the processes that are required to accomplish the task. Thus the children are provided with a conceptual model of the literacy task before they are asked to attempt to perform it independently. According to Collins et al. (1989, p. 456), a conceptual model gives the child:

- An advanced "organizer" for planning and performing a complex skill.
- A structure for making sense of the teacher's feedback, hints, and corrections.
- An internalized guide for supporting independent practice.

For example, during a writing aloud session at the overhead projector (see Chapter 5), Mrs. Watson models for the children the process of problem solving words as she composes her message. She comments, "When I come to a word I don't know, I can try it out on my practice board. First, I can think of some things I know about other words that can help me. Then I can write the word several ways to see which one looks right to me." Mrs. Watson realizes the relationship between language and action; thus she looks for productive examples to demonstrate the process of solving words. As she works on her practice board, she uses explicit language to describe her actions. During her demonstrations, she carefully observes how the children interpret her performance. From time to time, she offers particular prompts that focus their attention on her problem-solving solutions: "Help me check this. Does it look right to you? Did that help us with that tricky word?"

Being presented with simultaneous models of language and action enables children to observe the types of strategies and skills they need to apply as they problem-solve on their own. Without clear models, children may not be able to conceptualize the goal of instruction. That is, the task may be an abstraction for them, and as a result, they may develop an inappropriate definition of the task. Good models provide children with standards (or benchmarks) against which they can reflect and evaluate their own progress.

### Coaching

Coaching involves guided participation, whereby the teacher observes the children during literacy events and offers hints, reminders, feedback, modeling, and other types of support to ensure successful performance (Collins et al. 1989). Through language prompts, teachers assist the child in integrating various sources of information and applying strategies for working out new solutions.

The following example illustrates the role of language and action in coaching the child to initiate a checking behavior for confirming a visual response to a meaningful substitution during guided reading. When Derrick comes to the word *fast*, he responds with the word *quick*. Mrs. Jones recognizes the importance of this meaningful response, but she wants Derrick to use first-letter cues more efficiently. So she prompts him directly to the source of information he needs to attend to in order to accomplish the expected action: "*Quick* makes sense, but does that word look like *quick*? Read it again and think of a word that would make sense and start with an *f*." With this prompt, Derrick is able to integrate meaning and visual cues in a successful and fluent action. However, were Derrick still unable to accomplish the action, Mrs. Jones needs to be ready to coach him further with a higher level of support. For instance, she might say, "Try the word *fast* and see if it works there," and then prompts him to confirm the response and to apply the knowledge to a new situation: "Did that work? Did it make sense and start with the right letter? I want to see you try that the next time you come to a word you don't know." The goal of coaching is to help the child understand a new concept, *and understanding derives from a meaningful and successful performance.*

As children acquire more problem-solving strategies, the teacher relinquishes more control. For instance, in early learning, the teacher's language is much more explicit and direct; once children understand the significance of the behavior as a way to help them problem-solve, the teacher's language becomes more general: "Try that again," or "Something isn't quite right." As the child learns how to monitor his own reading, the teacher must be careful that her language does not find the error for the child, thus denying him an opportuni-

ty to problem-solve on his own. One question teachers might ask is, Am I requiring the child to correct his mistake before he has found it? If so, the teacher's language may be inhibiting the child's ability to develop effective searching and problem-solving behavior. In apprenticeship, the teacher's language is critical for guiding successful experiences that shape higher-level understanding.

During shared reading (see Chapter 3) and interactive writing (see Chapter 5), the teacher's language serves two purposes:

- To expose children to educational words and concepts that are used during literacy activities.
- To help children understand how the concept label relates to the reading and writing experiences.

Here are some examples of explicit language for teaching print concepts:

| Print Concept | Example of Teacher's Language |
| --- | --- |
| Title | Who can show me the <u>title</u> of our new book? |
| Pictures | What's happening in this <u>picture</u>? |
| Direction | Who can show us <u>where to start</u> reading? Where do we <u>go next</u>? |
| One-to-one matching | Let's <u>point</u> to the words as we read. |
| Words | Who can find the <u>word</u> *me* on this page? |
| Letters | Who can find a word that starts with the <u>letter</u> *b*? |
| Capital letters | Who can find the <u>word</u> *the* with a <u>capital letter</u>? |
| Lowercase letters | Who can find the <u>word</u> *the* with a <u>lowercase letter</u>? |

| | |
|---|---|
| Sequence | Turn to the <u>first page</u> in our story.<br>Turn to the <u>last page</u> in our story. |
| Punctuation | Let's read the <u>punctuation</u>. |

## Scaffolding

Assisting a child in the zone of proximal development is called scaffolding (Bruner 1984). During guided instruction, teachers provide children with varying degrees of support that enable them to accomplish specific tasks. As children become more competent, the scaffolding is removed and the children take over more of the responsibility. Scaffolding is *not* simply a case of breaking learning segments down into scope and sequence. Instead, it is a complex interactive process whereby the teacher regulates levels of support according to how well the children understand the task at hand. An essential quality of a scaffold is that it be self-destructive. By that we mean that the child's behavior signals the teacher, I don't need your help anymore. *I can do this all by myself.*

During scaffolded instruction, levels of support are determined by what the child brings to the task. In the beginning, the teacher may use explicit language and corresponding actions that specifically direct the child to the source of information needed to solve the problem at hand. As the child develops competence, the teacher's support is adjusted to accommodate the child's increasing control.

Consider, for example, how Mrs. Pool provides Tony with varying degrees of support for writing a known word. She first asks Tony to write the word *can,* and the child writes the word *is.* Mrs. Pool realizes that Tony has activated the wrong visual pattern for two known words. She says, "Take a good look at that

word. Is that word *can?*" "No," Tony says, "that's *is.*" Then Mrs. Pool prompts Tony to the source of information needed to activate the correct visual pattern: "Say *can.*" Tony repeats the word. The teacher says, "How would you start to write it?" Tony responds, "C." The teacher confirms, "Yes, it starts with a *c.*" Tony writes the letter *c* and exclaims, "Oh, I know how to do it!" Then he correctly writes the word.

The goal of scaffolding is to provide a temporary structure that enables the child to accomplish the action successfully. However, *the scaffold must provide the minimum amount of support needed by the child at the particular time.* In the previous example, Tony's regressive behavior may have been triggered by the interference of another known word (*is*) or by a new environmental context for writing the word. Whichever the case, Mrs. Pool provides just enough support to enable the child to sort out the confusion and resolve the problem.

The degree of support will depend on how much the child brings to the task. In order to promote self-checking behavior, the teacher should ask:

1. What source of information does the child need to attend to?
2. What is the least amount of support I can give him to ensure he will accomplish the task?

## Articulation

Articulation is any language prompt that encourages children to articulate their knowledge or problem-solving strategies during a particular task (Collins et al. 1989). The purpose of articulation is to make the child more aware of his own cognitive processes. Some examples of language prompts that promote articulation are:

- How did you know?
- What can you try?
- What did you notice?

For example, Mrs. Reed suspects that Sean, an emergent reader, is reading the four-word recurring pattern (I see a _____) based on his memory of the text. So she coaches Sean to locate and confirm first-letter cues. She uses language to help him notice the initial similarity between his name and an unknown word: "Can you find a word on this page that starts like your name?" After Sean successfully locates the word *see,* Mrs. Reed prompts him to articulate the reasoning behind his response: "How is it like your name?" Sean responds, "They both start with an *s.*"

Another way that teachers use articulation is to help children learn how to plan, organize, and reflect on their literacy performances. In this case, articulation is difficult to separate from models and reflection. For instance, before students edit their writing, the teacher says, "Now, what are some important things you need to do when you edit your story?" Or, after a guided reading group, the teacher prompts the children, "Tell me some strategies you used to help yourself when you were reading." In each case, the children must use language to describe good reading and writing practices. Articulation gives children a tool for guiding their own performance. However, in order for articulation to be effective, the children must know the *meaning of the language as it describes a way to help them accomplish the goals of the literacy task.*

There is a point when articulation is discouraged by the teacher. For instance, in Chapter 1, we discussed how an external behavior (speech) becomes an internal behavior (thought) after successful and prolonged practice. If internal speech is the goal, the teacher who insists on the child's verbalization

of well-known information may actually be inhibiting the child from developing automatic responses. At this point, it is more productive to increase the challenge within the child's zone of proximal development rather than spend unnecessary time on something the child no longer needs.

## Reflection

When children become reflective learners, they acquire an important skill that enables them to judge their performance in terms of external standards. This means that children should be taught how to analyze and reflect on their own progress. Some prompts that encourage such reflection are:

- How do you think you did on that?
- Where do you think you did your best work?
- Can you find a part that you would like to spend more time on?
- Did you have any problems with this part?
- Show me the hardest part.

Teachers promote reflection through questions that focus on personal accomplishments. For instance, during a conference with an emergent writer, the teacher might ask the child, "Show me your best letter," or, "Show me a good space." The child thus develops a personal model that can be used as a standard for future comparisons. After these prompts, the teacher might encourage the child to articulate his reasons in order to promote a more conscious awareness of the concept.

While writing aloud, the teacher can also model reflective language. For example, she might pause at a particular sentence and comment, "Does that sentence sound right to say it that way?" Or she might reflect on her story by rereading and evaluating it for clarity: "I need to hear my story to make sure that I have included the most important points for the reader." Through modeling, the teacher demonstrates the value of reflection. Soon, children begin to internalize the teacher's language and use the same prompts to guide their own work.

Finally, teachers can promote reflective activity by introducing editing charts. During assisted writing activities, the teacher guides the children to construct a checklist of relevant areas for monitoring their independent work (some examples of these charts are provided in Chapter 5). Remember, an editing chart is a temporary scaffold that helps promote reflec-

tion. Like all scaffolds, when it has outlived its usefulness, it becomes an unnecessary tool and is eliminated.

## Closing Thoughts

Although we have discussed each language form used in an apprenticeship approach to literacy in isolation, it is wrong to think of language so simplisticly. During any given literacy activity, teachers must employ a range of language forms and provide interactive and adjustable degrees of support for each one.

# Learning to Read

Teaching and learning interactions related to reading need to be examined in four contexts: (a) reading books to children, (b) independent reading of familiar materials, (c) shared reading, and (d) guided reading. We discuss the first three in this chapter; guided reading has its own chapter, Chapter 4. Throughout our discussions, we emphasize the importance of the teacher in creating literacy opportunities that focus on three important learning principles:

- Building on the strengths of learners.
- Using language as an instructional tool.
- Promoting problem-solving processes.

## Deficits Versus Strengths

Recently, Linda asked a group of teachers in a college course how they taught reading to their lowest-achieving children. From their responses, it was clear that their theory was a deficit one guided by their concern about how much the children did not know. Traditionally, we have tested children to identify their weak areas and then designed instruction based on what they do not know. This theory of learning is in direct opposition to what research tells us about how the brain acquires information and then organizes related information into larger networks. Cognitive apprenticeship emphasizes the importance of using known information as a bridge to acquire new knowledge (Rogoff 1990). From this point of view, the old knowledge has the potential to activate new connections and to stimulate higher-level processes in the brain.

Let's apply this theory to our own learning experiences. Think of a topic you feel uncomfortable with (i.e., you don't have the background experiences for making sense of it) and imagine yourself in a class where you are expected to learn new information that relates directly to this topic. You might compensate for your inadequate background by recording and memorizing the basic information and thus be able to satisfy the teacher's requirements. But memorizing information that the brain does not understand forces you to use lower-level systems (Luria 1982; Healy 1990).

In Chapter 1, we discussed the importance of building self-regulatory systems that enable young learners to use their current skills and strategies to initiate new learning. So we can assume that a solid foundation based on conceptual understanding is the tool for promoting higher-level processing in the brain. In contrast, instruction that is based on inadequate background is grounded in a deficit model, which may force young learners to rely on low-level processes.

An important assumption underlying this theory is that teachers must identify the strengths of young children and use this information as the basis for designing rich learning experiences that emphasize problem-solving. Clay (1991) describes how all teachers have a general theory about reading that guides their instructional interactions with their children. She explains that if a teacher's theory is in conflict with her observations of children, the teacher should be prepared to change the theory.

Children need us to be knowledgeable about the reading process. The teacher's role focuses on helping children become self-regulated readers with a repertoire of strategies for independent reading. Instructional interactions are based on the theory that children become proficient readers as they engage in strategic activity for integrating the semantic, syntactic, and graphophonetic sources of information in the text. The teacher's ability to observe the children's processing behavior and to respond contingently are critical forces in developing strategic readers.

## Cues: Sources of Information

A reader who is reading independently is attending to many sources of information—or cues—in the text:

- *Meaning, or semantic, cues.* These derive from the reader's background knowledge and understanding of particular concepts as they relate to the author's purpose and intended message. Reading should always be message driven. An underlying question will be, Does my reading make sense in accordance with what the author is trying to tell me?
- *Structural, or syntactical, cues.* These derive from the reader's control of oral language and exposure to book language. Grammatical substitutions are the most common cue used by young readers. This is not surprising when we remember the ease with which young children manipulate the structures of oral language when learning to talk. While reading, the reader applies structural cues to the text by asking, Does it sound right if I say it this way?
- *Graphophonetic cues.* These derive from the letters and their corresponding sounds. If the reader's response shows evidence of attention to visual cues, then we can assume that the reader has accessed some level of the visual information present in the text. Attention to visual cues may be triggered by a leading question: What have I noticed about this word?

A successful reader integrates all the cues as he reads fluently and expressively with a focus on meaning. The struggling reader has not learned how to integrate multiple sources of information. Instead, he views reading as an isolated process whereby he overly relies on one source of information at the expense of others and is deprived of important feedback from these other sources. The struggling reader must therefore build networks of information and learn how to use these mental storehouses for checking and confirming his or her responses to the text.

## Strategies: Mental Problem-Solving Behavior

Strategies are cognitive actions initiated by the reader to construct meaning from the text. We cannot observe strategies (i.e., in-the-head processes), but we can collect evidence of reading behavior that indicates a child is engaging in mental problem-solving. Children who are employing strategies as they read are engaged in what Clay (1991) refers to as "reading work." From Clay's research with young readers, we know that effective readers are constantly

- Predicting upcoming actions.
- Using pictures to support meaning.
- Anticipating language structures.
- Making links to their own personal knowledge.
- Monitoring by rereading.
- Cross-checking one source of information with another.
- Searching to extract further information from the text to help them with new learning.
- Correcting themselves when cues do not match.
- Reading fluently and expressively.
- Problem-solving flexibly according to different purposes and changing contexts.

All of these processes are brought into play efficiently and automatically by the strategic reader. However, the low-progress reader has developed a processing system that is either ineffective or inefficient. In planning the child's literacy program, it is critical that the teacher observe and take notice of which strategic operations the child is initiating and which ones she or he is neglecting.

To examine strategic use, the teacher will analyze the running record and look closely at cues that were used or ignored by the reader (see Clay's [1993] *Observation Survey* for how to use running records; also, Johnston 1992). The teacher must determine whether the child employed a strategy to help her actively make predictions and confirm or reject the predictions based on other information. To that end the teacher examines the running record for evidence of what the child did at the point of difficulty:

- Did the child stop at an unknown word and make no attempt?
- Did the child appeal for help?
- Did the child reread to gather more information?
- Did the child articulate the first letter of the problem word?
- Was the child using meaning cues (semantics), structural cues (syntax), visual cues (graphophonics), or some combination of these?
(Clay 1993; Fountas and Pinnell 1996)

## What Strategic Reading Looks Like

Each of the following examples of reading behavior demonstrates that the child is well on her way to becoming a proficient reader. In each case, the child is actively involved in the process of constructing meaning based on her own prior knowledge and personal language structures. In order to move the child to a higher level of processing, the teacher uses language to promote cue integration and reading strategies. Reading for meaning is the ultimate goal.

✓ ✓ ✓ big     ✓     ✓     ✓     right ✓ ✓
I saw a — brown horse looking — at me.

Here the child is using his language structures to make sense of the text. He is aware that reading must make sense. However, the teacher knows that the child must gain control of one-to-one matching. So the teacher prompts the child to "read it with your finger and make the words match." If the child experiences difficulty, the teacher assists with the matching process.

   ✓   ✓   ✓  <u>a</u>   ✓
The lion and the giraffe
   ✓  <u>a</u>   ✓   ✓   ✓   ✓
and the elephant wanted the radio.

Here the student introduces a substitution that makes sense with the text. Since the miscue is insignificant, the teacher chooses to ignore it.

   ✓   ✓   ✓   ✓   ✓
And the pumpkin seed grew
   ✓   ✓   <u>sprig</u>
a pumpkin sprout.

Here the reader substitutes a word that is meaningful and structurally appropriate and also contains some visual similarities. Based on previous observations, the teacher realizes that the child possesses visual knowledge for investigating the word *sprout* further. Therefore she uses the miscue as an opportunity to direct the child's attention to searching behavior, prompting, "Try this again." The *accuracy* of the word is not the issue; rather, it is the *opportunity* the word offers the beginning reader to apply problem-solving strategies.

  ✓  ✓  ✓  ✓  ✓ ✓  ✓ ✓
"I've made some cookies for tea," said Ma.
  ✓  ✓  ✓  ✓  ✓
"Good," said Victoria and Sam.

  ✓  <u>hungry / starting / SC</u>
"We're starving."         R

In this final example, the reader uses a range of problem-solving strategies as she works diligently to create a match between meaning, structural, and visual cues. First, she makes a prediction that is based on meaning and language structures but quickly rejects this information because of the inappropriate visual match. Next, the reader taps into her visual storehouse (her knowledge of *st* and *ing* patterns) and uses this knowledge to initiate a new response to the text. When the reader realizes this second attempt does not make sense in the story, she searches further for a new word that will satisfy her expectations for meaning and visual matches. This process results in self-correcting (SC) activity. In a final transaction with the text, the reader repeats the pattern "We're starving" with an emphasis that indicates a full understanding of the author's intended message. During this short process, we see the reader engaged in self-monitoring, searching, and self-correcting behavior that is driven by the desire to create a meaningful story.

These readers all made miscues, but the errors in each sample preserved the meaning of the text. Each reader used a strategic process to anticipate what the text would say, but each one was at a different level in his or her control of the reading process. In order to move the child to a higher level of reading development (a) the teacher must be a good observer of the child's processing behavior and (b) the teacher must have a good understanding of the reading process.

## Accuracy Versus Problem-Solving

The language a teacher uses when responding to a child's miscues should help beginning readers build effective processing systems for learning how to read. When teachers pose questions to young readers, they should consider the value of today's prompts for tomorrow's problem-solving actions: How can I prompt the child in such a way that he can use this information as a tool to help himself later when he encounters an unknown word?

The type of prompts used by a teacher can be a determining factor in how the child perceives the reading process. The reading behavior in the previous examples is evidence that these children view reading as a process of gaining meaning from the text. In contrast, the following example emphasizes "word level" response at the expense of constructing meaning.

> A child is reading a predictable story with a cumulative pattern that builds on the actions of several animals who swim to a rock to take a nap. The story ends when the crocodile swims to the rock and eats the animals for lunch. As the child reads the text, he comes to the unknown word *lunch* and hesitates. The teacher prompts the child with an off-task question that focuses on getting the word correct: "What are we getting ready to eat?" The child exclaims, "Lunch!" The teacher praises the child's response with her comment, "Yes! Lunch! Good job."

The trouble with this interaction is that the child has missed an opportunity to predict a meaningful event based on logical expectations for how this story might end. At the same time, ineffective behavior has been reinforced so that the child develops an inappropriate definition of reading that will influence his reading behavior tomorrow. In this example, the child did not apply *any* textual information to help solve the unknown word. The prompt "What are we getting ready to eat?" has absolutely nothing to do with the story and has no value for decoding the visual information.

How can we prompt beginning readers to use visual information in a productive process that leads to new learning? We know that reading is a process of integrating multiple cues from text in order to construct meaning for the author's message. We also know that we must pay attention to visual information, for the printed symbols on the page are graphic signals whereby the message is communicated. Without the visual information, reading cannot occur. Teachers must therefore help young readers learn how to use visual information in fluent and flexible ways.

## Problem-Solving with Analogies

The children in Cathy's guided reading group have just finished reading a story about a baby bird. Cathy observes that several children are having difficulty with the word *something*. She decides this word is a nice example for helping children learn how to problem-solve with analysis, analogy, and integration.

In preparation, Cathy passes out small dry-erase boards for each child in the reading group. Then she records the sentence from the story—"I must get something for my baby bird to eat"—on a large dry-erase board at the front of the reading table. As she points to the word *something*, she remarks, "I noticed that several of you were having a little trouble with this word when you were reading." As she runs her finger under the word, she adds, "Let's take a good look at some things you already know that will help you solve this tricky word."

Cathy then guides the children so that they will learn how to access known information and use it to help them decipher unknown words. First she instructs the children to write the word *come* (a known word) on their individual boards. Then she asks them to erase the *c* from *come* and put an *s* in front of it. Simultaneously, Cathy performs this simple analogy at the large board so the children can confirm their attempts with her work. "What new word did you make?" she asks. "Some!" the group responds. Then Cathy says, "Jeremy, frame the word *some* in the sentence at the board." Next she models for the children how to learn a new word (*thing*) by manipulating two known parts (*th* and *ing*) from two other known words (*the* and *going*). She uses precise language and clear demonstrations to make the process of learning new words through analysis and integration explicit. After the demonstration, Cathy tells the children, "Now read the sentence and see if the word makes sense and looks right to you."

## A Balanced Reading Program

A balanced reading program includes a range of literacy activities, carefully selected materials for each activity, and a responsive teacher who knows how to structure literacy interactions that move children to higher levels of understanding. In an apprenticeship approach, the teacher asks the following questions:

- What can the children do alone? What can the children do with my help?
- What types of materials will support the children in applying their current knowledge, strategies, and skills?
- How does each type of literacy activity support the children in building effective reading systems?
- What sort of guidance do I provide the children in each activity?

The components of a balanced reading program would include many opportunities for children to learn about the reading process through the following:

- *Being read to.* This allows children to hear more complex language patterns that

would be too difficult for them to read by themselves. As the teacher reads, the children listen and respond to the story.

- *Rereading familiar books.* This allows children independently to practice cue integration and strategy application on familiar materials. Teacher support can be lessened because the familiar texts provide their own support system.
- *Shared reading.* This allows children to learn important concepts about reading and to practice effective behavior in a group assisted activity. As the teacher shares an enlarged text with a small group of children, she creates instructional conversations that guide the children to apply their knowledge and strategies to the reading situation.
- *Guided reading.* This allows children to practice effective reading strategies on texts at their instructional level with the guidance of their teacher. As the children read supportive texts with a minimum of new challenges, the teacher observes their processing behavior and adjusts her degree of support to accommodate their problem-solving actions.

The overlapping and reciprocal benefits of the four types of reading events are illustrated in Figure 3.1. The rest of this chapter and Chapter 4 examine the teacher's role in each of these components.

## Reading Stories to Children

A well-balanced literacy program includes opportunities for children to hear stories that they are unable to read for themselves. Reading aloud to children appears to be the single most important factor for building critical concepts about reading (McCormick 1977; Teale 1984). We know that young children who

**Figure 3.1** The reciprocal relationship between four reading events.

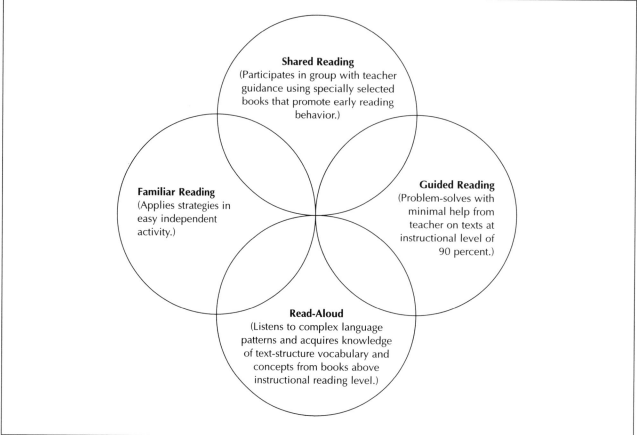

Shared Reading
(Participates in group with teacher guidance using specially selected books that promote early reading behavior.)

Familiar Reading
(Applies strategies in easy independent activity.)

Guided Reading
(Problem-solves with minimal help from teacher on texts at instructional level of 90 percent.)

Read-Aloud
(Listens to complex language patterns and acquires knowledge of text-structure vocabulary and concepts from books above instructional reading level.)

are exposed to book experiences in interactive literacy settings develop a complex range of attitudes, concepts, and skills that form the foundation of school-based literacy.

Reading to children introduces them to the language of books, which is different from speech and conversation. As children hear stories read to them, they acquire knowledge about book concepts, story structures, literary language, and specialized vocabulary and begin to anticipate that particular structures will occur within written language. They discover recurring relationships between various texts and discourse patterns. This knowledge gives children a personal foundation for making meaningful predictions as they read stories on their own.

Hill (1989) explains that reading stories aloud to children provides the following opportunities for reading development:

- It opens up their world to new and exciting knowledge.
- It helps them learn concepts without having to worry about words.
- It exposes them to books they may want to read at a later time.
- It bridges the gap between oral and written language.
- It helps them overcome any fear of words they may have.

The purposes of reading aloud to children are to:

- Provide a good model of fluent and expressive reading.
- Expose children to a wide variety of story structures, genres, characters, and writing styles.
- Provide opportunities for writing.
- Provide opportunities for retelling.
- Increase children's concept and vocabulary knowledge.
- Promote an enjoyable experience with books.

You should prepare very carefully before you read a story. First, include a brief introduction that answers any questions about the characters, plot, or setting. Second, read the story expressively and with evident enjoyment. At appropriate points in the story, invite the children to respond to particular events. Afterward, engage the children in an interactive discussion; let them ask questions and solicit their feelings and comments.

Teale (1984) describes reading books aloud as "one type of social interactional activity from which the child can internalize features necessary for reading and writing" (p. 118). Listening to stories provides the child with important tools for building bridges to new learning.

## Familiar Reading

As children read familiar materials, they learn how to become successful readers. The familiar context of the story provides opportunities to apply strategies in an integrated process. With each rereading, the child is able to anticipate the textual response more quickly, simultaneously freeing the brain to focus attention on constructing higher-level understanding about the story.

The familiarity of an easy book allows the child to practice fluent processing behavior. Clay (1991) describes it this way:

When readers are allowed to reread familiar material, they are being allowed to learn to be readers, to read in ways which draw on all their language resources and knowledge of the world, to put this very complex recall and sequencing behavior into a fluent rendering of the text. The orchestration of these complex behaviors cannot be achieved on a hard book. (p. 184)

The teacher can use the context of a familiar book to teach the child how to search for graphophonetic information. For example, the teacher can direct an emergent reader's attention to frequently encountered words with prompts such as, Can you find the word *the* on this page? Can you find the word *The* with a capital letter? To help children connect reading and writing, the teacher can prompt the child to notice links: Can you find a word on this page that you know how to write in your stories? After the child has written the word, the teacher might ask the child to compare the two words: Take a good look at the word in your story and look at the word you just wrote. Do they look the same? In this way, the teacher enables the child to develop a more conscious awareness of the reciprocal relationship between reading and writing.

In summary, the reading of familiar materials enables the child to:

- Make meaningful predictions that can be checked against visual information.
- Practice effective strategies on easy material.
- Read with fluency and expression.
- Experience the pleasure of revisiting favorite stories.
- Become more knowledgeable about story structure and vocabulary.
- Problem-solve independently.

The teacher's role in organizing familiar reading is crucial. Books should be selected based on observations of the children's processing behavior across time, not left to chance or based entirely on the children's preferences. Children must have appropriate materials that build on their current knowledge and promote successful reading strategies. So the teacher prepares baskets of familiar books that include specially selected texts that the children can read with at least 90 percent accuracy. The children then select their familiar reading books from this collection of texts. As the children read, the teacher circulates and observes.

Some examples of familiar reading material include chart stories, alphabet books, poems, Big Books, and reproductions of shared stories that may be hanging around the room. The only selection criteria are that the children are familiar with the texts and that they enjoy reading them.

# Shared Reading

Shared reading is an apprenticeship: the teacher reads with the children, and the children actively contribute to the reading with the teacher's guidance. As the children become more familiar with the story, the teacher's support fluctuates in response to her observations of the children's developing control. She uses the familiar context of the shared book as a tool for directing the children's attention to new problem-solving activity.

Children enjoy shared reading because it enables them to begin reading successfully from their first day of school. It is an important experience for less able readers who enter school with limited exposures to books and print. It is a nonthreatening and enjoyable way to strengthen the language skills of struggling readers. When children read familiar texts over and over, they build literacy skills without boring, repetitive worksheet drills.

## Choosing Texts

Choosing the right text is important: it needs to provide a supportive context that helps young children learn about the reading process. Many teachers use a variety of materials for shared reading:

- Big Books.
- Poems on charts.
- Poems on transparencies.
- Enlarged texts.
- Nursery rhyme charts.
- Raps.
- Favorite songs.
- Finger plays.
- Wall stories written during interactive or writing aloud activities.

Choosing a text that both the teacher and children will enjoy should be the first consideration. Books that have predictable story lines, make use of repeated phrases, include rhythm or rhyme, and incorporate natural spoken language are the ones children will want to read over and over again. Overall, teachers need to create a relaxing, supportive reading experience for young readers.

Another crucial consideration when choosing texts is the size of the print. Ideally, children should gather closely around the teacher in an effort to simulate the intimacy of parents reading to their children. However, the text must be enlarged so that each child will be able to follow the print. Too often, teachers gather their entire class around a commercial Big Book that has tiny print rather than oversize print, too many lines of text per page, or unusual placement of text on the page. This hinders the children's ability to build their knowledge of print conventions. It is important that teachers keep in mind the needs of the children and the purpose of reading as they select texts.

## A Specific Example of Shared Reading

This example involves a small group of six children in a first-grade class. As the teacher works with the group, the remaining children in the class pursue a range of independent activities: familiar reading, illustrating the text of a class-written book, writing stories on the computer, and listening to books on tape.

The teacher has carefully selected *Goodnight, Goodnight* (Parkes 1989) and has examined the book for supportive and challenging features in relation to the strengths and needs of the children. (The amount of teacher support required during a first reading varies, depending on the number of experiences that the children have had with books, the type of text, and the particular concepts about print on which the teacher intends to focus.)

The teacher introduces the children to the book by setting the scene. First, she reads the title and asks the children to look at the picture on the cover. "What will happen in this story?" she wonders. Several children respond, "The little girl is going to bed." The teacher validates this response and encourages the children to make further predictions as they look at the pictures and discuss the story's development:

**Teacher:** She's going to bed, isn't she? Because she has her nightgown on and she's in the bedroom. Do you see anything else in the picture?
**James:** She has her teddy bear in bed.
**Sheena:** She's reading a book to her animals.
**Teacher:** In this story, the little girl is reading some bedtime stories and she has a dream about some of her nursery rhyme friends who come out to play with her. Let's look at the first two pages and see who might come out of the storybook.
**Thomas:** There's a lady in her room!
**Teacher:** Yes, there is a lady. Where do you think she might be looking?

**Sheena:** In that door.
**Tanisha:** That's a closet!
**Thomas:** She's looking on the floor in the closet!
**Teacher:** Those are all good guesses from looking at the pictures. Let's read and see if we can find more clues about who this lady is and what she is doing in the story.

The teacher reads several of the pages with expression and without interruption. As she reads, she points to each word, thus modeling the relationship of spoken to written language. After hearing the repetitive pattern only two or three times, the children are able to initiate some of the reading on subsequent pages. The teacher helps this along by pausing at predictable points in the story, inviting the children to take over. She continues to direct their attention to the pictures and the rhyming patterns of the language as ways they can predict and confirm their responses:

**Teacher:** (*Reading story*)
"I love to read in bed at night.
Then Teddy and I turn out the light.
And as we dream the night away,
our storybook friends come out to play.
Who's that looking in my cupboard?
It's my friend Old…"
**Tanisha:** Mother Hubbard!
**Teacher:** What makes you think it might be Old Mother Hubbard?
**Tanisha:** Because it said *cupboard*. That's like *Hubbard.*
**Teacher:** Let's try it together.
**All:** "Who's that looking in my cupboard? It's my friend Old Mother Hubbard!"
**Teacher:** Were you right?
**Children:** Yes!

The next page gives the children another opportunity to predict a word that sounds the same:

**Teacher:** "Jump on the bed and join the fun. There's lots of room for…"
**All:** Everyone!
**Teacher:** Aren't you smart!! You thought of a word that makes sense and rhymes with *fun*! *Everyone.* Let's read it together.

Similar interactions occur throughout the reading of the text. The children's repeated exposure to the structure of the story enables them to make faster predictions. They are learning how to apply two important strategies to their reading: (a) predicting from picture cues and language structures and (b) listening to the rhyming patterns of words. The teacher guides the reading so that the children can practice fluent and expressive phrasing of language, thus serving as a personal model for how reading should sound.

## Teaching for Strategies

The teacher uses the supportive context of shared reading to:

- Model and teach early concepts about print, such as directionality and one-to one matching.
- Locate some known words and letters.
- Predict some letter/sound correspondence.
- Teach reading strategies such as rereading to monitor, predicting and confirming responses, cross-checking one cue against another, and searching for additional information to resolve conflict.
- Teach book conventions such as title, table of contents, author, and illustrator.

In addition to multiple rereadings, the teacher uses quick, focused activities to direct the children's attention to specific features of the text and to show them how to apply problem-solving strategies. The following tools are helpful here:

- A pointer.
- Framing cards.
- Masking questions.
- Cloze procedures.
- Sentence strips.
- Word cards.

These activities should be done sparingly and quickly; the teacher will choose only two or three teaching points for each shared reading.

## Framing Cards and Masking Questions

Framing cards and masking questions (Fisher 1991) help children notice specific concepts about print. Masking questions are prompts the teacher uses to direct the children's attention to a particular aspect of the text, which they then isolate with a framing card (a card with a "window" in the middle of it). The windows in framing cards are of different sizes in order to isolate different visual aspects of the text (one letter, a two-letter word, a four-letter word, a phrase, etc.). In the excerpt below, the teacher uses this technique to help the children apply their knowledge of beginning sounds (*onset*) and ending patterns (*rime*) to locate a new word in the text. (See Chapter 7 for an explanation of onset and rime.)

**Teacher:** Who can find a word that starts like *house* and rhymes with *dad*? (*Andrew raises his hand*) Okay, Andrew. Use the framing card to tell us the answer.
**Andrew:** (*Framing had*) *Had.*
**Teacher:** Great job! *Had* starts like *house* and rhymes with *dad*. Now let's read it in the story.

Frames can be used to locate:

**Figure 3.2** Using framing cards to isolate specific aspects of the text.

- Known words.
- Rhyming words.
- Specific letters.
- Frequenctly encountered words.
- Punctuation.
- Word endings.

## Cloze Procedure

Sometimes teachers use a cloze procedure to help children predict a word based on meaning or to apply cross-checking strategies. A simple way to do this is by placing a sticky note on top of words at various points in the text. The teacher reads the story up to that point and asks the children to make a prediction that makes sense. Then she asks the children to predict the letter they would expect to see at the beginning of their word. The teacher writes all the letter predictions on the board. Next she uncovers the first letter of the word, and the children confirm or reject their predic-

tion based on this additional information. Then the teacher articulates the word slowly and encourages the children to make further predictions based on the sounds within the word. Throughout this process, the teacher guides the children to apply predicting, confirming, cross-checking, and searching strategies. Here's a specific example using a poem:

**Teacher and Children:** (*Reading together*)
"Rabbit
My rabbit has two big ears
And a funny little _____.
He likes to nibble c_____
And he hops wherever he goes."
**Teacher:** "My rabbit has two big ears and a funny little…" Who wants to make a guess on something that might make sense in this sentence?
**Terry:** Nose!
**Justin:** Tail!
**Eli:** Mouth!
**Teacher:** Those are good guesses because they all make sense.
"And a funny little nose."
"And a funny little tail."
"And a funny little mouth."

Notice how the teacher validates the children's responses in two ways: (a) she praises them for making good guesses and (b) she repeats each response so that the children can hear how they all make sense. As the dialogue continues, the teacher pushes the learning to a new level by prompting the children to use first-letter cues to confirm or reject their initial response:

**Teacher:** What letter would you expect to see at the beginning of the word *nose*?
**All:** *N.*
**Teacher:** What letter would you expect to see at the beginning of the word *tail*?

**All:** *T.*

**Teacher:** What letter would you expect to see at the beginning of the word *mouth*?

**All:** *M.*

**Teacher:** Well, you all made good guesses based on what would make sense in the poem. Now we need to check further by looking at the first letter in the word.

At this point, the teacher uncovers the first letter of the word and the children apply strategies for confirming or rejecting their initial responses.

**James:** Oh, mine's not right!

**Eli:** Neither is mine.

**Teacher:** How do you know?

**Eli:** Because it doesn't start with an *n*.

**James:** Because there's no *t* in it.

**Teacher:** Could this word be *nose*?

**Terry:** Yes!

After the children confirm the word based on first-letter cues, the teacher prompts them to check their choice with meaning cues. She asks, "Can anyone think of another word that starts with an *n* and would make sense in the sentence? 'My rabbit has two big ears and a funny little *n- n- n-*...'" When the children say no, the teacher highlights the importance of using multiple sources of information during reading: "So the word *nose* makes sense in our story and it starts with the right letter. You found two ways to check on the word."

The dialogue below focuses on helping the children listen to the sounds within the word and predict the letters associated with these sounds.

**Teacher:** Before I uncover the whole word, can you tell me any other letters that you might expect to see in the word *nose*?

**Terry:** *S.*

**Eli:** *O.*

**Teacher:** Let's look. (*Uncovering the word and reading*) "My rabbit has two big ears and a funny little nose." Were you right?

All: Yes.

## Reading an Alphabet Chart

A common activity in kindergarten or early in first grade is for the teacher and children to participate in a shared reading of an enlarged alphabet chart. The purpose is to help the children acquire letter-sound alphabet cues they can use when they are reading and writing. Each child has a reduced version of the chart, which is also used during independent writing.

The children and the teacher gather around the chart, and the teacher leads the children in saying the name of each upper- and lowercase letter and pointing to an adjacent drawing of something beginning with that letter (A, a, apple, B, b, ball, etc.). The letters are read fluently, and the teacher pauses

**Figure 3.3** Using word cards to match the text of a familiar poem.

occasionally to allow the children to say the letters or the name of the picture symbol. As the children become more competent, the teacher increases the difficulty of the task:

- "Read the tall letters only."
- "Read the lowercase letters only."
- "Read the picture cues only."
- "Read the rounded letters only."

## Sentence Strips and Word Cards

Teachers use sentence strips and word cards to extend the shared reading experience. The text of a familiar story is gradually rebuilt as the teacher prompts the children to match the text fragments to the story by placing sentence strips into pockets on a chart. First the teacher passes out strips of paper containing individual sentences from the story. Then she asks, "Who has the first line of our story?" The child with this line of text goes to the chart and places her line in the first pocket. After each line is added, the teacher guides the children in rereading the sentence strips to see what

should come next. Each child contributes his or her sentence until the story is completed. Finally the teacher prompts the children to reread the story on the chart and to check it against the published version.

The same activity can be adapted for word cards. First, the teacher and children read a sentence from the shared book; then, the teacher passes out cards containing individual words from the sentence. The children rebuild the words into the sentence. Each time a word is added, it is important that the teacher and children reread the sentence to predict the next word needed.

## Cut-Up Poems

Poems are frequently used for shared reading. Once children have heard a poem many times, the teacher can photocopy the poem and cut it into meaningful chunks that can be "rebuilt." Children reassemble the poem by using the familiar language structure to predict and con-

**Figure 3.5** Learning how to build sentences and stories by assembling cut-up words from familiar texts.

**Figure 3.4** A shared reading of an alphabet chart.

firm the visual features of print. The jigsaw format is self-correcting. (The cut-up poems can be stored in Zip-lock plastic baggies and placed in poetry centers where children can work independently.)

## More on Shared Reading with Poetry

Poetry provides young children with rich opportunities to hear the rhythm of language and to develop phonological awareness of sound patterns. Oral language is a natural foundation for learning how to read. When children expect particular language patterns to occur in text, they have a reliable means of relating the structure of language to its visual features. The teacher guides the process by using prompts that direct the children's attention to cue integration. (Chapter 7 discusses the use of poetry in more detail.)

In most kindergarten and first-grade classrooms, shared reading of poetry is a daily activity. We encourage teachers to expose young children to hundreds of poems, thus building a rich storehouse of language patterns for supporting reading development.

## Shared Reading in a First-Grade Class

We close this section by eavesdropping on Angela as she conducts a shared reading with her first graders. She gathers the children around her to introduce them to a new book. *The Enormous Watermelon* (Parkes 1986) recounts the antics of nursery rhyme characters who work together trying to pull an enormous watermelon out of the ground. Angela begins by talking about nursery rhymes.

**Angela:** What do we know about nursery rhymes?
**Suzy:** They always rhyme.
**Angela:** That's right. What is an example of a nursery rhyme? Who knows?

**George:** "Jack jumped over the candlestick."
**Angela:** (*Validating George's knowledge and prompting him to remember the language pattern*) "Jack be nimble. . ."
**George:** (*Chanting in rhythm*) "Jack be nimble. Jack be quick. Jack jumped over the candlestick."

Angela and George share the experience of reciting the poem. Angela's supportive language helps maintain the integrity of the rhythm and rhyme associated with poetry.

**Angela:** "Jack jumped high…"
**George:** "And Jack jumped low.
Jack jumped over and bumped his toe."

Angela next invites other children to share favorite nursery rhymes. She modulates her voice and pauses at appropriate points so that the children can predict upcoming language patterns.

**Angela:** Do you have a favorite nursery rhyme, Dexter?
**Dexter:** "Hey, Diddle Diddle."
**Angela:** "Hey, Diddle Diddle, the cat and the…" (*Pausing with a slight rise in her voice to stimulate the next response*)
**Dexter:** "…fiddle!"
**Angela:** "The cow jumped over the moon."
**All:** "The little dog laughed to see such a sight. And the dish ran away with the spoon."

During the lesson, Angela pulls out familiar poems that have been written on large colorful posters and leads the children in fluent rereadings. The children are exposed to poetry's specialized vocabulary and literary patterns. For example, when the children read the line "rapping at the windows," Suzy asks, "What does *rapping* mean?" Dexter responds, "It's just another word for *knocking*." "Old

Mother Hubbard" provides another opportunity for vocabulary development. When the word *bare* is read in text, the children develop a new understanding of its significance in regard to the fate of the characters:

**CC:** What does *bare* mean?
**Dexter:** It means empty.
**Angela:** Yes, the cupboard was empty. There was nothing in it.
**Suzy:** What did she eat?
**Angela:** I guess nothing. The cupboard was bare, so she didn't have anything to eat, and neither did the dog.
**George:** They're probably starving.

Remembering these familiar nursery rhyme characters has set the stage for the shared reading of the new book. Angela now holds up the book; the cover has a picture of an old woman pulling a large watermelon out of the ground.

**Angela:** Let me show you what today's book is going to be about. It's called *The Enormous Watermelon*. We've been talking about nursery rhymes, so what do you think this book is going to be about?
**Suzy:** A watermelon.
**Angela:** (*Confirming Suzy's prediction while encouraging more ideas*) Well, it has a watermelon on the cover. What else do you think this book is going to be about?
**Dexter:** I think they are going to try and get it out.
**Angela:** Who?
**CC:** Some people.
**Angela:** (*Continuing to prompt for more information*) Do you have any idea who the people might be?
**George:** Some nursery rhyme people!
**Suzy:** (*Leaning forward and pointing to the old woman on the cover*) She's going to pull it out.

**Angela:** (*Prompting Suzy to justify her prediction*) How can you tell?
**Suzy:** Because she's got some water there on her face.
**Angela:** Because she's sweating? Is she pulling so hard that she's sweating?
**Several children in unison:** Yeah!

The dialogue above is characteristic of an apprenticeship approach to literacy. Angela prompts the children to use clues from the cover and from their background experiences to establish a predictable framework for the story.

**Angela:** This story is called *The Enormous Watermelon*. What does *enormous* mean?
**CC:** It means bad.
**George:** No. It means *really, really* big.
**Angela:** (*Prompting the children to explain their predictions*) Well, how do you know what the word means?
**Suzy:** (*Pointing to the large watermelon on the cover of the book*) Because it's *really* big. Because big means big!
**Angela:** Yes. That is a *really* big watermelon! So, we can call it an *enormous* watermelon.

Next Angela introduces the concept of "retelling."

**Angela:** This story is retold by Brenda Parkes.
**Brandon:** Retold?? What's retold?
**Angela:** Retold means that someone else wrote it a long time ago, and Brenda Parkes decided to redo it herself. So she retold the story in her own words.
**CC:** She just put in some words? And put some things in it?
**Angela:** Well, maybe she just changed the story a little bit, retold it in her own words. Like if you wanted to tell the story to a friend or write about it in your jour-

nal, you might use your own words to tell about it. (*Prompting the children to listen carefully to her next question, which focuses on the main character*) Now here's a really important question. (*Points to the old woman on the cover*) Who do think this old woman is? Who have we been talking about today that this might be?

**Brandon:** Old Mother Hubbard!

**Angela:** Do you think this could be Old Mother Hubbard planting a watermelon seed?

**Suzy:** (*Aware that an author may pull from different sources when retelling a story*) She probably got that out of a nursery rhyme.

**George:** Or Old Mother Goose.

As the shared reading continues, the children focus on creative ways for helping Old Mother Hubbard pull the enormous watermelon out of the ground. They express excitement as familiar characters from nursery rhymes appear in the pages of the story. Brandon comments that Humpty Dumpty looks different in this book. Angela explains, "That's not the important thing in the story. Because every illustrator draws their pictures a little different." When a pail of water appears in one corner of the page, Suzy points to the bucket and comments, "That's Jack. That gives us a clue." Angela reinforces this behavior, saying, "Yes, that does give us a clue, doesn't it. On every page, we have a pattern of clues. Let's look for more clues as we turn the pages."

As the story ends and the enormous watermelon remains in the ground, the children offer advice. Suzy indicates her impatience with the characters' efforts to continue with a plan that seems to be getting them nowhere. In a slightly irritated voice, she exclaims, "They need to try something a little bit better than that!" About that time the watermelon comes out of the ground, and all the children seem relieved. As the characters return to the house with the watermelon, Angela asks, "What do you think they are going to do when they get inside?" Several children respond, "Try to eat it," but Brandon remarks, "Get a drink of water." This response is a logical prediction because the characters have worked so hard to get the watermelon out of the ground; a drink of water might be the first thing on their mind! However, as the last page of the story is turned, the children confirm their predictions and the group exclaims in unison, "They ate it!" Brandon remarks, "I would eat it, too!"

# Guided Reading

Recently a great deal of attention has been focused on the importance of grouping children according to their instructional needs. At the same time, we want to be careful not to repeat the errors of the past—that is, placing children in static groups that remain the same year after year. Individual children make progress at different rates; thus we need to group (and regroup) them for guided reading based on careful observations of how they are applying their skills, knowledge, and strategies while they are reading and writing. In their excellent book on learning how to conduct guided reading groups within the context of a balanced literacy program, Fountas and Pinnell (1996) also emphasize flexible grouping based on children's developing control of the reading process.

In guided reading, the teacher works with a small group of children with similar instructional needs. The teacher's role is to predict the type and amount of support the group needs in order to be able to read and understand the book or story. She prompts them to apply reading strategies, regulating her assis-

tance according to the developing control of the individual children in the group. She intervenes only when a student is unlikely to problem-solve independently, is frustrated, or is in jeopardy of losing meaning and does so by asking questions that relate to the reading process. She also provides specific feedback that praises an appropriate processing behavior: for example, "That's good that you went back to the beginning and reread that part. That helped you to figure it out."

Guided reading helps children develop an appreciation and understanding of the story and at the same time stimulates problem-solving conversations about how to apply reading strategies in context. Competence as well as independence is encouraged as the teacher models ways of responding when one encounters difficulty in text.

## When Do I Begin Guided Reading in My Classroom?

Although there isn't a pat answer to this question, there are observable characteristics that indicate children are ready to participate in these more formal groupings:

- Do they have many of the early concepts of print almost under control (i.e., can they distinguish between text and illustration)?
- Do they have some understanding of directionality?
- Do they have some knowledge of one-to-one matching?
- Do they know the difference between letters and words?
- Do they know the letters of the alphabet and a few frequently encountered words (e.g., *I*, *the*, *a*)?
- Do they actively participate in shared reading by predicting events and language structures that show an awareness of comprehension, rhythm, and rhyme?
- Do they spend time reading and noticing a few details of print?
- Do they explore the print on the classroom's walls?
- Do they notice that the same words appear in many different contexts?
- Do they link sounds with symbols when they write?
- Do they articulate words slowly as they write?

If the answer to some of these questions is yes, chances are children are ready to learn more about how printed language works. Some children are ready to begin guided reading in kindergarten, while others need many more opportunities and experiences with print before reading a book in a small group.

## Elements of a Guided Reading Lesson

### Book Selection

Book selection is critical. Books need to be chosen based on children's interests, prior knowl-

edge, and competency. When selecting books for young readers, teachers should consider important factors such as text layout, specialized vocabulary or concepts, the child's oral language facility, and his potential to apply problem-solving strategies to figure out the words he is unlikely to know. A carefully selected book enables a child to learn more about reading each time he reads.

The book selected needs to be able to be read at 90 percent accuracy or better. Analyzing running records of previously read texts (see Clay 1993) will help you with this judgment call. When reading accuracy falls below 90 percent, the child may be unable to retain the meaning of the story.

Many books that might be considered easy for some children can be too difficult for others. Reading is a problem-solving process by which the reader creates meaning through interacting with the text. Meaning is created as the reader brings prior knowledge and personal experience to the page. The physical design of books and the way their stories are constructed are critical elements in the process. Children begin school with varied literacy backgrounds—some have so little experience that they may not even understand that the print conveys the message. Limited experiences in a child's environment may hinder his or her understanding of the content (e.g., if a child has never been to a zoo, he may be unfamiliar with some of the animals in a zoo book). Therefore, teachers must be very careful to select books for beginning readers that not only meet the goal of instruction but also support the children's level of knowledge and experience: are the picture cues clear? is the type large enough? is the layout of the text easy to follow? does it require knowing about certain concepts?

For a child to be able to read a book effectively, the book needs to contain more supportive features than challenging ones. Answering the following questions should help you select an appropriate book for guided reading:

1. Does the book allow the child to construct meaning?
2. Does the book contain structural patterns that are within the child's language control?
3. Does the book include letters and some words that the child can use to monitor his or her reading?
4. Does the book allow the child to use his or her current strategies and skills to problem-solve?
5. Does the book promote fluency?
6. What are the supportive features of the book?
7. What are the challenging features of the book?

## Setting the Focus

In cognitive apprenticeship, the teacher is the more capable person. Through sensitive observation, she is always aware of the cutting edge of her children's development. The focus of a guided reading lesson is determined by the strengths and needs of the children in the group. The teacher can use the following questions (Clay 1991; Fountas and Pinnell 1996) to help her set the proper focus for instruction:

1. Can the child match one-to-one?
2. What strategies is the child using (e.g., rereading, searching pictures, using first-letter cues, noticing chunks in words)?
3. What strategies does the child not use?
4. What does the child do at point of difficulty (e.g., appeal to the teacher, sound out the word, reread, correct himself)?

As children become competent readers, the focus of instruction may shift to deepening their understanding of the story. For example, the teacher may ask questions about the characters and the plot, the author's writing style, characteristics of the genre, or literary devices used by the writer to express meaning.

## Book Introduction

Before a group reads a new book, the teacher introduces the book. The introduction prepares children to read the story by creating a supportive context for building meaning. The teacher relates the story to the children's personal experiences, invites them to make predictions about the book based on its cover, and identifies the title, author, and illustrator. In her orientation, the teacher prompts the children to integrate meaning, structural, and visual cues. She helps the children build *meaning* by giving a brief overview of the story and prompting them to discuss the pictures. She exposes them to *structure* by identifying recurring language phrases and patterns, being careful to use the precise vocabulary of the story as she and the children talk about it. She introduces the children to visual or *graphophonetic* cues by having them find a frequently encountered word they know or predict a letter at the beginning of an unknown word. As the children gain more control, she can ask them to predict letters in ending and medial positions as well. As the children become more competent readers, the introductory discussion can include a conversation about the content, characters, setting, plot, and writing style.

The book orientation provides a framework for children to use as they explore the written text. The teacher sets the purpose for reading and quickly discusses with the group how to overcome possible challenges within the text. This gentle reminder encourages the children to consider alternatives and to make informed decisions in order to gain meaning. Their attention is freed so they can concentrate more closely on the visual details of words and letters when they need to.

The level of support in the introduction diminishes as the children move toward self-regulated reading. During the emergent reading stage, the teacher provides a rich introduction with active discussions around the pictures and the story line. As the children move into subsequent stages, the introduction may be reduced to a summary statement and a few selective questions about the story. When the children have become fluent, self-regulated readers, they introduce the books themselves, with only a little help from the teacher. Figure 4.1 illustrates how the teacher adjusts her degree of support as children develop control of the reading process. As the children become more competent readers, they are able to introduce new books to themselves, a necessary skill for independent reading.

## First Reading

Once the story has been introduced, the children have the background for constructing meaning. The first reading is an opportunity for them to use the skills and strategies they know with the assistance of a supportive and responsive teacher. Each child begins reading at his or her own pace. Instructional interactions with the children are varied and are determined by individual strengths and needs. Many times the teacher helps children apply problem-solving strategies to visual information in context, such as letters, chunks, rhyming patterns, whole words, affixes, roots, or sound sequences.

After everyone has read the book, the teacher selects one or two important teaching points that will boost the children's learning to a higher level. These points are based on careful observation of the children's processing behavior during the first reading.

**Figure 4.1** Levels of teacher/child support in introducing books during guided reading.

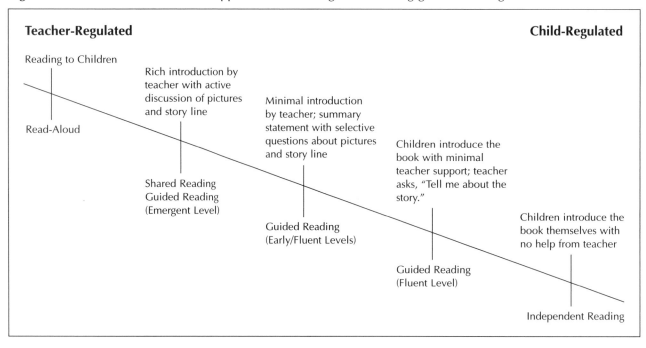

As children become more competent readers, they are asked to do the first reading silently. The teacher's questions focus on enhancing the children's comprehension and initiating thoughtful discussions. She can ask them to respond personally to specific events in the story: "What would you do if you were all alone during a storm?" She can ask them to locate specific information: "Read and find the part in the story that describes how the girl felt when the storm hit the island." She can use the text to initiate new learning opportunities: "Where can we go to find out more information about storms?"

In second and third grades, partner prompting can be a useful technique. At this level, children are usually competent readers who know flexible ways to help themselves read. In this approach, after the book is briefly introduced by the teacher, each child selects a reading partner and the two of them find a quiet corner where they can read the text together silently. Afterwards they discuss the story together. They can also help each other problem-solve tricky words, but a general rule is that one partner can't simply give the word to another.

## Subsequent Readings

Subsequent readings of a story give children opportunities to strengthen newly made connections, thus fostering higher-level thinking. Rereading familiar stories allows children to practice reading strategies comfortably, promotes reflection, and frees the attention to be able to notice new information. All these things promote a deeper understanding of the story.

During the days immediately following the guided reading lesson, the children are encouraged to reread the story several times. The children who read independently during the first reading are ready to share their book with a partner or to read it by themselves. The teacher can also use these now-familiar texts for mini-lessons or for writing activities.

## Levels of Guided Reading

Below we provide examples of guided reading interactions at the emergent, early, and fluent levels. Remember: successful guided reading interactions depend on the teacher's ability to (a) observe the children's processing behavior and respond accordingly, (b) use language prompts that focus on cue integration and effective processing strategies, and (c) select appropriate materials that support reading development.

## Emergent Guided Reading

Children in kindergarten and the first half of first grade are typically emergent readers. They are used to "making sense." Their oral language provides additional cues, and the things they remember about the story guide their interactions with the text. The observant teacher uses information from the *Observation Survey* (Clay 1993) and ongoing documentation of children's processing behavior (as recorded during shared reading, interactive writing, and journal writing and on running records) to determine the aspects of print to which children are attending and thus come up with an appropriate focus for small-group instruction. Although at this level the pictures provide major cues to reading books, the teacher wants the children to realize that the story resides in the text. So she directs their attention to the print by asking them to point to the words, locate known words, and search for unknown words based on their knowledge of a beginning-letter/sound relationship. The children's behavior is observable evidence that they are learning about the processes of reading: they send signals that they are aware something is wrong and they begin to search for alternatives to resolve the problem. The sensitive teacher is alert to these signals and responds accordingly.

## Book Selection

For a guided reading group at the emergent level, the teacher uses ongoing assessments such as running records and samples of children's writing to help her select a new book that is within the children's zone of proximal development. As the teacher analyzes the children's processing behavior in both reading and writing, she is collecting data that will drive her instructional focus during guided reading, assisted writing, and word-building activities. Figure 4.2 lists the typical reading and writing behavior of a child at the emergent level.

Let's look at a typical emergent guided reading group. Lynn, the teacher, realizes the importance of selecting books that will help the children gain control of early reading behavior. She is aware that the children are still relying primarily on the picture. Looking through the books that have been identified as being at the emergent level, Lynn notices that most of them have only one sentence or line per page. The sentence usually matches what is seen in the picture. She also observes that most of the texts have a picture on both the left-hand and right-hand pages, with a single line of print positioned at the bottom of the page. Lynn knows that the position of the text is critical for emergent readers: when they open a book, the first thing they should notice is the print on the left-hand page. Therefore, she searches through the books for ones with

**Figure 4.2** Reading and writing behavior at the emergent level.

| Reading Behavior | Writing Behavior |
|---|---|
| Relies on pictures | Writes one or two letters to represent one word or phrase |
| Attempts at one-to-one word matching are inconsistent | Can retell a story after hearing it, but does not consistently use one-to-one matching with print |
| Enjoys the rhythm and rhyme of language | Knows how to form most letters and knows that letters represent language |
| Can read one-line text with strong picture support | Can writes a simple sentence with supportive drawing |

the print on the left-hand page and the picture on the right-hand page. She wants the children to discover that the message is in the print, not the picture.

Continuing to analyze the books, Lynn looks for those in which the spacing of the letters and words on the page will give the children room to move their finger from word to word as they read. In some emergent-level books the spacing between words is so small that the children cannot practice the speech-to-print match successfully. Lynn believes this supportive feature will serve as a conceptual model the children can apply to other reading and writing contexts.

Narrowing her choice still further, she looks carefully at specific words and letters. She has observed that the children are becoming more aware of particular letter forms as they write and read daily. She wants to select a text that will give them the opportunity to use their limited knowledge of print to check on their own reading. Finally, Lynn selects a book that contains the following features:

- Print begins in the upper-left corner. This directs children's attention to an appropriate starting point.
- Pictures are placed on the right-hand pages. Children will look at the print first, then at the picture.
- Print is large and spaces are bold. The children will be able to pay attention to one-to-one matching.
- A simple repetitive language pattern occurs on each page. The one-word change is supported by the picture.
- One or two frequently encountered words are repeated throughout the text.
- Several known letters are used in the context of the repetitive pattern.

Setting the Focus

After carefully analyzing the children's reading and writing behavior, Lynn sets an overall focus for the group that will take them to a higher level of cognitive development. She knows that the children must learn how to use what they know to check on their own reading progress. She realizes the children are inconsistent with their one-to-one matching. For instance, instead of using known words in texts to monitor their responses, the children rely on their oral language and their memory. Lynn wants the children to use their finger to guide their speech-to-print matches. With these goals in mind, Lynn is ready to introduce the new book to the emergent reading group.

Book Introduction

During the book orientation, Lynn introduces the children to specific concepts they will encounter in the story. Her aim is to create anticipation and to construct a meaningful framework for the story. First she shares the cover of the book, *Me* (Randell 1996), and gives a brief summary of the story: "Today we are going to read a story called *Me*. The little girl in this story tells us about the things that she can do." By encouraging the children to share some things they can do, Lynn activates their background knowledge. Next, she gets them to discuss the pictures in the book, simultaneously planting the language of the text in their minds: "Let's look at the pictures and see what the little girl can do." Several children exclaim, "She can eat!" Lynn validates these responses and at the same time adjusts the language to accommodate the words in the text. "Yes," she comments, pointing to the words as she says them, "I am eating."

Finally Lynn passes out individual copies of the book to the children and prompts them to apply phonological skills for predicting a first-letter cue in an unknown word:

**Lynn:** (*Stressing the initial sound of the word* sleeping *during pronunciation*) Who can tell me what letter *sleeping* begins with?
**Children:** *S*!
**Lynn:** Yes. Can you find the word *sleeping* in your book?

As the children locate the word and frame it with their fingers, Lynn watches to see whether they are successful. When Sarah experiences difficulty, Lynn increases her level of support: "Find the word that starts with an *s*." She is prepared to pull out a magnetic letter *s* if Sarah needs additional support. After all the children have located the word, Lynn prompts them to confirm their response: "Check it with your finger to be sure it is the word *sleeping*." Confirmation is a critical part of the reading process.

To promote further attention to visual information, Lynn puts magnetic letters on the overhead projector and shows the children the word *am* (see Figure 4.3). Then she instructs them to locate the word *am* in the story. She selects *am*, a partially known word, for two important reasons. First, the word is encountered frequently and she wants the children to notice it. Second, she believes the structural position of the word (it falls in the middle of a three-word repeated pattern) will give the children a strong anchor for one-to-one matching. The children already have control of the word *I*, which is the first word on each page of the story, and they can use a strong picture cue to get the last word of the repeated pattern.

After the children locate the word *am*, Lynn says, "This is an important word in your story. I want you to use it to help yourself when you are reading." With this prompt, Lynn is sending a critical message: the children must use known words as anchors in the text to monitor and guide their reading.

## First Reading

Before asking the children to read the text, Lynn tells them, "Use your pointing finger to help you as you read." Then she circulates among them while they read. She observes their behavior and prompts them toward constructive activity: "What is happening in the

**Figure 4.3** Lynn uses the overhead projector and magnetic letters to show the children an important word from the text.

picture?" "Can you find a word that you know?" When the reading is completed, Lynn uses her observations of the children's reading behavior to emphasize three carefully selected teaching points:

- *Teaching point 1 (validating a previously learned response):* "That's good that you used your finger to point to the words while you were reading. That helped you to match your words, didn't it?" Here Lynn acknowledges the children's attempts at one-to-one matching.
- *Teaching point 2 (activating a new response):* "Also, I noticed that when several of you came to the word *laughing* on page 3, you started to say *smiling.* How did you know the word was not *smiling*?" Here and in the next teaching point, Lynn illustrates the importance of using first-letter cues to monitor one's reading.
- *Teaching point 3 (activating a new response):* "You all know that the word *smiling* starts with an *s*, don't you? Like *sleeping.* Let's take a look at some other words that start with *s.*"

## Subsequent Readings

The books are now placed in the children's "familiar reading" baskets, and over the next few days they are encouraged to reread the story several times. The children who read independently during the first reading are ready to share their book with a partner or to read it by themselves.

## Early Guided Reading

As children develop and refine their reading skills, they integrate cues and apply flexible strategies for solving new words. They exhibit behavior that indicates they are using visual information to check on the printed message (e.g., they rely less on the pictures). They are less dependent on the finger for matching speech to print, and the teacher encourages this greater control, prompting them to "read it with your eyes." Precise and deliberate matching is replaced by more fluent reading. The breaks between the words disappear, and groups of words are read with correct phrasing and intonation. The stories are read more naturally and sound more like the language that children use every day. Let's look at a group of first graders who are participating in an early guided reading group.

## Book Selection

Sandy, the teacher, selects *The Seed* (Cowley 1996) as an appropriate text for a guided reading group at the early level. Her choice is based on a careful analysis of the children's processing behavior as documented on previous running records, her observations of their reading strategies during independent and guided reading, and her observations of their problem-solving strategies during assisted and independent writing.

Figure 4.4 lists reading and writing behavior typical of children in this group. These characteristics are important criteria for selecting an appropriate text.

## Setting the Focus

Based on her analysis of their reading and writing behavior, Sandy concludes that the children need more opportunities to apply problem-solving strategies for examining words during reading. She knows that it is critical for the children to have flexible ways to analyze unknown words at points of difficulty. This same focus will be emphasized during

**Figure 4.4** Reading and writing behavior at the early level.

| Reading Behavior | Writing Behavior |
| --- | --- |
| Displays knowledge of several frequently encountered words and uses them to monitor reading | Writes several frequently encountered words with fluency and ease |
| Uses first-letter cues to cross-check against meaning and structure cues | Articulates words slowly when writing |
| Initiates some problem-solving actions on unknown words | Hears and records beginning, ending, and some medial consonant sounds in sequence; also some vowels |
| Displays understanding of one-to-one matching and does not need to use the finger during most reading | Shows consistent control of spacing between words |
| Rereads to confirm meaning and pick up new information for solving problems | Rereads to confirm meaning and expand the message |
| Corrects errors by matching sources of information | Applies early revision strategies, such as crossing out words and making new attempts |

writing activities (see Chapters 5 and 6) and word-building activities (see Chapter 7).

## Book Introduction

Sandy introduces the book to the children by engaging them in a discussion that draws on their background knowledge:

**Sandy:** What do you think our story is going to be about?
**Child:** Planting seeds.
**Sandy:** Yes, we can tell from the picture on the cover that the man is going to plant some seeds. Have any of you ever planted seeds?

Several children share personal experiences with planting seeds. Sandy acknowledges their contributions and gently guides them back to the story.

**Sandy:** When you planted your seeds, what are some things that your seeds needed in order for them to grow?
**Child:** Water!
**Another child:** Sunshine.
**Sandy:** Yes, water and sunshine are very important for seeds to grow. When you planted your seeds, did you wait and watch for them to grow?
**Children:** Yes!
**Sandy:** Well, in this story Bobbie and Annie planted some seeds, but they were afraid their seeds wouldn't grow.

At this point Sandy invites Leigh to read the title of the story, giving the group an opportunity to think about the importance of using things they know about words to solve new words.

**Sandy:** Leigh, read the title for us.
**Leigh:** *Seeds…Seeds.*
**Sandy:** What helped you with that word *seeds*?
**Leigh:** *See.*
**Sandy:** Right, the word *see* helped you with the word *seeds*. Now, let's go inside the story and see what Bobbie and Annie are going to do with seeds.

Here Sandy and the children have a short conversation about the story, making predictions based on the pictures and the story line. When Jason predicts the word *hoe* for *rake,* the teacher accepts the response because it will give the group an opportunity to cross-check meaning and visual cues when they read the text.

Next, Sandy directs the children's attention to a visual feature of the text and models how to use a known word to get to an unknown word:

**Sandy:** If you were going to read the word *away,* what chunk would you see at the end of the word?
**All:** *Way.*
**Sandy:** (*Makes the word* way *with magnetic letters on the overhead, then puts the letter* a *in front of it*) That's right. If I put the letter *a* in front of *way,* what new word did I make?
**Children:** *Away.*
**Sandy:** Yes, there are other words that start like *away—about, around, across.* Now, I need everybody to look on page 7 and find the word *away.* (*Placing the word in the context of the story*) What did Bobbie and Annie do? They went where?
**Children:** They went away.
**Sandy:** That's right. They went away!

First Reading

As the children read the story independently, Sandy moves among them and listens. Willis comes to the word *forgot* in his story and hesitates. First, Sandy prompts him to use meaning cues: "What did Bobbie and Annie do after they planted the seed?" Willis responds, "They went away." Since this prompt has not helped Willis with the problem word, Sandy tries a visual cue. When she frames the two parts of the word with a masking card, Willis is able to produce the correct response. Last, Sandy asks

Willis to reread the line and check to see if the word makes sense.

After the children finish reading the story, Sandy praises them for specific strategies they used. She leads them in a quick review of things to do to help themselves when they are reading.

**Sandy:** What are some things that you can do when you get stuck on a word?
**Child:** Go back and reread.
**Another child:** Think about the story and look all the way through the word.
**Another child:** See if there is a part of the word you know.
**Sandy:** Yes, it helps you to do those things as you read. Now, I want you to take your book and read your story with a partner. When you have both read the book, please put it in your familiar-reading basket.

Subsequent Readings

During subsequent readings, the children might reread the book with a partner or read it alone. The important thing is that children be given the opportunity to practice fluent rereading behavior.

## Fluent Guided Reading

At this level, children are competent readers and can apply strategies to help themselves read text within their instructional range. Reading becomes more silent, which enables children to increase their speed. Children need lots of time to read independently, because they continue to improve with each book they read. Reading now takes on a new focus: reading to learn. As children read a much wider range of material, they use their knowledge of *how* to read nonfiction and fiction material anywhere they find it. Children respond emotionally and read with increasingly deeper understanding of the author's intended message.

In order to examine the children's processing behavior and determine reading group placements, the teacher may occasionally ask the children to read aloud for a running record. It is expected that fluent readers' processing will be more refined and automatic. When they encounter difficulty, children use the text as the main source for solving the difficulty. Errors tend to be single, isolated words, and substitutions are often visually similar words. Self-corrections diminish as the children apply preprocessing strategies to solve words before errors occur.

## Book Selection

Selecting books for the fluent reader is based on a much wider range of criteria: interest, content, thematic units, and story genre. Books at this level have complex structures, which are generally characterized as (a) repetitive, (b) cumulative, (c) cultural, (d) chronological, (e) problem-centered, and (f) rhythm and rhyme. At this level, readers must be able to deal with diverse material that includes various organizational structures, multiple writing styles, and specialized vocabulary. Figure 4.5 lists reading and writing behavior typical of children at this level.

## Setting the Focus

The fluent reader can already integrate cues and flexibly adapt reading strategies to fulfill a range of purposes. Therefore, the focus of instruction varies according to the topic or subject matter. The focus may include (but is not limited to) learning how information is presented in a variety of ways, (maps, drawings, charts, tables of contents, indexes, glos-

**Figure 4.5** Reading and writing behavior at the fluent level.

| Reading Behavior | Writing Behavior |
| --- | --- |
| Acquires rapidly expanding vocabulary and concept knowledge through reading | Writes complex sentence structures about varied topics with ease |
| Applies flexible strategies with good control of visual patterns | Shows good control of visual patterns; spelling is generally at the conventional and transitional stages |
| | Applies a range of editing and revising techniques |
| Adjusts reading to accommodate author's message and intended purpose | Knows how to write for different audiences and different purposes |
| Selects books independently and enjoys reading | Chooses to write often and enjoys writing |
| Reads with expression and fluency | Incorporates various punctuation and literary devices |
| Preprocesses information before making errors (self-corrections are less obvious) | Understands the writing process and the purpose of first drafts, revising, editing, and final drafts |

saries, headings, subtopics, diagrams, and labels); making comparisons and contrasting information between texts; exploring the author's style of writing; developing an increasing range of comprehension skills (oral and written retellings) or increasing mastery of story elements (setting, main characters, plot, problem, resolution). The range of possibilities in setting a focus for a fluent guided reading group is immense, as are the opportunities for moving children forward to a higher level of competency. Let's look at two examples of how to conduct a guided reading group with fluent readers.

### *The Tale of Peter Rabbit:* Book Introduction

Judy, the teacher, introduces *The Tale of Peter Rabbit* (Potter 1993) by building on background experience: "Have any of you ever done something your mother or father told you not to do?" Several children relate their personal experiences. Next, Judy presents a brief overview of what the story is about: "Well, in this story, Mother Rabbit warns Flopsy, Mopsy, Cottontail, and Peter not to go into Mr. Mcgregor's garden, or something terrible might happen to them, like it did to their father." Then she encourages the children to make predictions:

**Judy:** What do you think might happen if the rabbits go into the garden?
**Ryan:** The scarecrow might scare them.
**Lisa:** They might get poisoned from bug spray or fertilizer.
**Jarred:** No! I think another animal will eat them, like a dog or a cat.
**Judy:** (*Praising the children's predictions*) Those are all terrible things that might happen to the little rabbits if they don't mind their mother.

Next Judy provides the children with enough detail to stimulate their interest and leave them wondering about what will happen to the rabbit: "Well, unfortunately, one of the rabbits disobeyed Mother Rabbit and went into Mr. Mcgregor's garden anyway. Needless to say, he ran into a lot of trouble. Several things happened to him that really frightened him and made him wish he had listened to his mother."

### *The Tale of Peter Rabbit:* First Reading

Now that the children are familiar with the overall theme of the story, they are eager to begin, and Judy prepares them for a silent reading. First, she sets a purpose for reading: "I want you to read pages 2 and 3 with your eyes and find out why Mother Rabbit didn't want the young rabbits to go into Mr. Mcgregor's garden." After the children silently read the pages, Judy asks, "Who can find the part that tells why Mother Rabbit didn't want her bunnies to go into Mr. Mcgregor's garden?" Lisa reads, "Your father had an accident there; he was put in a pie by Mrs. Mcgregor." Judy responds: "Well, no wonder Mother Rabbit didn't want her babies to go in there."

Next Judy prompts the children to read pages 4 through 7 to find out what happened to one of the rabbits as he squeezed under the gate of Mr. Mcgregor's garden. After they've read these pages silently, Judy starts a discussion:

**Judy:** On page 4, what did Peter do when he entered the garden?
**Children:** He ate the vegetables in the garden.
**Judy:** Read the part that describes what happened to Peter in the garden.
**Ryan:** "First he ate some lettuces and some French beans; and then he ate some radishes. And then, feeling rather sick, he went to look for some parsley."
**Judy:** (*Coaching the children to think beyond the story*) Why do you think that Peter went to look for some parsley?
**Lisa:** He ate so much that he got a tummy ache.
**Nicholas:** Yeah, and the parsley will make him feel better.

The children continue to predict their way through the text and use rereading to confirm or discount their predictions. At appropriate places, Judy guides the children to make further inferences: for example "How do you think Peter felt when he had to face his mother?" She prompts them to relate these textual events to life: "Have you ever disobeyed like Peter and had to face your actions? What happened to you? How did you feel? What lesson did you learn?" These questions are selective and are naturally interspersed with extended stretches of reading.

The discussion during the first reading does not deter the children from comprehension or the sheer enjoyment of reading. It simply engages them in the reading process as they learn to read for the author's intended meaning. As children gain experience and expertise in silent reading, they are encouraged to read increasingly longer passages at one time, until a whole book can be managed.

After the first reading, the teacher may focus on some problem-solving strategies if the children have encountered any troublesome spots. For instance, she might select one or two appropriate words from the story for extending the children's knowledge about words and use magnetic letters or a whiteboard to illustrate appropriate problem-solving techniques. This is in direct contrast to introducing vocabulary words or potentially difficult words before reading the story. Waiting until after the first reading before discussing the tricky parts gives the children the opportunity to meet and overcome the challenges independently.

*Frog and Toad Are Friends:*
Book Introduction

Mrs. Vest introduces the book *Frog and Toad Are Friends* (Lobel 1970) to a guided reading group. Together, they read the title and the name of the author and illustrator on the cover. Mrs. Vest explains that the book is an anthology of adventures about two very good friends named Frog and Toad. She turns to the table of contents and briefly notes the different stories in the book. Then she informs the children that today they will be reading the first story, "Spring."

Next Mrs. Vest taps into the children's prior knowledge by initiating a discussion about hibernation. The children talk about animals who sleep during the winter months and awaken in the springtime from their long winter naps. This provides a nice framework to introduce the story. Mrs. Vest says, "In today's story, Frog tricks Toad into waking up too soon from his long winter nap." Then she coaches the children to think of ways Frog might trick Toad to do this. Mrs. Vest records the children's predictions on a chart and comments, "After you read the story, we will check to see if you were right."

Next Mrs. Vest sets a purpose for reading the story: "I want you to read the story silently and find out how Frog convinced Toad to believe it was about half past May and time to get up." She is careful to plant the language chunk "half past May" in the introduction, so that the children can hear this unfamiliar phrase. "What do you think is so important about 'half past May'?" Several children exclaim, "That's when it's time for Toad to get up from hibernation."

Before the children begin reading, Mrs. Vest also initiates a brief conversation about ways the children can problem-solve independently: "When you come to a hard word, what are some things you can do to help yourself?" The children's responses indicate their understanding of problem-solving strategies: "Search for chunks in words." "Notice how the word starts and check to see if the word makes sense and looks right." Mrs. Vest reminds the children to try various ways to solve the problem but tells them that if they are unsuccessful in their attempts, they can mark the word with a sticky note: "We will help you figure the word out after you finish reading the story."

### *Frog and Toad Are Friends:* First Reading

To set the scene and establish a fluent pace, Mrs. Vest reads the first two pages of the story. Then she says, "Now, I want you to read the next six pages to yourself." Next she guides the children to view the characters from different perspectives: she asks some children to focus on the feelings of Frog and others to focus on the feelings of Toad. After the reading, Mrs. Vest guides the children in a short discussion around the emotions of Frog and Toad. She accepts all responses, occasionally inviting children to read passages that support their interpretations of the characters' feelings. As the first reading comes to an end, Mrs. Vest says, "Now, finish reading the story to yourself to find out how Frog finally got Toad out of bed."

After the children finish the story, Mrs. Vest directs them back to their original predictions from the chart. They confirm or discount their initial predictions with supportive passages from the text. Next, she asks them to locate any word that they had difficulty with during the first reading. She selects one or two words for group problem-solving. Mrs. Vest coaches the children to apply strategies for solving the problem. When appropriate, she uses magnetic letters or the chalkboard to illustrate strategies for analyzing words. Afterward, the children are encouraged to return to the text and read the problematic part within the context of the story. Then, taking the textual experience to a new level, Mrs. Vest asks the children to debate whether they feel the trick was fair and to predict what they think will happen if Toad ever finds out it really was not "half past May." These lively discussions lead to writing connections that allow the children to explore feelings and story elements.

## Closing Thoughts

In the apprenticeship approach to guided reading, the following characteristics need to be emphasized:

- The teacher designs instructional interactions that build on the knowledge children bring to the reading task.
- The teacher provides adjustable scaffolds that reflect ongoing observations of the children's skills, strategies, and knowledge of the story.
- The teacher moves the children into higher-level guided reading groups as they become more competent readers.
- The teacher uses language techniques such as modeling, coaching, scaffolding, articulating, and reflecting to enable the children to experience successful interactions with the text.

# Assisted Writing

An apprenticeship approach to literacy requires that we spend time observing changes that indicate children are moving in appropriate directions. These are the data we need to make informed decisions about what types of assisted writing activities will promote advanced learning.

As teachers of young writers, we recognize the vast range of experience and ability children bring to the task of writing. In apprenticeship settings, teachers provide children with guided opportunities to learn how to use things they know (skills, strategies, facts) to initiate problem-solving activity in different situations. During assisted activities, the teacher uses language prompts and adjustable levels of support to enable children to accomplish writing tasks they would be unable to accomplish alone. During follow-up writing activities, children are given important opportunities to apply their personal knowledge to independent work. As a child's understanding of the writing process increases, responsibility is transferred from the teacher to the child. Simultaneously, the child moves to a higher level of intellectual development. Clear

demonstrations and guided practice are the basis of apprenticeship learning.

Teachers must therefore keep ongoing documentation of what children know and can do. With this information they can validate children's knowledge and activate the problem-solving processes we want them to access each time they pick up a pen. This process of *validation* and *activation* is an important concept in helping children acquire higher-level understanding about the writing process.

The following writing conference illustrates the complementary relationship between validating and activating knowledge. Mrs. Pool and LaShala are talking about LaShala's story (see Figure 5.1).

Mrs. Pool observes that LaShala is able to write the words *He* and *burned* independently. She also notes that LaShala is hearing consonant sounds (*c, n* in *couldn't; g, t* in *get*). She feels that LaShala should be able to hear the *t* in *couldn't*. She thinks that perhaps the middle figure in *get* may be an attempt to self-correct the *t* to *e*. Mrs. Pool's teaching conference focuses on praising (validating) and lifting (activating) LaShala's knowledge about writ-

**Figure 5.1** LaShala's story. ("He couldn't get burned.")

ing. Mrs. Pool validates LaShala's knowledge by using explicit feedback to point out the words and letters that LaShala wrote independently. Then she activates new problem-solving activity by asking LaShala to listen to the ending of *couldn't* and to practice writing the word *get*. LaShala is able to accomplish both activities successfully. However, if LaShala had experienced any difficulty, Mrs. Pool was prepared to increase the level of support to ensure a successful response.

**Mrs. Pool's AP\* 1:** Say the word *couldn't* slowly. What can you hear at the end of the word?

**LaShala:** *T.*

**Mrs. Pool's AP\* 2:** Yes, say *couldn't* and *get* (*stresses the* t *sound*). How do they sound alike?

**LaShala:** They both end with *t.*

**Mrs. Pool's AP\* 3:** Now, take a good look at the word *get.* You heard the *g* and you heard the *t;* but there's something about it that doesn't look quite right. Can you find it?

**LaShala:** That needs to be an *e.*

**Mrs. Pool's AP\* 4:** Write it on your board and see if you can make it look right. (*Writes the word* get *correctly on her marker board.*)

\* Activating prompt

Children's writing development is shaped by experiencing different types of writing activities in assisted situations, which are then followed by independent practice. Using an apprenticeship approach, the teacher designs instructional interactions that evolve around children's current knowledge, skills, and strategies. The goal of assisted instruction is achieved when the children apply this knowledge to guide and regulate their independent writing.

This is accomplished by instructing children in numerous writing activities aimed at their zone of proximal development. The teacher provides the children with opportunities to practice things they know (at their independent level), while simultaneously supporting them as she guides them down new learning paths (in their zone of proximal development).

An early literacy writing program should incorporate a range of assisted activities, each one designed to help young children reach higher levels of understanding about the writing process. An observant teacher documents children's progress and plans transitional moves that reflect children's increasing control. The continuum of assisted writing includes:

- Interactive writing.
- Writing aloud.
- Revising and editing.

Teacher support and explicit instruction are essential elements woven throughout all levels and types. However, the teacher glides in and out, depending on how much the children can control or get to with their present abilities and what new learning must be introduced in order to activate the children's processing abilities.

## What Is Interactive Writing?

A common characteristic of struggling writers is their reluctance to take risks with their writing. Their stories are often controlled by the words and letters they know, rather than the message they want to share. This overdependency on a limited number of words and letters does not give children enough opportunity to try out new learning and to confirm or reject their responses based on old knowledge. John Dewey (1935) reminds us: "The old and the new have forever to be integrated with each other so that the values of the old experiences may become the servants and instruments of new desires and aims" (p. 62). This is a lesson that struggling writers have not yet learned. These children need us, as their teachers, to help them acquire problem-solving strategies that they can use to advance their own learning to higher levels.

The goal of writing is to communicate a message; however, writing consists of putting conventional marks on paper in order to express this message. During instructional interactions with a more knowledgeable person, children acquire important learning that they can use to communicate their thoughts in a readable context. The purposes of early writing activities are:

- To create a situation that promotes risk taking.
- To demonstrate effective writing strategies.
- To help children learn how to apply their existing knowledge to problem-solving in different places and on new information.

One form of assisted writing is a collaborative writing technique known as interactive writing (Pinnell and McCarrier 1994; Button et al. 1996; Fountas and Pinnell 1996). For the past six years, we have successfully used this technique in primary classrooms and with kindergarten and first-grade students in a literacy group program. Interactive writing is one of the most powerful tools there is for helping young children acquire critical reading and writing concepts.

Interactive writing helps beginning writers develop reading and writing strategies. It is a shared experience between the teacher and a small group of children who collaboratively write a text. Each child uses his or her colored marker to contribute known letters and words, and the teacher writes the rest. The personalized markers provide the teacher with ongoing documentation of the children's growth.

For the technique to be most productive, the teacher must know the children's strengths and give them opportunities to use this knowledge in the writing process. In this way the teacher is able to validate the children's current understanding and provide specific and explicit feedback to further that understanding. The teacher's interactions with the children focus on developing early reading and writing behavior:

- Directional movement and one-to-one matching.
- Concepts of letter, word, and punctuation.
- Sounds in words.
- Letter knowledge.
- Familiarity with some frequently encountered words.
- Rereading and predicting strategies.

The teacher's conversation throughout these interactions moves children forward. The teacher is continually using the children's strengths, never doing anything for them that they can do alone. Furthermore, the teacher demonstrates and models powerful strategies that will carry over into children's individual writing.

## Organizing for Interactive Writing

A small-group interactive writing lesson should take approximately ten minutes. The length of a whole-class session will vary with the size of the class and the teacher's decisions about the children's instructional needs. In either case, the quality of the interaction, not the amount of time spent, is the key to a productive lesson. Examples of writing formats include a simple sentence, a dialogue bubble, a menu, a recipe, a list, a weather report, or a short description of an event in the morning news.

Typically, the materials needed include an easel holding unlined chart paper, a black marker, correction tape, a pointer, a large alphabet chart, reduced copies of the alphabet chart, and a set of colored markers. Each child uses the same-color marker each day, thus allowing the teacher to document individual progress across time. The most manageable size for a group is between five and ten children with similar instructional needs.

Risk taking is encouraged if children are able to try things out. Many teachers place a dry-erase board next to the interactive writing chart; children can practice something on the board before writing it in the group story. In addition, we encourage our teachers to give each child a dry-erase magnetic lapboard, dry-erase marker, and magnetic letters for individual problem-solving. This is important for two reasons: (a) the teacher has an opportunity to see how different children are processing print, and (b) the teacher is able to guide an individual child toward an appropriate

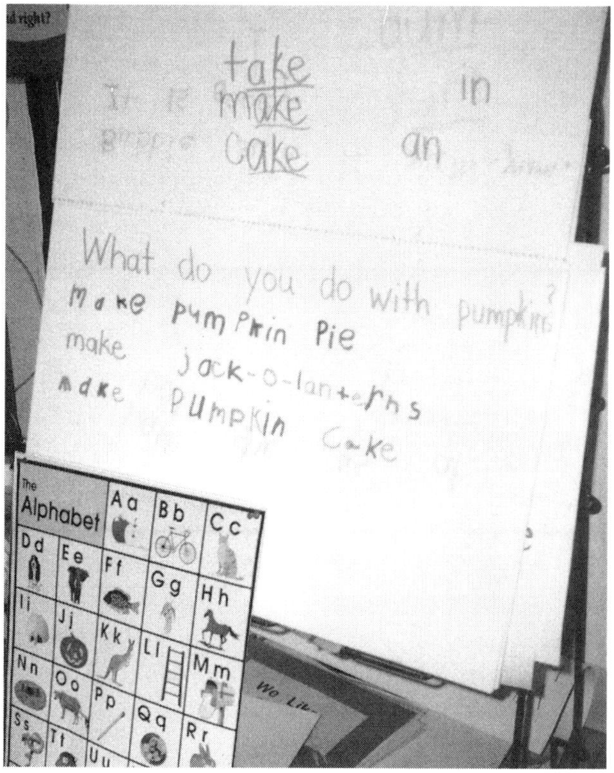

**Figure 5.2** A piece of interactive writing, along with a practice page and an ABC chart.

response before a wrong letter or word is written in the group story. Children's approximations are praised. However, because the stories will be reread, it is important that the words are spelled conventionally. Therefore, correction tape is occasionally used to mask any preconventional attempts.

## Interactive Writing with Emergent Readers

### Generating a Message

After reading the predictable text *I Like...* (Cutting 1988), Harriet, the teacher, guides a small group of children in constructing a story. (In emergent writing, a story may consist of a single sentence.) Harriet uses each child's personal knowledge and oral-language background as well as the language of the book as the group jointly constructs a story based on things they like to eat.

**Harriet:** What are some of the foods you like to eat?
**Paul:** Pizza!
**Damion:** Candy!
**Melissa:** Ice cream!
**Julie:** Hot dogs!
**Larry:** French fries!
**Harriet:** Yum! Those all taste good. Which one do you like best?
**All:** Pizza!
**Harriet:** Me too! So, in our story, we can write, "I like…"
**All:** "Pizza!!"

Next Harriet gives the children an opportunity to hear and rehearse the language of the story, thus supporting the students' memory of the language pattern for future predictions. This remembered message is critical, because the children will use it to self-monitor their writing.

**Harriet:** "I like pizza." Let's all say the story together.
**All:** "I like pizza."

## Writing the Story

Harriet repeats the language phrase fluently, then prompts the children to attend to the concepts "first" and "word":

**Harriet:** "I like pizza." What is the first word in our story?
**All:** *I.*

Next Harriet focuses the children's attention on where to begin writing and the left-to-right directional movement across print:

**Harriet:** Where do I start to write the word *I?*
**Damion:** Right there (*pointing to the left side*).
**Harriet:** I want everyone to point on your own board where to write the word *I.* (*The children point to the appropriate starting points on their dry-erase lapboards.*) Which way do I go now? Show me on your board. (*The children demonstrate left-to-right movement on their lapboards.*)

Harriet now repeats the language phrase and gives the children an opportunity to write a known word:

**Harriet:** "I like pizza." You all know how to write the word *I.* Damion, come up and write *I* in our story. Everyone else can practice writing *I* on your board.

Harriet goes on to prompt the children to recall the story, confirm their knowledge, and demonstrate the process of slow articulation of sounds within a word:

**Harriet:** What does our story say?
**All:** "I like pizza."
**Harriet:** Yes, "I like pizza." L—i—ke. Now, everyone say the word with me very slowly and let's listen to the sounds we can hear in the word.
**All:** L—i—ke.

Harriet now prompts the children to monitor their writing by rereading to recall their story (a message level) and then asks them to think about the next word (a word level) in the story. She again demonstrates the process of slow articulation of sounds within a word (emphasizing but not segmenting the sounds). The children must now predict the letter for the sound they hear (a graphophonemic level). She also helps the children attend to important conventions of print: word, space, letter formation, first, next.

**Harriet:** After writing the word, we have to go back and reread our story and think about what we want our story to say.

**All:** "I like pizza."

**Harriet:** What word are we writing next? I… (*Pausing to invite the correct response*)

**All:** Like!

**Harriet:** Yes. The next word in our story is *like.* Where do I need to write the word *like*? Julie, can you come up and show us? (*Julie comes up to the chart and points to the space beside the word* I.) Good for you! Before we write the next word, we need to leave a space like it looks in books. That makes it easier for us to read. Julie, can you make us a good space with your finger?

Next Harriet concentrates on hearing and recording sounds in words. She validates the children's contribution of the ending sound of *k* while simultaneously directing their attention to the importance of listening to the sounds in sequence. She emphasizes the beginning sound, that of the letter *l,* in three ways: (a) she stresses on the first letter, (b) she compares it to the beginning letter in Larry's name, and (c) she links it to the appropriate letter on the alphabet chart.

**Harriet:** Say the word *like* very slowly. Let's stretch the sounds.

**All:** L—i—ke!

**Harriet:** What can you hear in *like*? Write the sounds you hear on your lapboard. Paul, come up and tell me what you can hear.

**Paul:** *K*!

**Harriet:** Good for you! There is a *k.* You hear it at the end. Now, everyone say the word *like* and listen to what you hear at the beginning. L-l-l-l-ike.

**Larry:** *L*! Like my name!

**Harriet:** Yes, it starts like Larry! Can everyone hear it? Can you feel it in your mouth?

L-l-l-ike. L-L-Larry. (*Harriet and the children say the two words together.*) Now who can find a picture on our ABC chart that starts like *Larry* and *like*?

**Damion:** Ladder!

**Harriet:** That's right. *Larry, like,* and *ladder* all start with *l.* Damion, will you come to the chart and point to the *l* so everyone can see how it looks? (*Locates the* l *for* ladder *and chants the letter and picture cue.*) Now Larry can write the *l* in our story. The rest of you can write it on your lapboard. (*She quickly adds the letter* i *in the word, than calls Paul up to the chart to add the* k.) Paul, you heard the *k* at the end of *like* so come up and write it in our story.

Analyzing new words by saying them slowly and predicting the sequence of sounds is a productive activity for helping children learn how to create links between sounds, letters, and words. In this lesson, Harriet makes it easy for the children to hear known sounds within the articulation of a new word. In other lessons, she will look for opportunities to help the children generalize their knowledge about sounds to beginning, middle, and ending positions within a variety of words. In the current lesson, Harriet only held the children accountable for things they already knew—she incidentally supplied the *i* in *like* because it was an unknown item, and she added the ending of the word. However, as she contributed the unknown ending, she used language that channeled the children's attention toward noticing a new feature about print: "Now, I'll write the *e* on the end of the word *like.* We don't hear that sound but we need it to make the word look right."

Through repeated readings of this simple text, the children are exposed to the visual features of the word *like.* Their ability to analyze the beginning and ending consonants form a framework for learning the visual features (the *i* and *e*) that are needed to make the word look right.

Because Harriet realizes children need to become familiar with some frequently encountered words, she follows up this activity with another the next day. First, she activates the children's perceptual awareness of the word *like* by having them locate it within the familiar context of their story. Next, she encourages them to take a good look at the word in their story, then shut their eyes and look at the word in their head. When Melissa enthusiastically exclaims, "I see the *l*," Harriet prompts her to locate its position point within the word: "Where do you see it?" Julie exclaims, "I see a *k* at the end." Finally, Harriet says, "Now open your eyes and check to be sure that your word *like* looks the same as the word *like* in your story." After the children confirm their response, Harriet passes out the appropriate magnetic letters for constructing the word *like* on their individual lapboards.

**Harriet:** Make the word *like* with your magnetic letters. After you have made the word, what do you need to do?
**All:** Check it with your finger. And say it.
**Harriet:** That's right. Check it with your finger and say the word as you check it. That will help you remember the word.

In the apprenticeship approach, it is critical that all children be actively involved in the literacy event. When an individual child contributes a letter or word to the group story, the teacher simultaneously engages the other children with appropriate prompts: (a) "Say the word slowly" (b) "Locate the letter on your alphabet chart" (c) "Write the letter on your lapboard" (d) "Trace the letter with your finger on the carpet." Throughout the lesson, Harriet guides the children to participate

actively in the learning experience. Her flexible prompts are based on her understanding of how the brain organizes information and provides feedback by which children can confirm their response (see Chapter 1). In the previous example, the children were not only learning a frequently encountered word (*like*), they were also acquiring an effective strategy for learning *how* to learn new words.

We use interactive writing for a special purpose: to support the development of early reading and writing behavior. The literacy demonstrations are very clear and focused in order not to overwhelm the children with new learning. As soon as the children demonstrate that they can use the behavior in their independent reading and writing, the assisted writing lessons are adjusted to reflect this increasing control.

Interactive writing gives children opportunities to practice critical aspects of print under the guidance of an observant and responsive teacher. They work within their zone of proximal development—that is, they are able to apply knowledge and strategies with the help of the teacher that they would be unable to accomplish alone. Children develop higher-level understanding as they become more aware of the power of their own knowledge in solving new problems. The teacher must therefore know how to adjust her assisted activities to accommodate the child's understanding of the literacy process. In the next section, the teacher "raises the ante" in interactive writing to reflect the children's new understanding about written language.

## Interactive Writing with Emergent to Early Writers

Having learned how to brainstorm ideas and generate simple messages gives children a very supportive framework for acquiring critical concepts about written language. An important shift occurs at this point: children become more conscious of their own mental processes and begin to use early checking strategies to guide and confirm their initial response to print. To keep children working at the simple sentence level would inhibit opportunities to learn more about the writing process. Children now need experiences in creating longer discourse similar to that used in texts.

In the following example, Judy is working with a small group of first graders. Her observations of the children's independent reading and writing behavior indicates they are ready to begin constructing longer texts. On this particular day, the children are very excited because they have just finished cooking a large pot of chili for a class project. This a perfect context for learning how to add details to a story while simultaneously providing opportunities to practice problem-solving.

Judy initiates the conversation. "I could smell your chili cooking this morning. Tell me how you made it!" Several voices join together as the children describe the ingredients. As the children talk, Judy records key ingredients on a chart: t*omatoes, hamburger meat, beans, V-8.* This list will become a resource when the story is written.

Now Judy guides the children to begin composing: "How do we need to start our story? What is the most important thing about the story?" Again, a chorus of voices exclaims, "We made chili." Judy confirms this fact while encouraging the children to expand on this simple statement: "That's right. Where did you make the chili? When did you make the chili?" Through guided participation, the children construct this message: "Today at school we made chili. We put in tomatoes, beans, hamburger meat, and V-8. It was so good! Yum, yum!"

With this simple text, Judy has elevated the assisted writing to a new level by introducing the children to key words—*when, what, where,* and *how*—they will use in their independent and group writing. Next Judy introduces simple analogies. First she asks the children to locate and frame (with a framing card) the word *we* in the story. When Darin notices that there are two *we*'s in the story, Judy confirms this fact and makes certain everyone is looking at the same word: "Yes, there are two *we*'s— one with a capital letter and one with a lowercase letter. Who can find the word *we* with a lowercase letter?" Next Judy distributes the appropriate magnetic letters and asks the children to change the first letter of this known word to make a new word:

**Judy:** Make the word *we* with your letters. Now I want you to take away the first letter from *we*. What letter are you going to take away?

**All:** *W.*

**Judy:** Yes, put an *h* in front of the *e*. You have just made a new word. Who can tell us what this word is?

**Several children:** *He*!

**Judy:** What would I do if I wanted to make the word *we*?

**Several children:** Take away the *h* and put back the *w.*

**Judy:** Let's try that and check it to see if it works.

Now Judy prompts the children to make another word: "I want you to make a word that starts like *mouse* and ends like *he*." Because Judy knows that *mouse* is a familiar cue—it is on the ABC shared reading chart—she believes the children will have no trouble making this new word. Although the prompt represents higher-level processing, Judy provides the children with strong external support—the appropriate magnetic letters and the letter/picture cue for *m*. The goal of the activity is to ensure a meaningful and successful performance.

After numerous experiences with interactive writing, children should demonstrate control of early concepts about print: starting position, spacing, letters, and so forth. In addition, children should know how to analyze and record sounds within words. They should be able to write several important frequently encountered words and apply simple analogies for using what they know about a known word to write an unknown word. Finally, children should be writing two- and three-sentence messages that demonstrate they are able to use punctuation to support meaning. Their writing should reflect their early understanding about how print works.

## Making the Transition to Writing Aloud

At this point the teacher introduces the "writing aloud" concept (Routman 1991). In this type of assisted writing, the teacher vocalizes her thoughts as she composes text, inviting the children to contribute at selected points. Her invitations are grounded in her knowledge of children's processing behavior, and her focus is on promoting effective problem-solving that will carry over to new situations. While writing aloud, the teacher's primary goal is to demonstrate the importance of composing a meaningful, coherent message for a particular audience and a specific purpose. Taking an apprenticeship approach, the teacher gives the children clear demonstrations and good models that they can use as standards when they direct their own writing activities. Through guided participation in these assisted demonstrations, the children acquire important tools for learning how to write more sophisticated and conventional messages.

## Organizing for Writing Aloud

The teacher gathers a small group of between five and ten children with similar instructional needs around her in front of a large flipchart. The length of the lesson depends on the purposes and the teaching environment. A small-group writing aloud activity might span several days, each session lasting ten or fifteen minutes. However, if the teacher is working with the entire class, she may want to complete an entire story in one longer session. Again, the quality of the demonstrations and the responsiveness of the children are more important than the time spent.

In this activity individual colored markers are no longer needed, because the teacher is the primary scribe. She also leads the discussion. She deliberately encourages children to contribute, expand, and sequence their ideas logically, because her goal is to help them develop an understanding of the composing process. Writing aloud also gives children opportunities to learn effective strategies for solving unfamiliar words.

To begin, the teacher takes a moment to describe the purpose of the activity and the teacher-student roles:

- She emphasizes that her main reason for writing is to create a story that others will enjoy. She tells the children they will help her compose her story and add details. As she writes, she asks clarifying and extending questions that focus on building meaning.
- She tells the children that her first copy is her "sloppy copy," that her main concern is the quality of her message, and that when the story is completed, she will reread it to ensure that she has communicated her message in an effective and descriptive way. She informs the children that they will help her with this process.

- She tells the children that she will show them some important ways to solve particular words as she writes the story: she will use her practice board to work on a few selected words, and they will help her.
- She instructs the children to listen to how she applies a wide range of problem-solving strategies and resources as she composes her message.
- She emphasizes that the main purpose of writing is to construct a meaningful (and interesting) message, so she will reread her story after she has worked on a new word or added a new detail in order to keep her mind on the composing process. She tells the children they will help with this rereading and make predictions about logical events that could occur next in her story.

Writing aloud provides children with shared opportunities to learn how to construct and organize ideas for particular purposes and how to solve words on the spot. It can emerge from read-alouds, storytelling, hands-on experiences, shared readings, and content-related books. The extensiveness of the prewriting discussions will depend on the type of writing.

## Writing Aloud Lesson with a Small Group of Early Writers

### Prewriting Discussion

Carla has chosen an enjoyable topic that will maintain the children's attention. Using the book *The Very Quiet Cricket* (Carle 1990), her own personal experience, and the children's background knowledge about fishing and crickets, Carla invites her students to help her write a story about the night she searched for crickets.

### Composing and Writing the Story

**Carla:** I want you to help me write my story. When do you think I went out to look for crickets?
**DeMario:** One night.
**Russell:** One dark night!
**Carla:** (*Writing*) "One dark night…" What did I do?
**Kevin:** Went walking.
**Carla:** (*Rereading*) "One dark night (*Writing new text*) I went walking…"

Since Carla's emphasis is on the message, she writes the story fluently. There is active discussion throughout, and the children contribute; however, Carla is the primary scribe. She focuses on composing and also on thinking aloud as she models conventions of writing and strategies for solving new words. Her mini-lessons foster writing proficiency. They are brief, on the spot, and purposeful attempts to call attention to a particular source of knowledge the children possess that can be used to solve new problems. Early in the lesson Carla reminds the children of a word they have recorded in their writing dictionary.

**Carla:** Yesterday we put the word *light* in our dictionary. Do you remember the chunk that was at the end of *light*? It can help us with this word *night*.
**Tania:** *I*.
**Carla:** *I* what?
**All:** *G - h - t*!
**Carla:** *I - g - h - t*. (*Writing* light *on the practice board next to the story.*) Now if I erase the *l*, what do I need to make the word *night*?
**All:** *N*.
**Carla:** (*Writing* night) So if I know *light*, that can help me to write *night*.

Carla now directs the children to reread and predict what could happen next in the story. She encourages them to expand the story and uses revising techniques to illustrate the process. She directs the children's attention to the importance of using things they know from one situation to help them in a new situation.

**Carla:** Help me read what we have written so far.
**All:** "One dark night I went walking."
**Carla:** Where?
**DeMario:** By a pond.
**Carla:** "By a pond." (*Writing this quickly.*) Now, let's read it again.
**All:** "One dark night I went walking by a pond."
**Carla:** What did I have with me when I was walking by the pond?
**All:** A flashlight!
**Carla:** Do I need to add that in there? Would that make my story better?
**Kevin:** Yes, because it was dark and we need to know you had a flashlight.
**Carla:** Okay, what do I need to cross out to add that?
**All:** The period.
**Carla:** The period, because I'm not finished. (*Rereading*) "One dark night I went walking by a pond with…" Adrianna, you can help me with that word *with*. You made that a while ago with the magnetic letters. (*As Adrianna spells the word, Carla writes it in the story.*)

## Negotiating the Text

Carla has the students monitor the message by rereading the text after each new addition. She encourages story expansion with questions that provide a scaffold from which the children can develop a well-organized story. In the next negotiation, Carla leads the children to incorporate book language into the story. She

asks, "What kind of noises did I hear?" When the children respond "Cheeps" and "Chirps," Carla fluently writes, "I heard chirping noises" into the text.

Carla also looks for productive opportunities to direct the children's attention to strategies for analyzing words, always keeping her primary focus on the fluent construction of a meaningful story.

**Carla:** (*Prompting*) What did I do then?
**Kevin:** I flashed my…
**Carla:** (*Writing* I flash) What do I put on the end of *flash* to get *flashed*?
**All:** E-d.
**Carla:** (*Adding* ed *and rereading*) "I flashed my" (*writing* light) toward the what?
**Andy:** Problem.
**Carla:** (*Writing* problem. *Writing a new sentence*) I saw some crickets. (*Prompting*) What did I say I was going to do the next time?
**Tania:** Get a jar.
**Carla:** (*Writing* The next time I go walking I need to take a j—) *Jar* is like another word that I know. *Jar* is like the word…
**All:** *Car*!
**Carla:** (*Writing* car) So if I know *car*, I can change the *c* to a what?
**All:** *J. Jar*!
**Carla:** (*Rereading*) "I need to take a (*writing*) jar so I can…"
**All:** Go.
**Carla:** (*Prompting*) "So I can…" What am I going to do with that jar?
**DeMario:** Catch some crickets.
**Carla:** (*Rereading and writing*) "So I can catch some crickets." (*Slowly saying the word, emphasizing the* ck *chunk, and then writing the word* crickets.) Then what will I do?
**Kevin:** Go fishing.
**Carla:** (*Rereading and writing*) "Then I can go f…" Help me with *fishing*.

**All:** *I-s-h.*
**Carla:** (*Writing* fish) What's on the end of *fish* to make *fishing*?
**All:** *I-n-g!*
**Carla:** (*Writing* ing *and rereading*) "Then I can go fishing (*writing*) and catch a…"
**All:** Big fish!

Notice how Carla engages the children in a collaborative dialogue during which they jointly use problem-solving strategies at both the message and the word level. At the message level, she asks leading questions (*when? what? where? why?* prompts) that keep the composing process in motion. She balances this by fluently recording particular patches of language and asking questions that prompt the children to use their own knowledge of analogies and spelling patterns to solve specific words. This is social dialogue, in which Carla prompts the children to assume responsibility for whatever aspects of the writing process they are able to control. It is through these interactions that the children will gain strategies for their independent writing.

As today's story comes to an end, Carla returns to the goal of writing, which is to create a meaningful message for the reader. She directs the children's attention to the writing chart as a resource for their individual work.

**Carla:** Now before I do anything else, what do I need to do with my story?
**Andy:** Go back over it.
**DeMario:** Read it again.
**Carla:** I want to read my story and see that it makes sense (*Pointing to the first step on the writing chart*) and that somebody who reads my story will understand it. So, let's read my story to see if it makes sense.

The teacher and children reread the story in unison and agree that it makes sense.

However, in her final comments, Carla emphasizes that a story can be added to even after we think it is finished: "Tomorrow we can put this on the overhead and add to it to make it even more interesting." She writes the words "sloppy copy" on her story and says, "My sloppy copy just needs to make sense so that when I read it to somebody they will understand it."

## Revising and Editing

Revisions are perhaps the toughest activities to do with children who are programmed to make perfect attempts. We believe children should be taught how to solve words so that they will take risks in writing interesting and longer texts. One way to accomplish this is through teacher demonstrations of problem-solving. Explicit talk and action give children a good model for solving words while keeping the focus on composing a meaningful text. The emphasis should *not* be on the word itself; rather, the word is the means for demonstrating important strategies the child can apply to new situations when writing independently. The child thus moves from the interpsychological plane (group problem-solving) to the intrapsychological plane (individual problem-solving) as he internalizes generative processes for moving his development forward.

The first step in revision is to examine the message for meaning: the teacher and children reread the text to see whether the story makes sense. The teacher instructs the children to listen for key words that move the story forward:

**Carla:** How many key words did you hear?
**Kevin:** There are three. *Next, so, then.*
**Carla:** Everybody read it together, and Kevin can circle them.

As revision continues, the teacher and children cross out or change words and insert words or phrases. Carla channels the children's attention toward the relationship between an appropriate title and the text:

**Carla:** What do I need to put at the top?
**DeMario:** Night Crickets
**Carla:** Is that what you think would be a good title? Yes, it is. (*Writing the title*) That is a very good title. It tells me exactly what is going to be in the story. I know that when I read "Night Crickets" that somebody is going to be out at night and what are they going to see?
**All:** Crickets!

At the end of the session, Carla tells the children she will make a copy of the story for future revision. Her explicit demonstrations of writing behavior and her gentle scaffolding at the children's level of understanding have helped them learn *how* to revise their work. She has not followed a script. Instead, she's made a number of flexible decisions based on her observations of and her interactions with the children. Her teaching priorities will promote gradual shifts in the children's writing behavior over time. Through critical teaching decisions such as these, children gain control of and take more responsibility for their own writing. The goal of assisted writing is achieved when the children begin to use the skills and strategies they've encountered in group demonstrations to monitor and regulate their own cognitive activity when writing independently.

Children need frequent opportunities early on to revise and edit their work. Crossing out words when you have changed your mind and using carets to insert missing words and phrases are just some of the revision techniques children need to acquire. They also need to learn how to edit their writing for grammar and spelling. This crucial behavior is taught during instructional interactions with an observant and responsive teacher. With more experience, emergent writers become fluent writers willing to work on an evolving piece of writing.

When children revise a piece of their own writing, they:

- Add meaningful information to clarify content.
- Add missing words to make the sentence sound right.
- Add details to expand and enhance the message.
- Cross out unnecessary words.
- Use appropriate punctuation.
- Capitalize the first letter of every sentence.
- Circle misspelled words.
- Add spacing between words.

Through mini-lessons and teacher and small-group conferences children learn that writing is not something that is done at only one time or in only one place. Their confidence and writing ability increases as the result of specific feedback. The successful teacher:

- Stimulates additional content ideas.
- Prompts for clarity and meaning.
- Elicits details and colorful words to make the story more interesting.
- Models questions writers need to ask themselves when writing.
- Demonstrates proofreading and self-correcting skills.

## Revision with a Group of Early Writers

During early revision sessions, we suggest placing a child's story on an overhead transparency and modeling how to reread the story in order to clarify it. Listening to a rereading gives the writer personal feedback for monitoring meaning: the author will often hear a gap in her story that she did not notice while she was writing it.

Carla's opening remarks establish the importance of creating a meaningful text:

**Carla:** Today we are going to use Andy's story on the overhead. We all know that writers miss things when they read their own work and that they need listeners to help them. When we look at Andy's story, we are going to think about whether it makes sense and whether Andy has made clear what he wants to share with us. Andy, read your story to us.

**Andy:** (*Reading*) "Last night I went outside and I saw some frogs and I picked them up and I put them in a box."

**Carla:** That is a wonderful story! Does Andy's story make sense?

**Children:** Yes.

**Carla:** Is there anything about Andy's story that you want to know more about?

**James:** Where did he find the frogs?

**Carla:** Yes, that's a very good question. Andy, where did you find the frogs?

**Andy:** At the pond.

**Carla:** Where would we add this in your story?

**Andy:** (*Rereading and adding new information*) "Last night I went outside and I saw some frogs by the pond." (*Carla adds a caret to the text and inserts the phrase* by the pond *into Andy's story.*)

**Carla:** Is there anything else you would like to know about Andy's story?

**DeMario:** I wonder if he is going to let them go so that they can go back home.

**Carla:** Andy, would you like to tell us about that in your story?

**Andy:** Yes, I could say that at the end. (*Rereading and adding new information*) "Last night I went outside and I saw some

frogs by the pond. And I picked them up, then I put them in a box. Then I let them go."

**Carla:** (*Asking for confirmation before making any additions on the overhead*) Is that where you want to put it? (*Then, prompting for further expansion and clarification*) Is there anything else you want to ask Andy about his story?

**Tania:** When did you go outside?

**Andy:** It was night.

**Carla:** What was it like outside?

**Andy:** Dark.

**Carla:** Where are we talking about "outside"? Where could we add the new information, Tania?

**Tania:** After "last night."

**Carla:** Would that be a good place, Andy?

**Andy:** It needs to go after the part "I went outside."

**Carla:** Okay, let me add it right here (*after* outside) and let's read and see if it makes sense there.

Later Carla prompts the children to think of an appropriate title for Andy's story. After several children suggest titles, she says:

**Carla:** Those are all really good suggestions, but since this is Andy's story, we will let him decide what his title should be.

**Andy:** "Night Frogs."

**Carla:** Does that title tell us about the story?

Later in the conversation, DeMario comments that this is Andy's sloppy copy.

**Carla:** Yes, this is his sloppy copy. And what has Andy done to his sloppy copy?

**Tania:** First, he read it to see if it made sense.

**Carla:** Yes, Andy wants his readers to feel like they are right there with him at the pond. How does his story make you feel?

**James:** I could see that in my imagination.
**Carla:** Yes, you were seeing his story in your head.

Finally Carla invites the group to reread the story together and praises Andy for writing a great story. The support offered by the members of this writing group is obvious, for everyone has played a role in working on Andy's story. However, the rules of ownership have been honored: each new suggestion was presented to Andy for his approval. This collaborative approach to revision is used daily until Carla observes that children are using these techniques when writing independently. After that, she holds more individual conferences. However, flexibility is important; Carla convenes a group conference whenever a common difficulty arises.

## Editing for Spelling with a Group of Early Writers

In this example, Esther uses the overhead projector and a transparency of Shanika's writing to direct her students' attention to proofreading techniques:

**Esther:** Shanika has written a wonderful story that she would like to read to us; and she would like us to help her get her story ready for publication. What are some things we need to check for before we publish any of our work?
**Mya:** We need to be sure we have capital letters and the right punctuation.
**Roshon:** Be sure to check the spelling.

Esther agrees with these suggestions and asks Shanika which one she wants help with today.

**Shanika:** I need help with my spelling.

**Esther:** What can we do first?
**Kevin:** We need to search for misspelled words and circle them.
**Esther:** That's right. We have to find them first, don't we? Shanika, read the first sentence and everyone else check with your eyes to see if the words look right.

The point of group editing is to help the children identify misspelled words and then apply some problem-solving techniques on *selected* words. This is more productive than correcting all the misspelled words at once. As Shanika reads her sentences from the overhead transparency, Esther circles the words the children identify as being misspelled. Then:

**Esther:** Let's look at the word *brothr*. You noticed something about it that is not exactly right. What did you notice?
**James:** There should be an *er* on the end.
**Esther:** Let's write it and see how it looks. (*Writing the word* brother) What do you think? Does it look right, Shanika?
**Shanika:** Yes.
**Esther:** Good, let's think of other words that look like *brother* on the end.

The children generate a short list of similar words and Esther records them under *brother*. The goal is not achieved until the children apply their learning beyond correcting the initial word.

At the end of the session, Esther reminds the children of other places to go for help:

**Esther:** You still have some words circled that we didn't work on today. Let's look at these words and think about where Shanika can go for help.
**James:** The word *was* is in the class dictionary.
**Tania:** Say *went* slowly. There's a letter missing in the middle.

**Kevin:** She could try the word wall.

**Esther:** These are all very good things to do to help with spelling. Shanika, after you have worked on your spellings some more, come see me and I will help you with the rest of the words.

## Checklists for Revising and Editing

Editing charts are a beginning tool for helping young writers learn how to monitor and evaluate their personal writing accomplishments according to conventional standards. Editing charts are introduced during assisted writing activities and also applied during independent journal writing.

For the charts to be effective, they should focus on assessing how well children are applying relevant skills and strategies to their independent work. As children develop control of particular behavior, the editing chart is revised to shift attention to a new area. For example, an early editing chart may emphasize the following areas: (a) include your name; (b) put good spaces between words; (c) start each sentence with a capital letter. When children can control this behavior, the old chart is discarded and a new one is stapled to their folders: (a) check for misspelled words; (b) reread for punctuation; (c) cross out unnecessary words. The editing charts change to reflect the children's increasing understanding of writing conventions. As children become more competent writers, they internalize these rules and become less dependent on a checklist to evaluate their work. The teacher looks for evidence that the children are making this shift to higher-level processing.

A writer's checklist is another supportive tool for beginning writers. Like the editing checklist, it is first introduced as a mini-lesson during assisted writing and is eliminated when it is no longer needed. Here's an example:

1. Write your story and make sure it makes sense.
2. Add to your story or cross out what you do not want.
3. Read your story to yourself or a friend.
4. Edit for misspelled words. Circle words that do not look right to you.
5. Look up words in your dictionary or try out spellings on your practice page.
6. Put in punctuation marks.
7. Write the final draft.

## Closing Thoughts

Two important principles contribute to successful group revision conferences:

- Children must be comfortable having their work displayed on the overhead for group revisions and editing.
- Teachers must ensure a supportive environment that focuses on collaboration and problem-solving.

Children's writing ability is directly influenced by three important factors:

- The appropriateness and the quality of the demonstrations provided by the teacher.
- The types of opportunities they have to apply revising and editing techniques.
- The teacher's feedback during group and individual conferences.

The teacher, as the more knowledgeable person, keeps the children working at the cutting edge of their intellectual development. As the children demonstrate they are moving to a higher plane of learning, the teacher creates new assisted writing situations that validate the old knowledge and activate new learning. At the same time, the teacher provides independent writing opportunities that allow the children to practice the skills and strategies they are acquiring from the assisted activities. Throughout, the teacher collects data that she uses to inform her next instructional move.

The social context is very important in developing new understanding. A balanced literacy program provides children with many opportunities to apply and expand their learning. The following principles are important factors in helping children become successful learners:

- Children acquire important concepts about writing during social and collaborative dialogues with more knowledgeable persons.

- Teachers use explicit language and action to model critical concepts about the writing process.
- Teachers hold children accountable for applying their existing knowledge in new problem-solving activity during assisted writing.
- Teachers constantly adjust their levels of support in accordance with their observations of children's developing control.
- Children's cognitive processes are validated and activated during meaningful collaborative writing.
- Literacy learning needs to take place in the children's zone of proximal development if they are to internalize, appropriate, and generalize these strategies.

# Independent Writing

An apprentice works beside a more knowledgeable person who helps him or her successfully carry out carefully structured tasks. Progress is measured according to two levels of performance: (a) what the child is able to accomplish in the zone of proximal development with the assistance of the more knowledgeable person, and (b) what the child is able to accomplish in the zone of actual development without the help of another person. Vygotsky (1978) would say that what the child is able to accomplish today with the teacher's assistance she or he will be able to accomplish independently tomorrow. If learning is not being generalized to new situations, the teacher must ask two questions:

- Did I provide clear and focused demonstrations that were based on the child's level of understanding?
- Did I step outside the child's zone of proximal development and hold the child accountable for unknown information?

A balanced writing program reflects three types of support that build on one another:

assisted writing with a group of children with similar needs (as described in Chapter 5), independent writing, and individual conferences about writing. A true measure of a learner's potential involves measuring both assisted and unassisted performances.

In assisted writing activities, the teacher provides instruction aimed at children's potential. Through guided participation, the teacher presents clear and memorable models that provide children with high-quality standards for writing. The goal of instruction has been achieved when the teacher observes that the children are applying this knowledge when writing independently.

Independent writing gives children personal opportunities to apply recently demonstrated techniques and strategies. The teacher has a chance to observe how the children use their skills, strategies, and conceptual knowledge on their own. By comparing the writing samples of a child across time, the teacher sees just how a child is regulating his or her own writing development. Questions the teacher might ask when looking at a range of independent writing are:

- What is the child beginning to notice about visual patterns?
- Does the child show consistent (or inconsistent) control of a spelling pattern?
- Does the child render frequently encountered words automatically?
- Is the child's writing moving toward more conventional styles?
- Does the child use punctuation to communicate meaning?
- Is the child using more complex sentence structures in his writing?
- Does the child write different types of messages for different purposes?

As the children write, the teacher observes how they problem-solve and apply what they know about writing. If a child doesn't apply a strategy the teacher believes he is capable of using, the teacher might stop by and nudge the child in a more productive direction: "Say it slowly as you write it" or "That word starts like your name." Or she might conduct a follow-up conference after the child has completed the story. In either case, she focuses on shifting his thinking to a higher level. In the early stages of development, new learning is somewhat shaky, so the child needs a sensitive teacher who is aware of what he can do and how she can support him in using this knowledge in a new situation.

## Writing and Spelling Development

In order to follow children's progress effectively and instruct them according to their needs, teachers must be able to analyze and interpret children's writing and spelling development. Children's writing samples reveal their progress across time.

Research shows that children move along a continuum of development reflecting increased control of written language and more conventional writing behavior. Heenman (1985) identifies five developmental stages that young children go through when they write:

1. *Scribble stage.* The child uses lines or scribbles to convey meaning. (See Figure 6.1.)
2. *Isolated letter stage.* The child strings together symbols, numbers, and letter forms with little or no sound-symbol correspondence. (See Figure 6.2.) Generally, there is no spacing between these forms. The child may be able to read the message, but only with the help of the picture.
3. *Transitional stage.* The child uses some correctly spelled words, but continues to use isolated letters, symbols, and numerals to represent meaning. (See Figure 6.3.)
4. *Stylized sentence stage.* The child begins to use repetitive patterns organized around known words. The child leaves spaces between words and shows evidence of letter-sound knowledge. The child can read the message without picture support. (See Figure 6.4.)
5. *Writing stage.* The child composes messages independently for a variety of purposes. The ideas are organized logically and chronologically. Sentences are more complex, varied punctuation appears, approximated and conventional spellings are used, and the writer's voice emerges. (See Figure 6.5.)

Gentry and Gillet (1993) identify five stages of spelling development that are closely aligned with the stages of writing development.

1. *Precommunicative stage.* The child uses random and recurring letters with no letter-sound correspondence. The letters are strung together without spacing. Most letters are uppercase. The child may have an

**Figure 6.1** Scribble writing. ("telephone")

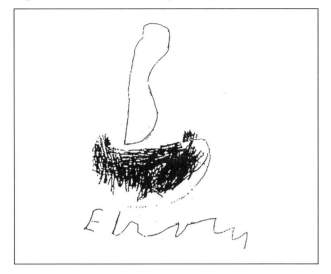

**Figure 6.2** Isolated letters representing the names of family members.

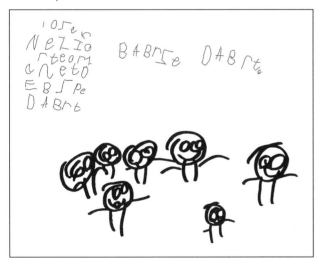

**Figure 6.3** Transitional writing. ("I live in a mobil home" "I live in a brick house.")

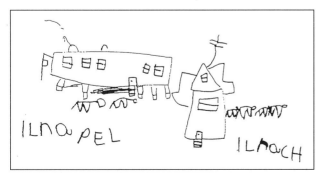

**Figure 6.4** Stylized writing. ("I like a car. The car is white. The car can move. The car can go. The car is big.")

**Figure 6.5** Writing stage.

Dear mrs. dorn,

you are a fast reader. I am sorry I got detenchchin-hall, my grandmother said she'd might come and pick me up from school. I hate to do that I feel like crying. but that is the rules, I hope times go by fast so, I can get out of here, and have a good day. But I don't think so. I might have a good day don't you think so

yes or no

pick your own choice

your friend,
Joe

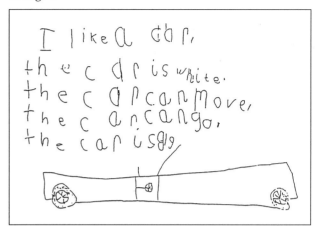

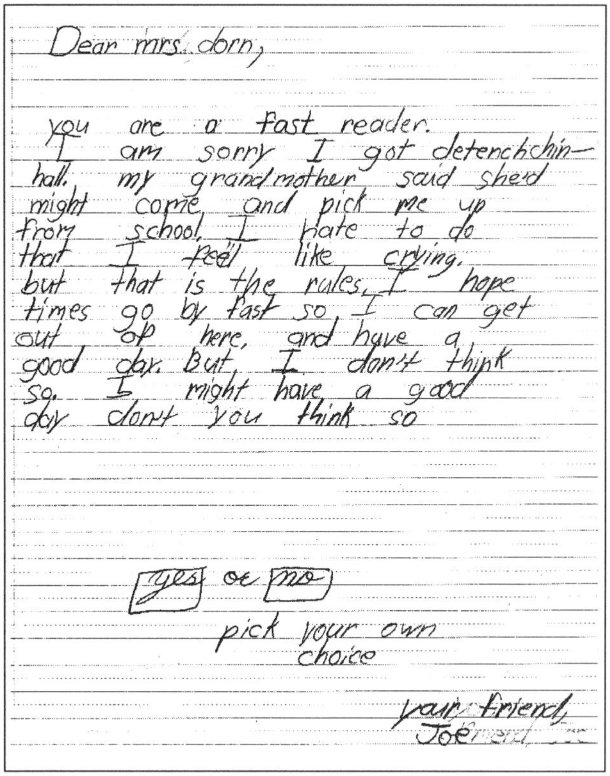

understanding of left-to-right directional movement in print. (See Figure 6.6.)

2. *Semiphonetic stage.* The child recognizes that letters have sounds, but may represent whole words with only one, two, or three letters. The writing shows a mixture of upper- and lowercase letters (with a preference for uppercase). Letter names are used to represent sounds or syllables (e.g., *b* for *be*, *r* for *are*, *u* for *you*). The child begins to use spacing between words. (See Figure 6.7.)

3. *Phonetic stage.* The child records letters for every sound within the word. Spacing and left-to-right directional movement are generally under control. The writing at this time may contain a mixture of semi-phonetically and phonetically spelled words, with some words spelled correctly. (See Figure 6.8.)

4. *Transitional stage.* The child begins to rely more on how words look visually rather than how they sound. The writing at this time may include alternate spellings for the same sound, reversed order of visual patterns (e.g., *ou* for *uo*), generous use of inflectional endings, vowels in every syllable, and flexible control of known words. (See Figure 6.9.)

5. *Correct stage.* The child's letter-sound knowledge is firmly established. The child uses a variety of word structures (prefixes, suffixes, compound words, etc.). The child is able to come up with alternative spellings when a word does not "look right" and is comfortable with using resources such as a dictionary and thesaurus for help. By now, the child has accumulated a large writing vocabulary. (See Figure 6.10.)

Of course, children's writing samples may indicate that several stages are occurring at one time. In Chapter 1, we discussed how children's progression through the zone of proximal development is characterized by both

**Figure 6.6** Precommunicative spelling.

**Figure 6.7** Semiphonetic spelling. ("I want to go to a house for Valentines. I going to eat for Valentines.")

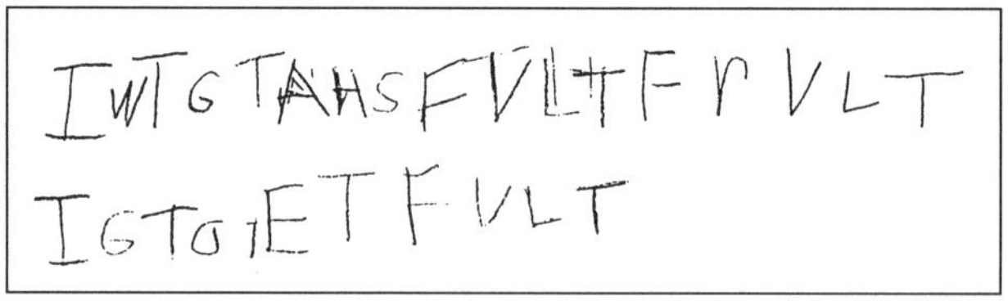

**Figure 6.8** Phonetic spelling. ("Then the fox said hop on my back. Get on my nose. And the gingerbread man was gone.")

**Figure 6.9** Transitional spelling. ("One day when I was at my house I saw a butterfly flying through the air. I tried to catch it but I couldn't.")

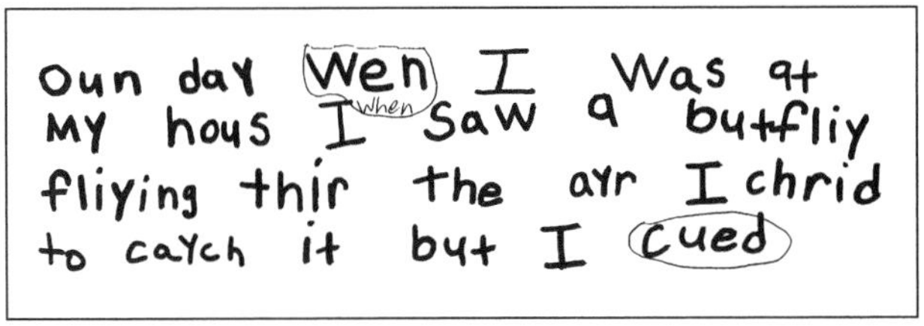

**Figure 6.10** Correct spelling.

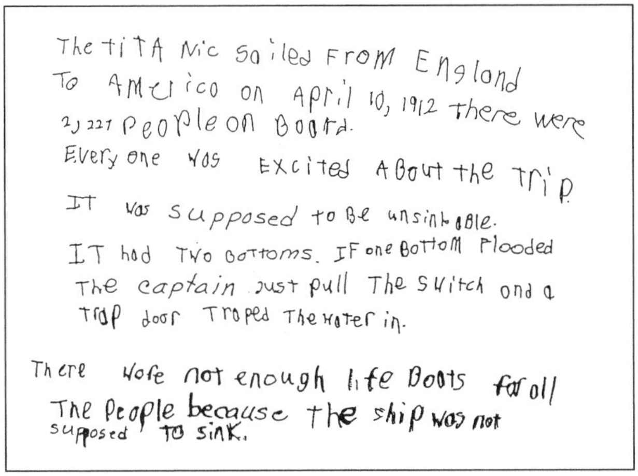

Some [of Destini's] attempts captured clear evidence of the learning process. For example, Destini attempted the word *and* nine times. Her first attempt was correctly spelled. On the next attempt, she recorded only the last letter. Next, she recorded two ending letters in the proper sequence. Destini recorded the beginning and ending letters on her fourth attempt. On the next attempt, only the final letter was written. Destini did not write any letters on the sixth trial, but on the final three attempts, she consistently spelled the word correctly. (p. 74)

In order to move children to higher levels of development, the teacher must understand the learning process. Teachers who work with struggling readers sometimes express concern because children know something one day but are unable to recognize the same information in a different situation or at another time. Too often, teachers view this behavior as a disability rather than as movement along a developmental continuum. The teacher's role is to observe where the child is in terms of graphophonemic awareness, spacing, directional movement, and letter formations, and use this knowledge to lift the child to a higher level.

Again we emphasize the relationship between assisted learning experiences and opportunities for independent practice. The teacher collects children's writing samples that indicate their current and potential levels of understanding and uses this information to plan constantly shifting instructional interactions that reflect the transitions in children's writing.

generative movements (where the child uses something known to learn something new) and recursive cycles (where the child temporarily ignores something known while problem-solving). During the recursive cycle, the child may divert his attention from something he has used before and spend his time thinking about a new challenge. Although this may appear to be regression, it is actually progress. The teacher needs to direct the child toward internalizing the concept (e.g., the spelling pattern, the known word), so that the response occurs automatically, without conscious attention.

Alice Humphrey (1997), a reading teacher working with first graders, found that her children did indeed go through generative-recursive cycles in acquiring word knowledge:

## Organizing Independent Writing with Emergent Writers

Teachers of emergent writers in kindergarten and early first grade generally follow their

daily assisted writing activities with ten or fifteen minutes of independent writing. If a
small group of children has been working on
interactive writing, the teacher might arrange
for follow-up independent work at literacy
corners or conference tables. (Chapter 8 discusses literacy corners in relation to independent work.) Throughout the day, the teacher
also provides these children with many opportunities to write for different purposes.

During small-group literacy lessons, emergent and early writers use an unlined journal
that is bound across the top. The children
write their story on the bottom section and use
the top section as a practice page for letter and
word work. When children's writing becomes
longer and more complex, the journal is
replaced with lined paper that is dated and
filed in writing folders. As the children write,
the teacher circulates among them and
observes their work. She focuses on the children's use of strategies that were emphasized
during assisted writing activities.

The following steps are used during journal writing:

- Generating and rehearsing the story in the
  group.
- Writing the story independently with minimal support from the teacher.
- Conducting an individual teacher-student
  conference after the story is complete.

Before children begin journal writing, the
teacher clearly models how to write in a journal. First she prepares a large chart divided
into two sections. Then she asks a student to
demonstrate on the chart where to write the
story and where the practice page is. Thinking
aloud, she talks about where to write her name
and the date. She discusses important strategies, hesitating on the word *get*, for example,
and saying, "I need to say that word really

slowly because that will help me hear the
sounds." She uses language to illustrate how to
space between words ("I'll put my finger
between these words so I can leave a big
space") and to model the importance of rereading to make predictions for the next word. She
uses clear, repetitive language and explicit
action to help children learn the process of
writing in their own journals. Following her
demonstration, she asks the children, "Who
can tell me some things I did to help myself
when I was writing my story?" As the children
respond, the teacher praises them and encourages them to use these types of strategies when
they are writing in their own journals.

Once children have learned how to use
their journals as repositories for productive
writing, the teacher sets expectations for them
based on her observations of the knowledge
they demonstrate and the strategies they use
during assisted writing. She uses this documentation in deciding when to shift the children to a higher level of assisted writing.

## Journal Writing with Emergent Writers Following Interactive Writing

### Generating and Rehearsing the Story

Children at the emergent level need to
rehearse their story orally before writing it in
order to have a language structure with which
to monitor their work as they construct the
story on paper independently. During the
weeks prior to this interactive writing session,
the teacher and children have read and discussed several books about being scared. The
teacher now guides the children to generate
and rehearse a short message:

**Harriet:** What are you scared of? Think a
  minute and then turn to your neighbor
  and tell him what you are scared of. (*The

*children whisper in each other's ear*) Who wants to be first to tell us what you are scared of?

**Marlin:** I am scared of a dinosaur.

**Harriet:** Me too! They are big and scary! Say it one more time, Marlin.

**Marlin:** I am scared of a dinosaur.

**Harriet:** Now, go get your journal and write your story.

Reading and writing are reciprocal processes. These simple and personal sentences introduce the children to important writing concepts that will simultaneously support their reading development. After the rehearsal, each child gets his or her basket of writing materials, which includes a journal, colored markers, an ABC chart, and a personal dictionary of known words. Working independently, each child helps herself or himself.

## Writing the Story

Harriet circulates among the children and records their use of strategies as they write their stories. She realizes the fragility of early learning and is ready to support a struggling child with gentle reminders of effective strategies to use at points of difficulty. Noticing that Marlin has made no attempt to record any sounds for the word *scared* in his story, Harriet reminds him of a helpful strategy for analyzing sounds:

**Harriet:** Say the word *scared* slowly. What can you hear?

**Marlin:** Sssccared. I can hear an *s*.

**Harriet:** Where do you hear it?

**Marlin:** At the beginning.

**Harriet:** That's good listening. It helps you to say the word slowly. Say it again and write the sounds you can hear.

## Conducting a Postwriting Conference

Besides conducting these "drop-in" conferences with the children as they write, Harriet also has follow-up conferences with different children each day. Children are always excited to have their work acknowledged in this way. These individual conferences allow the teacher to provide personal support for a child in a particular area. During early conferences, Harriet provides explicit praise by placing a light checkmark over the child's contributions (see Figure 6.11):

**Harriet:** Read me your story.

**Rashad:** "It was a vampire."

**Harriet:** (*Responding to the message*) Oh, that's a scary story! You are such a good writer. Look at all you did. You wrote the word *it* all by yourself. (*Writing the word* it *and placing a checkmark over Rashad's writing*) And you heard the *w* in *was*. That's good listening. And you knew there was an *s* in *was*, didn't you? (*Writing the word* was *and placing a light checkmark over the child's contributions.*)

**Figure 6.11** Rashad's journal writing sample, early literacy lesson, week 3. ("It was a vampire.")

Harriet builds on Rashad's partially correct attempt to write the word *was*, wondering whether it is based on a visual memory for how the word looks. She quickly makes the word from magnetic letters and says, "This is the word *was*. You wrote the *w* and the *s*, didn't you?" She then encourages Rashad to evaluate his own accomplishment: "Show me the letters you wrote by yourself." After this she asks Rashad to construct the word *was* two more times, carefully modeling how to check and confirm the word.

In this simple example, Harriet validates Rashad's contribution but also lifts him to a new level of perceptual attention. Her final teaching point is to instruct Rashad to point to the accurate version of the text and read the story with his finger, thus encouraging one-to-one matching on a familiar language pattern.

Rashad's independent work documents that he is able to hear and record consonant sounds in beginning (*w, v*), middle (*p*) and ending positions (*t, s, r*). His use of the chunk *ir* in the word *vampire* suggests he may be beginning to notice visual features within words. This will be an area where Harriet will need to collect further evidence. Rashad is also aware of two frequently encountered words (*it, was*), which he can add to his personal writing dictionary. Rashad's writing style is at the transitional stage: he is writing a simple sentence with isolated letters that represent letters and sounds. His spelling development is a mixture of semiphonetic and phonetic knowledge.

During tomorrow's interactive writing lesson, Harriet will need to focus Rashad's attention on spacing between words, a critical area for supporting his reading and writing progress. The explicit nature of interactive writing will continue to play a role in helping Rashad gain greater control of early literacy behavior. Through guided participation, Rashad will have opportunities to refine his understanding of letter-sound knowledge and to acquire some new words. Rashad's independent writing indicates that he is ready to progress to writing longer stories (at least two or three sentences) during interactive writing.

## Journal Writing with Emergent to Early Writers Following Interactive Writing

In order to communicate a message, children must be taught some important strategies for helping themselves when they write. First, they must learn how to listen to the sounds within words and assign an appropriate letter for the sound they hear. Also, they must learn how to retrieve a message by rereading the text after they have stopped to solve a word. During interactive writing at the emergent level, the context of a simple sentence provides a natural backdrop for helping young writers acquire these strategies.

However, children must learn that writing consists of more than just one sentence. So the teacher models the process of writing texts with two or three sentences. The topics for assisted writing are deliberately varied; for example, they may be generated by a read-aloud, a personal experience, a retelling, a letter, a recipe, or the daily news. Before asking students to write independently, the teacher invites them to stand in front of their classmates and tell their stories. This rehearsal serves two important purposes: (a) it places value on the child as a storyteller with a message to write about, and (2) it enables the child to practice the story's meaning, which he can then use to monitor the written version.

In the following example, the children have been instructed to write about something exciting that has recently happened to them. Blake, who is in first grade and has been in an early literacy program for four weeks, writes the journal entry shown in Figure 6.12. It reflects his understanding that sentences must come together in a coherent and sequential pattern to communicate a message. This is a characteristic of Heenman's (1985) writing stage in the continuum of children's writing development. Blake's writing from previous lessons has given no evidence of stylized writing. Instead, Blake writes in single sentences for nearly four weeks before his writing changes to a three-sentence story. Angela notes that the change occurred two days after the assisted writing demonstrations on constructing longer texts.

Blake's spelling is generally at the phonetic level: he's able to hear and record the sounds of most of the consonant letters and is able to spell several frequently encountered words correctly. He is also beginning to monitor his writing attempts (e.g., *went, saw, animals, one*) by crossing out the incorrect response and trying the word again. In the first sentence, Blake writes the word *went* correctly. In the second sentence, he writes the word *went* for *we*, then corrects his first attempt by crossing out the unnecessary letters (*nt*) to produce the accurate spelling of *we*.

Angela begins the follow-up conference by inviting Blake to read his story. Then she validates what he's written (the primary focus of the conference must be to respond to the child's message before attending to the words

**Figure 6.12** Blake's journal writing sample, week 4. ("Me and my dad went to the zoo. We saw lots of animals. My favorite one was the bear.")

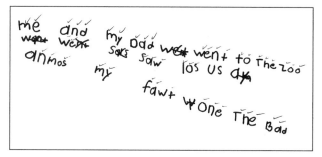

within the text): "I like bears too. I think they are such pretty animals." Blake responds by expanding on his original message: "They are my favorite animal because they have fur on them and they look like a big teddy bear." Angela says, "Well, tomorrow you might like to add that to your story."

Next Angela validates Blake's knowledge of words, praising him for the ones he is able to write correctly. Since she realizes Blake must be able to spell common words, she boosts his learning by using the words he already knows. First she says, "Find the word *the* in your story." Next she says, "Turn your paper over and write the word *the* quickly." Then she says, "If you know *the*, you can write the word *then*." She shows Blake how the two words are the same except for the *n*, which Blake is able to hear. Then she asks Blake to put an *m* on the end of the word *the* and read the new word. Blake reads the word *them*, but adds a little stress on the final sound as though he is using the *m* to help himself with the word. This teaching point shows Blake how to apply visual information from a known word (*the*) to auditory information from two known sounds (*n, m*) in order to create two new words (*then, them*). Blake is learning a strategy for working on new words during his writing. Before ending the conference, Angela makes a final comment about the story: "I hope you and your dad get to go back to the zoo again."

## Journal Writing with Early Writers Following a Writing Aloud

The primary purpose for writing aloud in an assisted situation is to help young writers learn how to compose longer stretches of text for different purposes and audiences. A secondary purpose is to demonstrate some strategies for solving selected words within the text.

As with any type of assisted writing, the teacher provides a follow-up opportunity to apply this learning in independent work (see Figure 6.13).

Following a writing aloud lesson, the children's stories become longer and more elaborate. They may contain examples of literary phrases and specialized vocabulary from stories they've heard their teacher read aloud or those they've encountered in guided reading. Their writing is more organized and contains a logical pattern, including a beginning, middle, and ending. Their focus is still on meaning; however, visual patterns may be evident in their attempts to write particular words.

The children are encouraged to write about anything of interest to them. During earlier writing aloud activities, the teacher and children have written about a favorite book, written a letter to a friend, and written about a personal experience. A specific time for story generation and rehearsal (as in interactive writing) is no longer needed.

## Writing the Story

As the children write in their journals, Carla circulates among them and responds to their messages. She observes how the children are expanding their stories independently using composing strategies that have been demonstrated in assisted activities. She has noticed that Kelly's stories are always about books she has read; yet that morning Kelly had told her a funny story about her baby sister. Carla drops in on Kelly and reminds her about this: "Kelly,

**Figure 6.13** Children writing independently while their teacher observes their progress.

you told me the funniest story this morning about your baby sister. Why don't you write about that today so everyone can read it. I know they will enjoy it." She and Kelly remember the story together and Kelly then begins writing about her baby sister.

Nick is able to regulate his topics according to specific needs and interests. The examples in Figures 6.14 and 6.15 accommodate different messages for different purposes. However, in each case, Nick's writing shows that he understands story organization. In the

example in Figure 6.14 Nick writes about losing his toy. His story follows a logical pattern that begins with one problem (the car won't start) and leads to another problem (he loses his toy). He includes details ("we went back to the car"), character dialogue ("'We will have to call dad so we can go home'"), language techniques for emphasis ("But no toy"), transitional words (*but, when*), and complex structural patterns. Nick's writing style can be classified at an early level of the writing stage (Heenman 1985).

**Figure 6.14** Nick's writing about a personal experience, first-grade early literacy lesson, week 8. ("Mom and I got in the car but the car would not go So we went to the phone to call the tow truck the tow truck came Mom said, 'We will have to call dad so we can go home dad came and we went home I forgot my toy We went back to see the car but when I went inside the car to look for my toy I looked for it all day but no toy We went inside the store I saw my toy Mr Fast had it I went home with my toy robot.")

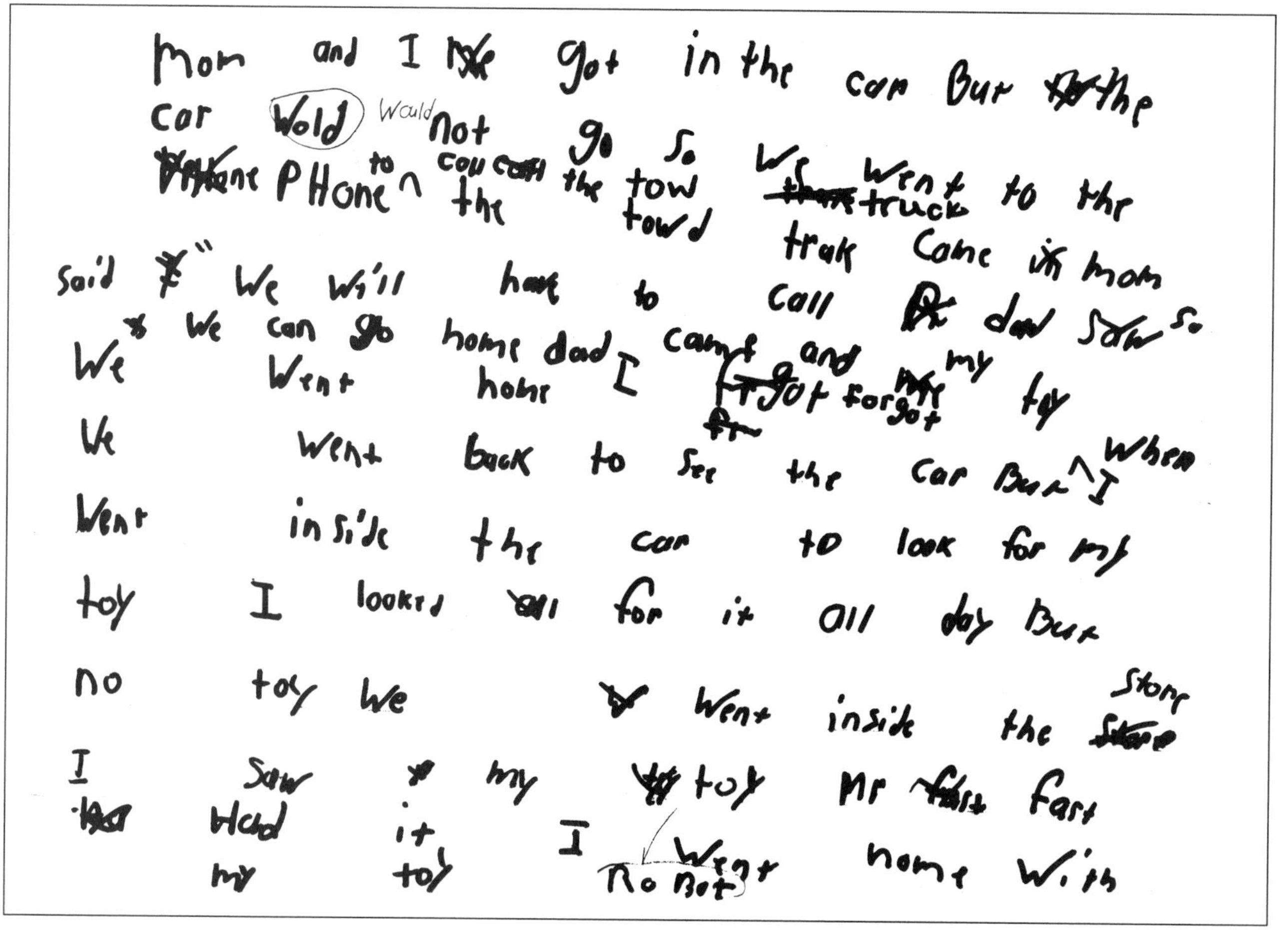

Two days later, in the example in Figure 6.15, Nick uses the same organizational techniques to retell a story from a guided reading lesson. In his version of *Late for Soccer* (Randell 1996), Nick describes the setting, the time, the problem, and the solution. He effectively uses dialogue to support meaning and literary phrasing for emphasis ("They got to soccer on time thanks to Michael's dad and Tim's mom").

In both examples, Nick writes his stories fluently and independently. He revises his message on the spot using techniques such as crossing out words and inserting carets. He edits his spelling by circling words he is unsure of and using the dictionary to check and revise them. After Nick corrects the word, he places a checkmark over the spelling for confirmation. On Gentry's spelling scale, Nick's writing reflects a mixture of transitional and correct spelling.

Carla's follow-up conference for both writing sessions is similar. In each case, she praises Nick for his message and asks him a few clarifying questions. Then she focuses on help-

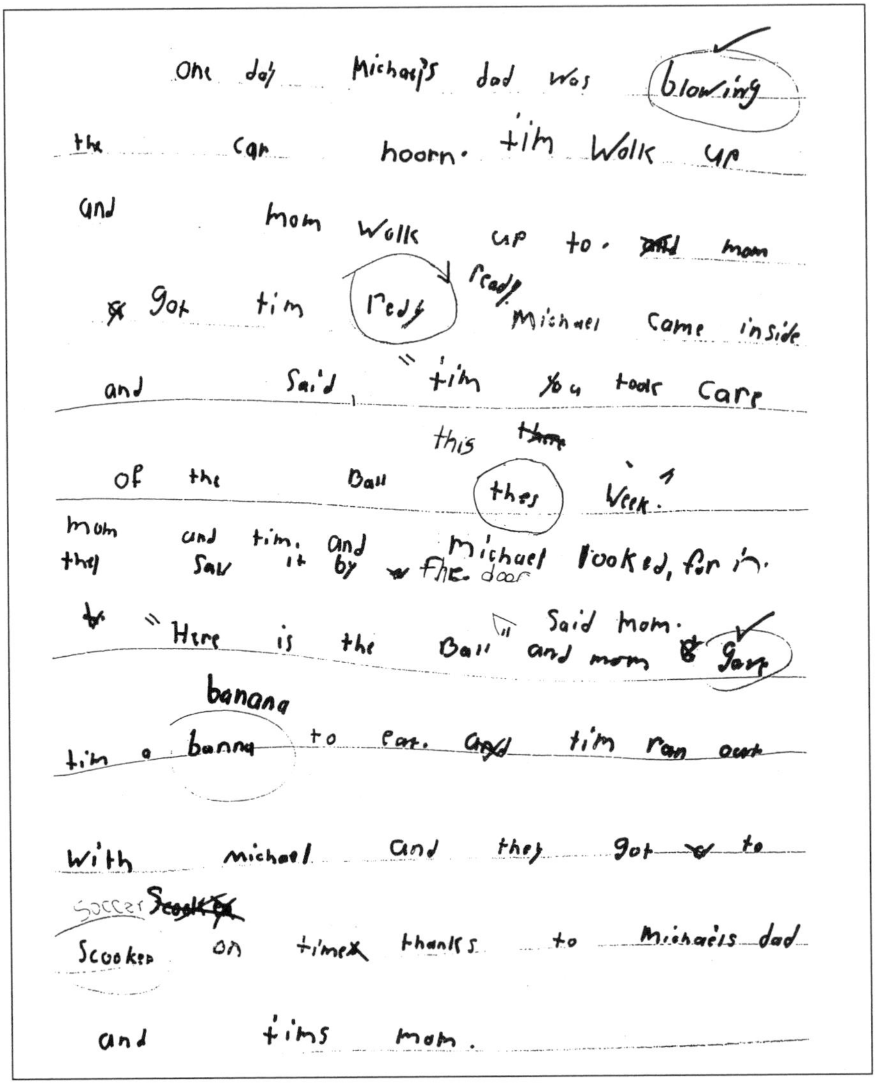

**Figure 6.15** Nick's story retelling, first-grade early literacy lesson, week 8. ("One day Michael's dad was blowing the car horn. Tim woke up and mom woke up too. Mom got tim ready Michael came inside and said, 'tim you took care of the ball this week.' Mom and tim and Michael looked for it they saw it by the door. 'Here is the ball' said Mom. and mom gave tim a banana to eat. tim ran out with Michael and they got to soccer on time thanks to Michael's dad and tim's mom.")

ing Nick refine his editing and revising skills, particularly relative to punctuation. His stories include expressive language, but he does not use consistent and appropriate punctuation marks to support that language.

In the classroom, Judy drops by Shane and invites him to read his story (see Figure 6.16). She observes the influence of book language ("One dark stormy night") and the natural sequence of events that lead up to his story's ending. Judy uses the story to focus Shane's attention on new problem-solving activity

**Figure 6.16** Shane's story, first-grade classroom. ("One dark stormy night I heard a loud noise and I looked outside and I saw a monster. I hit the monster with a brick and He fell down and I went back to sleep and the monster disappeared.")

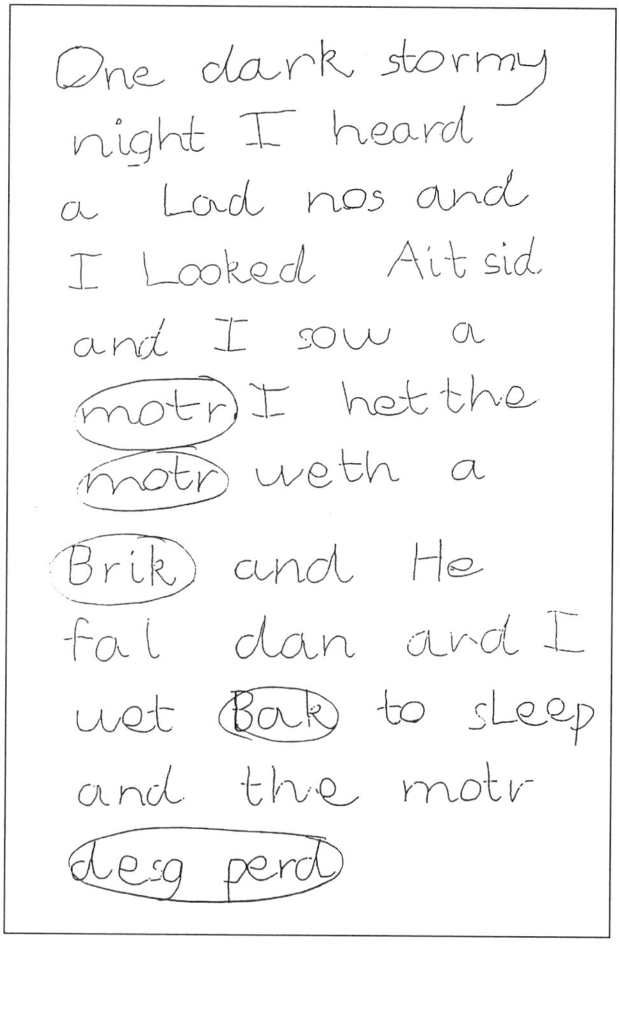
One dark stormy
night I heard
a Lod nos and
I Looked Ait sid
and I sow a
motr I het the
motr weth a
Brik and He
fal dan and I
wet Bak to sLeep
and the motr
desg perd

with the chunk *ck*: "Can you find the word *brick* in your story?" When Shane locates the word *brik*, she says, "Yes, you're right. That's the way the word sounds, but take a good look at the end of the word. Something doesn't look quite right. Can you find it?" Shane looks carefully at the word and exclaims, "That should be a *ck*, not a *k*!" Then Judy says, "Read your story again and see if you can find another word that ends like *brick*." Shane rereads the story, locates the word *back*, and comments, "That should be a *ck* too." Having observed that Shane is ready to move into further revision and editing, she instructs Shane to read over his story and circle the words that he will need to work on.

## Journal Writing Following Exposure to Revising and Editing

Although some simple editing techniques can be introduced when writing aloud, the teacher must not overwhelm the children with too much attention to them. Instead, she needs to keep her primary focus on the composition process. Even solving words is a temporary detour from the fluent construction of the message. Later, when revising and editing processes are introduced to the group, the focus of instruction shifts to include more attention on overt revisions and the specific editing techniques that result in publishable work.

### A Lesson with Early Writers

As children acquire more knowledge about the writing process, they exhibit a higher degree of control over their own work, applying independent strategies that were once demonstrated in a group setting. Their writing reflects revising and editing techniques that are necessary if their work is to be published.

The children are behaving like writers who have a message to share with an audience.

As the children write, Carla moves among them and makes occasional comments about their work. She records strategies used by individual students and identifies common areas that would make productive mini-lessons for the group. She allows time during each writing session to meet with at least two children for an individual conference.

Today Carla stops by Karrisa's desk and asks her to read her story (see the second draft in Figure 6.17), which she has been working on for the past two days. Afterward, Carla asks, "Is there anything else you would like to add?" Karrisa says, "I decided in my story I would not hit the people with my bommyknocker, even though they didn't find me any cats!" She continues, "I didn't want to be mean like the giant in the book." Karrisa is creating stories that link her personal and textual experiences.

Then Carla comments on Karrisa's independent editing skills. Although Karrisa shows progress in many areas, she needs support in using this knowledge more consistently and flexibly. Looking at Karrisa's story Carla observes that:

- She is beginning to edit as she writes (she has crossed out the word *oen* and changed it to *one*).

Figure 6.17 Karrisa's draft story.

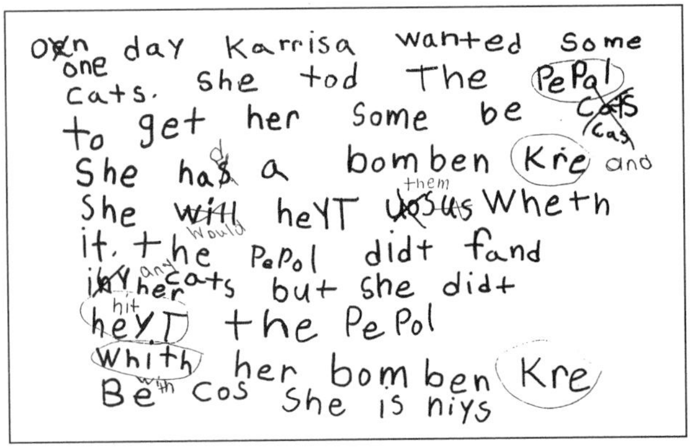

- She shows some evidence of monitoring structure (she has changed the verb tense of the word *has* to *had*).
- She is aware of some of her misspellings (she has circled *pepol*, *whith*, *kre*).
- She is starting to use periods with more consistency (all four sentences end with periods).
- She is somewhat aware that a sentence should begin with a capital letter (the second sentence begins with a capital letter).

During the follow-up conference, Carla praises Karrisa for her editing skills and focuses on helping her polish her work for publication. She encourages Karrisa to use available resources to correct her spellings for known words. She notes that Karrisa has written several of these words correctly in previous stories. Figure 6.18 is the published version of this story.

Figure 6.18 Karrisa's published story.

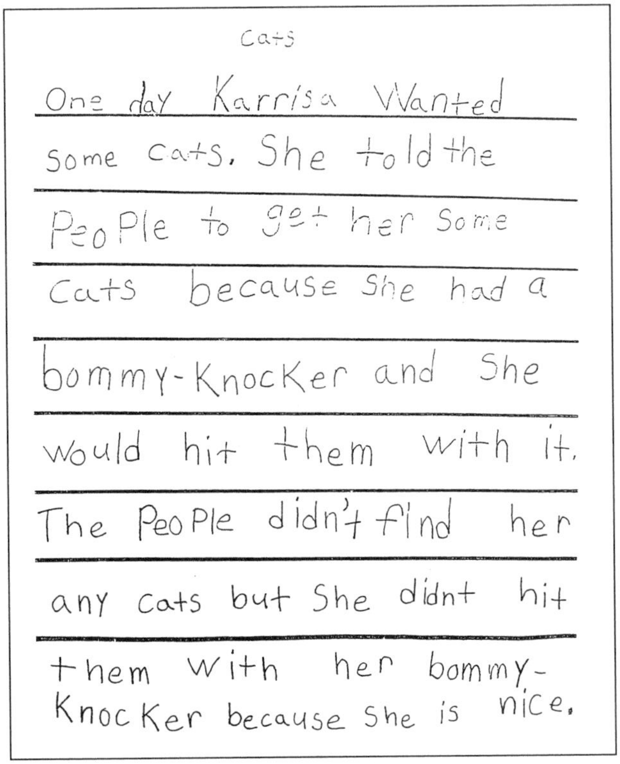

## A Lesson with Fluent Writers

The writing sample in Figure 6.19 is the first draft of a mystery story written by Tamarisk, a third grader. Comparing Tamarisk's work with Karrisa's, we see that both students are using their knowledge of text characteristics to create stories. Tamarisk has a more sophisticated style influenced by her more-varied experiences with texts. Her story is structured as a play with roles for herself and her friend Doris. Karrisa's story reveals her awareness that stories must adhere to a conventional set of rules that require a problem and a solution. In social interactions with a more knowledgeable person, both girls have acquired an understanding about written language that has carried over to their independent work. It is important that the teacher recognizes the individual needs of her students and designs conferences that address not only their current knowledge but also their potential level of development. The appendix examines the writing development of Laterica during the first ten weeks of her early literacy program. The transitions between lessons and the influence group assisted writing activities have on her independent writing are highlighted.

**Figure 6.19** Tamarisk's script.

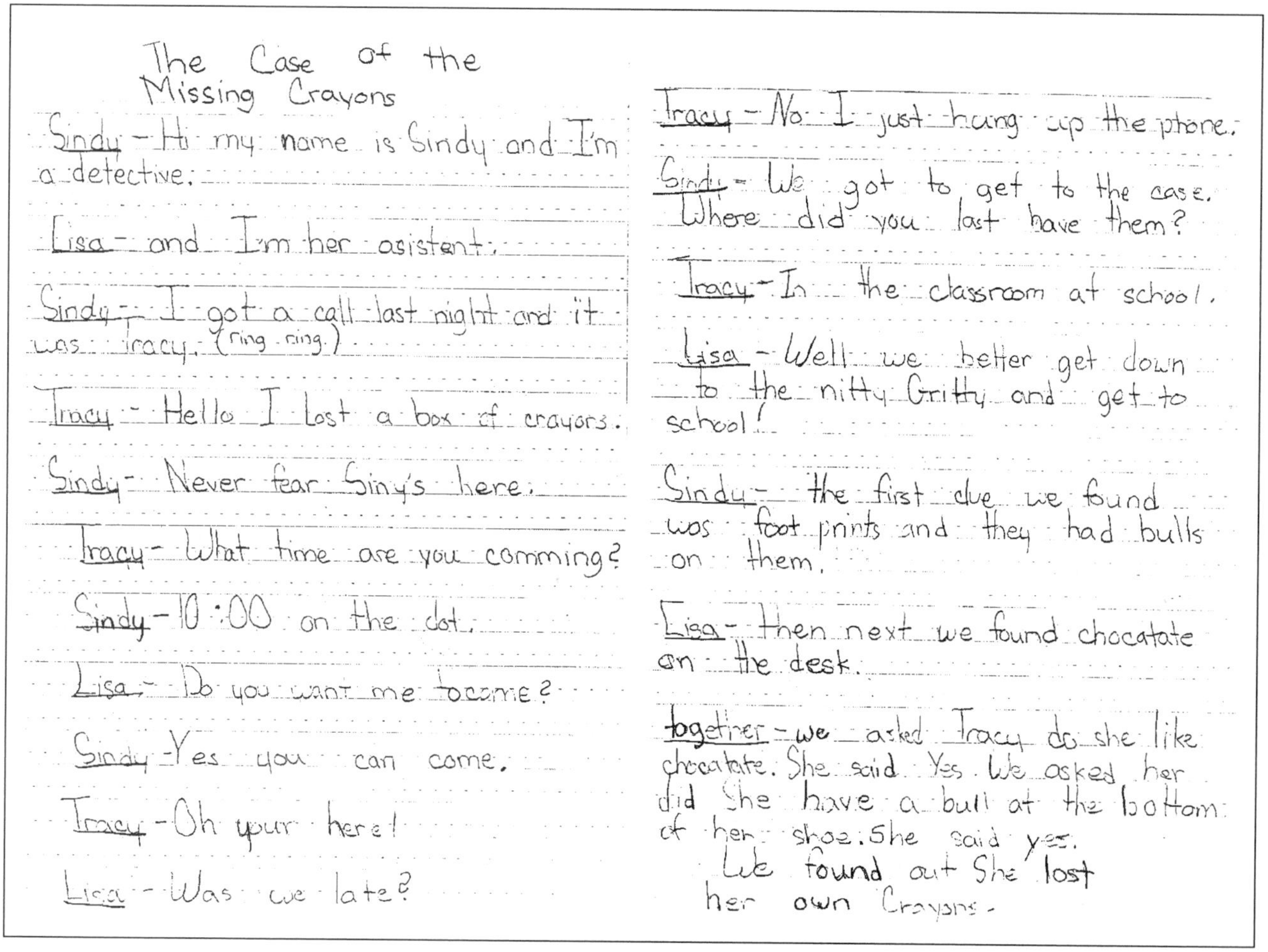
The Case of the Missing Crayons

Sindy - Hi my name is Sindy and I'm a detective.

Lisa - and I'm her asistent.

Sindy - I got a call last night and it was Tracy. (ring ring.)

Tracy - Hello I lost a box of crayons.

Sindy - Never fear Siny's here.

Tracy - What time are you comming?

Sindy - 10:00 on the dot.

Lisa - Do you want me to come?

Sindy - Yes you can come.

Tracy - Oh your here!

Lisa - Was we late?

Tracy - No. I just hung up the phone.

Sindy - We got to get to the case. Where did you last have them?

Tracy - In the classroom at school.

Lisa - Well we better get down to the nitty Gritty and get to school!

Sindy - the first clue we found was foot prints and they had bulls on them.

Lisa - then next we found chocatate on the desk.

together - we asked Tracy do she like chocatate. She said Yes. We asked her did She have a bull at the bottom of her shoe. She said yes. We found out She lost her own Crayons.

# Developing Phonetic Skills

Where does phonics instruction fit into an apprenticeship approach to literacy? Recently a great deal of attention has been focused on the teaching of phonics in the elementary grades, particularly first grade. Do we teach phonics in our program? Yes we do. Good teachers have always taught phonics. A child cannot learn to read without attending to letters and sounds.

We have already presented numerous examples of how teachers use phonetic activities during reading and writing. For instance, during assisted writing, children use ABC charts, magnetic letters, and practice boards to learn about letters, sounds, and words. While writing independently, children analyze the sequence of sounds within words and apply strategies for noting relationships between spelling patterns. To complement this learning, the teacher addresses phonetic skills during group and individual conferences. The teacher also prompts the children to locate, predict, confirm, and search for visual information while reading. All these activities occur within the context of meaningful read-ing and writing. In the process, children learn how to transfer their knowledge about letters, sounds, and words across varied and chang-ing circumstances.

This brings up a second question: do we teach phonics in isolation? Well, it depends on how you define isolation. In this chapter, we explore additional ways that knowledge of letters, sounds, and words are developed through mini-lessons. Learning about letters, sounds, and words is a strategic process, rather than memorization or drill. Thus we structure learning opportunities that focus on categorization, comparison, integration, and analysis of graphophonemic information. At the same time, we provide children with var-ied experiences that promote automatic and flexible control of letters and words. Although some of the information is presented in isola-tion from the text, it is *always* based on the knowledge, skills, and strategies the children bring to the task. As a result, the activities reinforce, link, and expand the children's learning through manipulation and explo-ration.

## Learning About Letters and Sounds

It is a mistake to think that because children know the names of letters, they will be successful readers. As teachers, we encounter children every day who can identify all the letters but are unable to read even the most simple text. Phonemic awareness, not letter knowledge, is a strong predictor of children's ability to read (Adams 1996). Yet, knowing the names of letters is valuable, because the names are labels for associating specific letters with their sounds. However, *children do* not *have to know all the letters or sounds before they can begin to read* (Clay 1991; Smith 1994). In a literacy apprenticeship, teachers design instructional interactions around continuous texts (both reading and writing) that help shape young children's development of phonemic knowledge.

As children develop letter knowledge, the teacher provides them with opportunities to learn the sound of the letter and how to construct the letter form. The process of learning letters, sounds, and graphic formations concurrently provides children with alternative feedback for checking and confirming each sensory system. This theory is supported by what we know about how the brain integrates multiple sources of information into a complex network of related knowledge (Sylwester 1995; Sousa 1995). Teachers enable children to access knowledge from various categories, thus strengthening the interconnections between related information.

Reading is a cognitive process whereby the brain applies a range of problem-solving strategies in order to make sense of the printed word. However, for the brain to process the visual information in print, we must have printed material in front of our eyes. The eyes (at the direction of the brain) pick up the visual information from print, and the brain classi-

fies the information according to existing categories (Smith 1994). Almost simultaneously, the brain integrates the visual information with other sources of knowledge—the auditory and physical characteristics of the letter, for example. Associations between multiple sources of data enable the child to make sense of an abstract form (i.e., the letter).

## Learning Words by Analogy

As soon as children have acquired some strategies for comparing letters, these strategies can be used to analyze the visual features of words. At the direction of the brain, the eyes search the word for distinguishable features—or known parts—which may or may not be associated with the entire word. Instead of searching for individual letter/sound categories (which is a slow process), the brain searches among its collection of logical word parts that can be used to problem-solve the unknown word. For example, if the unknown word is *stack,* and the brain has a category for words that start like *stop* and another category for words that end with *ack,* the brain integrates the visual information from these two known categories and responds with an appropriate choice for the unknown word. Searching six letter categories (*s-t-a-c-k*) individually is a much slower response. In *Becoming Literate: The Construction of Inner Control* (1991), Clay describes how "letter analysis is slow, requires more learning, allows for more error and is more difficult to re-instate as a word." Rather, children need to notice larger chunks of information: "the larger the pronounceable units a child can discover and use, the less learning effort will be required" (p. 290).

Goswami and Bryant (1990) and Moustafa (1997) discuss how beginning readers use onset and rime patterns as an analogy strategy for solving words. Take the word *stack.* The onset—any consonant sounds that precede the vowel—is *st,* and the rime—the vowel and any consonant sounds that come after it—is *ack.* Rimes are very useful for helping children develop phonological knowledge: nearly five hundred primary-grade-level words can be derived from a set of only thirty-seven rimes (Wiley and Durrell 1963, as quoted in Adams 1996). One of our colleagues, Kay Magness, has created a list of common onset and rime patterns that she uses to help her children learn how to manipulate word parts. Here are a few examples:

| Known Word Starts Like (onset) | Known Word Ends Like (rime) | New Word |
| --- | --- | --- |
| ball | sack | back |
| by | tall | ball |
| buy | me | be |
| boy | red | bed |
| book | pig | big |
| bat | cut | but |
| broke | mother | brother |
| cat | man | can |
| do | may | day |
| got | save | gave |
| good | hot | got |
| he | sad | had |

Teachers use sorting activities to help children acquire effective strategies for perceiving, concentrating, and remembering visual information. Using known sources as a cue, children develop classification strategies for organizing visual information into related groups. Through repeated practice, children internal-ize specific knowledge about printed language. As children become more competent, the teacher adjusts her level of support to accommodate this higher-level understanding.

In kindergarten, teachers promote this skill through picture-sorting activities in which children organize known pictures under a key letter. Before the lesson, Judy displays four letter cards (*b, c, d, f*) in a large pocket chart. The children are familiar with these letters, and each card contains a picture cue. To begin the lesson, Judy guides the children in a shared reading: they chant, "B, b, bat, C, c, cat, D, d, dog, F, f, fish." Then Judy holds up separate pictures of common objects that begin with one of the four letters in the chart. She prompts the children to identify the beginning letter by slightly stressing the initial sound: "What can you hear at the beginning of *fork*?" The children respond, "F!" Judy then asks a child to come to the chart and place the picture under the appropriate letter. This instructional conversation continues until all the cards have been placed in the appropriate pockets.

As children become more competent, this early skill is replaced by more complex strategies; sorting words according to multiple criteria, for example. Word-sorting activities are designed to help children acquire automatic control of orthographic patterns. This control is important because through it children have a ready storehouse of visual information that promotes fast and fluent responses to reading and writing. (Later in this chapter is an example of how Carla helps her first graders sort words according to child-generated categories.)

In literacy apprenticeship, there is no scope and sequence for learning particular letters and sounds; rather, the learning is guided by the knowledge that children bring to the task. The teacher designs instructional activities that are geared to validate old knowledge and activate new learning. As the children become more competent in certain areas, the teacher raises the ante.

## Mini-Lessons for Letter, Sound, and Word Knowledge

The teacher designs mini-lessons that help beginning readers learn about letters, sounds, spelling patterns, and words. The lessons take place with small groups or with an entire classroom of children.

In a whole-class setting, the lessons may last up to thirty minutes. The room arrangement enables the teacher to view the children's work with relative ease: the children sit in small groups, four or five children at a table, and the teacher circulates among them, observing their progress and prompting them as needed (see Figures 7.1 and Figures 7.2).

A small-group mini-lesson centers on a teaching point after guided reading or an interactive writing lesson. The children sit at a table or gather around the teacher in a small

**Figure 7.1** A small group of children sorts and analyzes letters.

circle on the floor. Since the children are grouped according to similar strengths, the teacher is able to focus on the needs of a smaller group. These mini-lessons generally do not last longer than five or six minutes. Obviously, the teacher is able to observe the children's progress in more detail in a small group.

Whatever the format, the teacher arranges the lesson in such a way that maximum learning can occur. Both whole-class and small-group lessons require a well-organized environment designed to promote successful experiences for all the children.

### Preparing Materials for Small-Group Mini-Lessons

In the following examples, Carla presents mini-lessons to a small group of first graders. For each child she has prepared:

- A small basket containing a set of preselected magnetic letters, one dry-erase marker, tissue for erasing, and one colored marker for recording words in the dictionary.
- A magnetic dry-erase lapboard (about nine inches by twelve inches).
- A small eight-by-ten ABC chart (a reduced version of the larger group chart).
- A letter-sound book for each letter of the alphabet (these can be purchased or made).
- A small blank personal dictionary that has the corresponding key word from the ABC chart at the top of each page.

Carla also gathers the following materials for her own use:

- A large magnetic dry-erase board sitting on an easel.
- Dry-erase markers.

**Figure 7.2** A teacher helps her students as they work together on letters and words.

- A large ABC chart identical to the children's copies.
- Magnetic letters.
- A large class dictionary.
- A commercially published children's dictionary.

## Multiple Ways of Learning About Print

In this lesson, for emergent to early readers, Carla gradually increases the task difficulty. Her instruction and language scaffold the children as the activities become more complex. She prompts them to think about how to categorize, associate, link, and generalize informa-

tion. The lesson begins with a simple-letter sorting activity and ends when the children record a new word in their dictionary.

Carla calls the children to a carpeted area of the room, and they sit in a small circle around her. Each individual lapboard contains three sets of lowercase letters *t*, *s*, and *o*, placed in the upper-left-hand corner. A circle has been drawn in the center of each child's board. Carla tells the children, "Look on your board at all the letters that are over to the side. I want you to find all the *t*s and put them in your circle and say the name of the letter as you bring it over." Since the children are already familiar with these letters, Carla knows this simple task will elicit fluent, quick responses. When the children have finished sorting, Carla prompts them to check their work: "I want you to check it really good. Look at the other letters and make sure there are no *t*s left."

Next Carla directs their attention to the formation of the letter. She says, "Now, let's trace over the letter *t* and let's say how we make it. Watch me first." Carla uses explicit language to describe her movement pattern ("Down, across") and matches the words with her action of creating the *t* form. "Now," she asks the children, "what is that letter?" The children respond, "*T*." When Carla is certain that the children understand her intentions, she instructs them to go to the side of their board and write the letter *t*. She reminds them, "Be sure to say how you make it as you write it." As the children write the *t*, Carla observes them carefully to be sure they are using the correct movement pattern and that they check and confirm their work.

Carla wants the children to know the letter in several ways:

- The letter name.
- The movement pattern for forming the letter.
- The sound of the letter.
- The feel of the sound in the mouth.
- The way the letter looks in a word.

Therefore, her next interaction focuses on guiding the children to associate letters with sounds. Through explicit language and coaching, Carla helps the children acquire some special cues for the letter-sound relationship. She uses the *t* letter-sound book and the ABC chart. First she asks, "What letter is on the cover of the book?" Then she prompts them to relate the letter to the picture cue: "What is the picture on the cover?" The children exclaim, "Tiger!" Carla goes on to link this information with the ABC chart:

**Carla:** Billy, go find a *t* on our ABC chart. What is the picture on the chart that starts with a *t*?

**Billy:** Tiger.

**Carla:** So we have tiger on the cover of the book and a tiger on our chart. Why do you think they put a picture of a tiger there?

**Kevin:** Because *tiger* starts with *t*.

Next Carla guides the children to use still other senses to reinforce and extend this information. She says, "Let's all say *tiger*; let your mouth feel the *t* sound." Carla says the word, stressing the beginning sound. As the children repeat the word, she encourages them to articulate their knowledge: "Where do you feel the *t*?" Several children comment, "The top of my mouth." Voices murmur throughout the room as the children practice this new learning.

Now Carla links the *t* sound with other words that start that way. Together, she and the children look through the pictures of colorful objects in the *t* book and name each object: *turtle, tiger, teeth, television*. From time to time, Carla asks, "Now, what letter is that? Can you find it? Check to be sure the word starts with a *t*."

**Carla:** How are all the words alike in this book?

**Children:** They all start with *t*.

**Carla:** Do we know anyone whose name starts with a *t*?

**Children:** Tanisha!

Carla moves on, getting the children to notice relationships between upper- and lowercase letter forms. She directs their attention to a large pocket chart that contains all the children's names, which have been cut apart into individual letters. She says, "Tanisha, bring the *T* from your name and let's see how it is different from the *t* in your book." Tanisha goes to the pocket chart, returns with the *T*, and points to the appropriate letters as she says, "This a capital *T* and this is a little *t*."

Next Carla directs the children's attention to the large ABC chart and the alphabetical placement of the *t* on the chart: "I want you to look at the ABC chart and tell me where the *t* is. Is it at the beginning or near the end of the alphabet?" "Near the end," the children respond.

**Carla:** Let's look at our class ABC book and put Tanisha's name in the book. Where do we need to open the book to—the beginning or the end?
**Children:** The end.
**Carla:** Why?
**Children:** Because the *t* is near the end of the alphabet.
**Carla:** Tanisha, can you find the *t* page and write your name in the book? (*Tanisha quickly does so.*)

Carla's final interaction focuses on learning a new word that starts with the letter *t*. She signals her intentions by saying, "Now I am going to teach you an important word that starts with the letter *t*. The word is *to*." Carla models how to make the word *to* on her magnetic board. After she makes the word, she reads it and checks it with her finger.

Then she tells the children to take a good look at the word and find the letters they need to make the word on their board. The children quickly search for the *t* and the *o* and make the word *to*. Carla emphasizes the importance of speed: "Okay, I want you to make it fast. Push the word over to the side and write the word real fast in your circle. What is the word you are writing?" When the children respond correctly, Carla asks a series of reinforcing questions: "What letter does it begin with? What

are other words that begin like *to*?" Then she has the children record the new word in their dictionary.

**Carla:** Now, we need to put the word *to* in our personal dictionaries. Where do you need to turn—at the beginning or the end?
**Nick:** Near the end.
**Carla:** Quickly, everyone find your *t* page. What are you going to write on the *t* page?
**Children:** *To*.

Next Carla has the children add the new word to other learning aids in the room: "Where else do we need to put our new word?" The children respond, "On the word

**Figure 7.3** Children practice learning a new word by making the word with magnetic letters and writing it several times.

wall under the *t.*" Carla hands Nick a blank index card: "Okay, Nick, write the word on this card and put it on the word wall." "Anywhere else?" Carla asks. "In our class dictionary," says Laterica. Carla hands a marker to Laterica, who quickly finds the *t* page and writes the new word.

Carla ends the lesson by asking the children to reflect on their learning: "Everybody, I want you to think a moment and tell me one thing you learned about the letter *t* today." Quickly, the children begin to articulate their new learning:

**Laterica:** Tanisha starts with *t,* but it is a capital *T.*
**Kevin:** *To* starts with *t.*
**Tanisha:** *T* is at the end of the alphabet.
**Billy:** *T* is at the top of our mouth.
**Nick:** We have three words on the word wall that start with *t.*

## Learning New Words

For this lesson, Carla has displayed the letters *e, y, b, o, b, t* across the top of the children's magnetic boards. Again, these are known letters, so she expects the children to respond quickly: "I want you to bring your letters down really fast and tell me the names of each letter. Ready? Go! Fast!" Afterward, the children push the letters back to the top of the board.

Her next instructional move is to use two of the letters to make a known word: "Make the word *be.* You know this word, so you should be able to make it really fast." Carla knows the children must gain automatic control of some frequently encountered words, which they can then use to monitor their reading and writing. She wants these words to enter their long-term memory so that they'll be

**Figure 7.4** Children record a new word in their personal dictionaries.

able to concentrate on more important reading tasks.

The children build the word rapidly, then check it with their fingers. Carla prompts them to reflect on their actions: "Were you fast? Did you check it to be sure you are right?" The children confirm their actions, and Carla moves on: "Now, bring down two letters and make the word *by*—right underneath *be.* How are they alike?" The children make the two words and explain, "They both start with *b.*" Carla uses this experience to activate old knowledge, coaching the children to think of other words that start with *b.* The children respond with various *b* words from previous experiences.

Carla then prompts the children to new learning: "Now I want you to take two more letters and make the word *to.* Put the word *to* right under your other two words. After you finish, read all three words. Be sure to check your work." As the children read all three words, Carla asks, "Which word starts differently?" In unison, the children respond with the word *to*. Next Carla instructs the children to turn their magnetic boards around to the dry-erase side. She says, "Pick one word that you can write really fast and write it." Carla concludes the lesson by encouraging the children to record the words in their personal dictionaries.

## Working with Known Words

The instructional interactions in this lesson are designed to emphasize letter-sound cues and fluency with known words. In preparation, Carla has organized the letters *b, t, e, h, e, h, e, e* across the top of the children's magnetic boards. She instructs, "Quickly pull your letters down and say their names." Then she says, "Use the letters and make three words you know." The children quickly make *be, the,* and *he*, in various orders. Carla has the children read their words. Then, activating new learning, she asks: "Which word starts like *balloon*?" Billy responds, "*Be*." Next she asks, "Do you know other words that start like *balloon* and *be*?" The children call out various responses: *Billy, bike,* and *bananas*. Then Carla says, "Take a good look at the words you made. Tell me how your words are the same." Laterica comments, "They all end with *e*."

Carla knows that the children must gain automatic control of frequently encountered words. So she prompts the children, "Turn your board over and get ready to write fast." Then she calls out the words *be* and *he*, which the children write fluently. Next she says, "Now write the word *the*." She observes that the children show no hesitancy in shifting their attention from similar patterns (*be* and *he*) to a new pattern (*the*).

Next Carla links the children's knowledge about *the* to a new situation: "If you add the word *the* to our dictionaries, what key word will help us with the first letters?" This is an easy question, because the *th* chunk is displayed on the ABC chart, which is read every day during shared reading. "*Thirty!*" Laterica and Nick exclaim with confidence.

Carla proceeds, guiding the children to associate the letters with other sensory information: "Everybody say *thirty*. Where is your tongue?" The children repeat the word and comment, "Touching my teeth—at the top of my mouth." Carla continues to prompt the children to new cognitive activity: "Where would you find *thirty* in your dictionary—in the beginning, middle, or end?" The children respond with confidence, "At the end."

"Now quickly," Carla says, "I want you to find the pages in your dictionaries where you can write the words *he* and *be*. You know where to look. I won't help you unless you need me." The children independently find the correct pages and record the new words.

## Simple Analogies with Onset and Rime

In the next lesson, Carla raises the ante. Instead of giving the children words to make, she prompts them to make their own words from a selection of magnetic letters. She has displayed *a, c, a, l, n, t, a, l* at the top of the children's magnetic boards. Quickly, the children pull down the appropriate letters and construct three known words, *can, all, at*.

Now Carla guides the children to manipulate onset and rime to make a new word: "Borrow the *c* from *can* and put it in front of *at*. What is the new word?" Carla watches the children to ensure they understand what she's said. Without hesitation, the children move the appropriate letter and respond with the correct word, *cat*. Then Billy points to the rime (*an*) that remains on his board from *can* and comments, "There's a new word, *an*." Carla acknowledges Billy's response and guides the children further: "Now take the *c* from *cat* and put it in front of *all*. Quickly, what is your new word?" "*Call*," the children exclaim.

Next Carla prompts the children to practice the same simple analogies in a different context. She says, "Turn your board over and write the word *at*." Since this is a known word, the children write the word quickly. "What word did you write?" Carla asks. The children say *at*, establishing auditory support for the rime. Then Carla directs the children's attention to the letter *f* and the identifying picture on the ABC chart: "Now borrow something from *fish* and put it in front of *at*. What is the new word?" The children quickly add an *f* to the word *at* and respond "*fat!*"

Then Carla prompts the children to articulate what they've done. She asks, "What did you do to make your new words?" In unison, several voices respond, "Put a new letter in front of the word." Since the children have demonstrated that they understand the concept of changing onsets to construct new words, Carla prompts them to provide their own examples: "Who can think of a letter that we can put in front of *all* to make a new word?" Several children respond with appropriate letters for making new words: *ball, hall,* and *tall*.

Now Carla shifts the mini-lesson emphasis to recording information in the class dictionary. Her goal is to promote fast and flexible use of the dictionary: "Look on the *a* page. Where is it?" "First!" the children exclaim. "*F* page?" Carla asks. "Middle!" the children say. Next Carla throws out a word cue: "Where will we put the word *all*? What page?" "*A* page. At the beginning," the children respond quickly.

"Okay," says Carla, "Find the *c* page." She wants to guide the children to apply the analogy strategy in a new context. The children quickly flip to the *c* page in their personal dictionaries. "Now listen. Borrow the *c* from *can* and put it in front of *all*. Write the new word in your dictionary." All the children record the word *call*. Carla prompts them to create one more word and then asks the children to read the new words.

## More Analogies with Onset and Rime

Now that the children understand the concept of analogies for making new words, Carla places a larger selection of magnetic letters—*b, h, e, c, t, a, u, p, m, e, r, p, j*—randomly at the top of the children's lapboards. She begins the lesson by prompting the children to make two familiar words, *jump* and *be*. Then she says, "Borrow the *b* from *be*. Now take away the ending chunk from *jump*. Make a new word." The children quickly construct the new word *bump*.

**Carla:** Push all the letters to the top of the board. Now pull down the letters you need to make *old*. Make it fast! Check it. Now make *cat*. You can make it fast, because you know that word really well. Now borrow something from *cat*. Put it in front of *old*. Make a new word. What is it?

As the children move the letters around, Carla carefully observes their behavior and is prepared to increase her support if needed. Without hesitation, the children construct the new word *cold*. After constructing the word, Nick comments, "If you put a *f* in front of it, you have *fold*." Clearly Nick is able to generate new examples from old experiences.

Carla continues to increase the complexity of the task: "Now make *her*." The children quickly pull down the necessary letters to construct the new word. Carla prompts the children to use their knowledge in a new activity: "What could you borrow from *her* and add to the end of *cold* to make a new word?" The children exclaim "*Er*." "That's right!" says Carla. "What is your new word?" The children add the *er* chunk to the end of *cold* and respond, "*Colder!*"

Carla ends the lesson by encouraging the children to articulate what they have done: "Tell me what you did to make new words." The children respond with several explanations that reflect their understanding of the analogy strategy for constructing new words.

## Using Poetry to Activate Knowledge of Spelling Patterns

By this time, the children have had many experiences built around analogy, always working in their zone of proximal development. In the next lesson Carla uses three poems to help them manipulate patterns in their heads. After Carla and the children read the first poem fluently, Carla prompts them to manipulate word patterns in their minds. She says, "Tell me two words that rhyme." Simultaneously, several children cry, "*An* and *pan!*" Carla prompts the children to quickly segment the rime and identify it: "If I take the *p* off *pan*, what chunk is left?" In unison, the children respond, "*An!*"

**Carla:** Tell me two more words that rhyme.
**Children:** *Mouse* and *house!*
**Carla:** If I take the *m* off *mouse*, what would the remaining chunk be?
**Children:** *Ouse!*
**Carla:** Put the *h* in front of the chunk and what is the new word?
**Children:** *House!*

Carla immediately introduces a new poem. Together she and the children read "Little Miss Muffet." Afterward Carla says, "Karrisa, tell me two words that rhyme." Without hesitation, Karrisa answers, "*Muffet* and *Tuffet!*" Carla uses explicit, redundant language to scaffold the children's actions: "If I take off the *t* from *tuffet*, what's the remaining chunk?" The children respond, "*Uffet!*" Again Carla coaches: "Take the *m* from *me*, put it in front of *uffet*, and tell me the new word." The children exclaim, "*Muffet!*"

Carla and the children read the third poem, "Little Boy Blue." As before, Carla prompts: "Tell me two words that rhyme." Laterica answers, "*I* and *cry*." As Carla points to the two words in the poem, she validates Laterica's response and activates a higher level of analysis: "Yes, they do sound alike. Now let's see if they look the same." In previous lessons, the children have sorted words according to spelling patterns; thus they are familiar with how sounds can be represented by different letters. Carla invites Laterica to come to the chart and circle the two words. After Laterica locates *I* and *cry*, Carla says, "Do they look the same?" "No," the children respond.

**Carla:** Who can think of a word that looks and sounds like *cry*.
**Nick:** *My!*
**Carla:** Write the words *cry* and *my* on your board. Quickly, what is the part that looks the same?
**Children:** The *y!*

Carla prompts the children for one more example: "Find two words that rhyme." Nick says, "Meadow," but hesitates when he realizes there is no rhyming word on the chart. Carla increases her support: "Let's read it again and listen to the rhyming words." After

**Figure 7.5**  Word charts and pocket charts are used to manipulate onset and rhyme patterns.

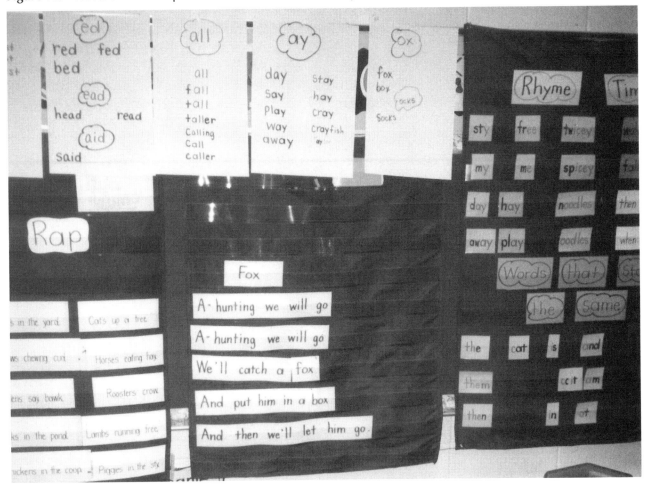

the second reading, Nick exclaims, *"Horn* and *corn!"*

## Organizing Words

For the next lesson, Carla randomly distributes a small pile of word tiles, approximately twenty words per child. She instructs the children, "Now you know many ways that words are alike and are different. So I want you to look through your words and group them together in any way you want to." She encourages the children to articulate some

ways that words can be classified: "What are some ways that we group the words together?" As the children call out various categories, Carla records their responses on a flipchart:

- Words that start the same.
- Words that end the same.
- Rhyming words.
- One-, two-, and three-syllable words.
- Words in the class dictionary.
- Words on the word wall.
- Words that end in *ed, ing, er.*

As the children organize their words, Carla observes the classifications they choose. The children extend their personal groupings by exchanging word tiles with other group members. For instance, Nick's category is words from his dictionary, and he recruits help from the other children in his group. He exclaims, "Hey, I know *they*! I need *they*! Who has *they*?" Laterica quickly scans her word pile and without comment picks up the word *they* and throws it into Nick's pile. Carla notes that Laterica has organized nine words into three categories: words that include the *at* chunk, words that start with *s*, and words with two letters. Laterica seems somewhat puzzled about how to manage the nine remaining words in her pile, which do not fit her other categories. Looking at Billy's pile, she sees a word that she needs. Pointing to the word *she*, Laterica says, "I'll give you these words for that word." And so the children bargain with one another as categories are established, negotiated, and expanded. Occasionally, Carla leans over and coaches a child to notice a new relationship.

Next Carla invites all the children to describe how they organized their words. As the lesson comes to an end, Carla picks up the small pile of remaining words and says, "Listen as I read these words and see if they fit anybody's categories." This activity comes to a fluent close as the children respond no to all words, with the exception of *my*, which is put into Laterica's two-word category.

## Activities for Promoting Familiarity with Frequently Encountered Words

Children must acquire a ready storehouse of common words. As the children encounter these words in authentic reading and writing, the teacher looks for memorable opportunities to focus the children's attention on the visual features.

In selecting appropriate words for mini-lessons, the teacher examines the children's reading materials and lists the most commonly occurring words. The children should know these words instantly and thus be able to focus on the real task of reading, which is to construct meaning. If children experience difficulty with these words, their reading fluency will be disrupted.

It is important to select words for mini-lessons that the children have already encountered in text or have already written in a story. However, children need repeated encounters with a word before it ceases to be a partially known word and enters their long-term memory. The textual experience is an entry point. The teacher can use the partially known information as a foundation for further visual analysis. Thus the teacher plans activities that enable the children to gain fast and unconscious control of important commonly occurring words. After such a mini-lesson, the teacher is careful to bring the children back to meaningful text. For instance, she might:

- Encourage the children to locate and read the word in the story.
- Have the children look for the word in other texts.
- Have the children locate the word in a story they are writing.

Some ways in which classroom teachers can help children learn frequently encountered words are by:

- Placing the words on word walls (see Cunningham 1996).
- Writing the words on narrow strips taped to the children's desks for easy reference.
- Recording the words in personal dictionaries.
- Recording the words in large class dictionaries.

- Filing the words in alphabetized word banks.
- Classifying the words on wall charts according to particular criteria (first letters, ending letters, number of letters, etc).

In addition, the teacher can provide the children with opportunities to practice word development on their own. We discuss this in more detail in Chapter 8, but some independent activities might include:

- Playing speed games with word cards.
- Circling words in familiar poems (which have been laminated).
- Constructing words with magnetic letters.
- Categorizing letter cards, word tiles, or other manipulatives according to teacher- or self-generated classification systems.
- Practicing writing the words quickly in a variety of places and with different media.

### Word Searches

Here's an example of using word searches with a group of third graders. The children are very familiar with how words work; they have manipulated words using magnetic letters, word cards, word walls, and word sorts. Linda has encouraged them to search for similar patterns in books, poems, or other reading materials.

Now she decides to introduce them to the *ation* ending. She begins by writing the following words on a large piece of chart paper and underlining the visual pattern: n*ation*, excla-m*ation*, imagin*ation*, observ*ation*, educ*ation*, determin*ation*, relax*ation*, and starv*ation*. She invites the children to chant the words with her, so that they can hear the similar sound in the ending chunk. Then she encourages the children, in small groups, to search their books for similar patterns. The new words they find are added to the word chart.

Linda expands the activity by including short definitions of the words and asking the children to incorporate the words and definitions into a class poem. Here's the result:

When rain falls from the sky, that's precipitation.
When you mix blue and yellow, that's a green combination.
When you write CA for California, that's an abbreviation.
When a seed begins to sprout, that's germination.
When someone really bugs you, that's aggravation.
When you work with your friends, that's participation.
When liquid turns to steam, that's evaporation.
When you finish high school, that's graduation.
When you take a short cut in addition, that's multiplication.
When you give life to something that's not living, that's personification.
When you put something in your brain, that's memorization.
When you are going someplace special, that's destination.
When you give thanks to someone, that's appreciation.
When people live and work together, that's civilization.
When Tamarisk starts to laugh, that's gigglelagation!!!

## Closing Thoughts

This chapter presents ways in which teachers can help young children acquire phonetic knowledge. Although the lessons take place in isolation, they originate from contact with meaningful texts. In a literacy apprenticeship, the teacher structures lessons that provide children with flexible opportunities to apply word-level strategies across repeated and varied circumstances. It is important to link new learning to old learning: the knowledge children already have about letters, sounds, spelling patterns, and words creates a personal foundation for noticing new relationships and forming generalizations about how written language works. The teacher plays a critical role, coaching the children through guided participation and scaffolded instruction.

# Establishing Routines and Organizing the Classroom

Throughout this book, we have emphasized the importance of two types of learning:

- That which occurs in the zone of proximal development (i.e., the children require the teacher's assistance).
- That which occurs in the zone of actual development (i.e., the children are able to work independently).

Children need opportunities to work both with assistance and unassistedly during a typical classroom day. Flexible grouping accommodates the learning zones of the children.

Recently a classroom teacher told us, "I keep hearing all this talk about grouping as though it is something new. For years we have grouped children—interest groups, writing groups, reading groups, literacy groups, flexible groups, literature groups, peer groups, center groups, whole groups, small groups." We agree that grouping has been around for many years; yet we also recognize that many of our past grouping practices have resulted in ineffective learning opportunities for young children. The renewed interest in small groups comes with a caution: *groups should be dynamic, flexible, changing structures based on an understanding that all children do not learn at the same pace and in the same way.* Children make connections based on their existing knowledge and acquire new learning at different rates. Teachers must be good observers of children's literacy behavior and know how to accommodate group placements based on children's progress.

In Chapter 4, we addressed guided reading groups; in Chapter 5, we described the instructional purposes of three types of writing groups. In this chapter, we examine the "nuts and bolts" of organizational structures by which classroom teachers provide their children with a balance of assisted and independent activities.

An important principle of apprenticeship learning is the role of routines in promoting literacy development. Teachers must create well-organized learning environments encompassing familiar routines that promote children's independence. It is important for children to participate in planning, rehearsing, and organizing the learning structure of the classroom. In doing so, they acquire important organizational skills that are directly linked to the development of self-regulation.

Let's apply this theory to Harriet and her first graders. Harriet is a reading specialist who provides supplemental literacy support to high-risk readers. Harriet believes that children must learn management skills for regulating their own activities during the day. At the beginning of the year, Harriet coaches the children in self-management techniques: retrieving and storing their own materials, recognizing the signals for moving into new instructional activities, and understanding the how and why of particular routines. Harriet models the expected behavior, uses explicit language to describe her actions, and guides the children through rehearsals of the expected routines. Thus the children have conceptual models of acceptable standards that they can use as benchmarks for evaluating their own performances in certain areas. When children internalize the concept of acceptable standards for particular classroom behavior, they have a scaffold that frees them to focus on the real issues of learning.

The process of teaching routines and high expectations is also evident in Angela's first-grade classroom. Angela arranges her classroom to accommodate the children's zones of learning. In a cozy corner enclosed with bookcases used to store reading and writing materials, small groups of children with similar needs gather for assisted reading and writing. The children are very familiar with their rotating schedule, they know when they will meet with Angela in small reading and writing groups. There are other literacy corners where children can practice their skills, strategies, and knowledge in independent work. In the center of the room, tables are pushed together in small clusters to enable the children to work with partners. At the front of the room is a large carpeted area surrounded by displays of familiar texts, including Big Books, poetry cards, and stapled collections of stories written during assisted writing. To one side of the room, next to the word wall, is a long writing table with several dictionaries, a thesaurus, letter and word books, and assorted publishing materials. A bathtub, a rocking chair, and comfortable cushions are cozy environments for familiar reading.

Carolyn also designed her first-grade classroom to facilitate assisted and unassisted learning experiences. Several years ago, she removed all the desks and replaced them with round tables and personal cubbies for storing the children's materials. This open space lets her assemble dynamic groups, which she constantly adjusts to reflect their members' changing needs. Everywhere there is the soft murmur of learning.

## Small Groups Versus the Whole Class

No two teachers incorporate literacy groups into their daily schedule in exactly the same way. Each takes the basic framework and molds it to fit her curriculum and her teaching style. Some elements of the framework are suitable for whole-group instruction, others require small groups.

Shared reading works well as a whole-class activity, provided the children are gathered closely around the teacher and she is using a text with large-enough print. Guided reading requires that children be placed in groups at their instructional level. These groups must be small enough so that the teacher can observe each child's reading strategies, because these observations allow her to extend the children's cognitive development. A teacher monitoring a whole class or large reading group often misses these opportunities.

The same holds true for assisted writing groups. Writing and spelling development is transitional: the teacher needs to structure writing experiences to validate the children's current abilities and to activate new learning. These opportunities are missed when children are part of a large instructional group that may not suit their current abilities. Responsive teaching depends on careful observations and spontaneous adjustments by the teacher.

Most teachers want all the children in their class to write in a journal every day. However, monitoring journal writing is a daunting task. The task becomes manageable when a teacher closely monitors the source of a selected group of children each day, usually one that has participated in an assisted writing activity that day.

Letter identification and word building can be done as a whole class or in small group, depending on the task. Beginning letter sorting with magnetic letters works best in a small group under the close supervision of the teacher, so she can scaffold the task. On the other hand, word building and manipulating letter patterns with magnetic letters or small letter cards can easily be accomplished with the whole class.

## Rotation Schedules

Perhaps some specific examples of how a literacy block might be broken down will give a better idea of how a teacher might manage both whole-class and small-group instruction. Schedule 1 (see Figure 8.1) is for a two-hour block devoted to reading and language arts. Teachers with more or less time will need to adjust the schedule accordingly. Incorporating things like opening activities, activity periods,

recess, and lunch may also alter the sequence of activities.

Following Schedule 1, the teacher begins her block with whole-class shared reading. From there, the children are assigned independent activities in different areas of the room, called literacy corners. (See below for more on literacy corners.)

While the children are working in the literacy corners, the teacher begins pulling out small groups for assisted instruction. Schedule 1 shows four small-group periods; two for guided reading and two for assisted writing. On Mondays and Wednesdays, the teacher meets with groups 1 and 3 for guided reading and groups 2 and 4 for assisted writing; the groups flip-flop on Tuesdays and Thursdays. Therefore, the teacher sees each child each day in either a reading or a writing group. The composition of the groups is adjusted to accommodate the children's progress over time and varies throughout the school year. Also, as children acquire more common understanding about the writing process, the need for small-group writing lessons may be reduced. When this happens, the teacher may choose to work with larger groups of children during assisted writing, thus allowing more time for independent writing and conferences. The point to keep in mind with any schedule is that as the children's strengths and needs change, the schedule is adjusted accordingly.

Immediately following the small-group segments, everyone returns to his or her desk for journal writing. While the children are writing, the teacher visits one small group of four, five, or six children to conduct journal conferences, meeting with a different group of writers each day.

Finally, the teacher works with the whole class on phonics and spelling activities. She uses both magnetic letters and letter cards (see Chapter 7) to ensure that each child has some

**Figure 8.1** Schedule 1 (for a two-hour literacy block).

| Time | Activity | Group Size |
|---|---|---|
| 15 minutes | Shared reading and read-aloud | Whole class |
| 20 minutes | Familiar reading and guided reading<br>**Mon/Wed:** *Group 1*<br>**Tues/Thurs:** *Group 2*<br>Take running record on 1–2 children<br>**Friday:** Book talks | Small homogeneous groups at instructional reading levels<br><br><br>Heterogeneous groups at interest levels |
| 20 minutes | Familiar reading and guided reading<br>**Mon/Wed:** *Group 3*<br>**Tues/Thurs:** *Group 4*<br>Take running record on 1–2 children<br>**Friday:** Book talks | Small homogeneous groups at instructional reading levels<br><br><br>Heterogeneous groups at interest levels |
| 15 minutes | Assisted writing (interactive, writing aloud, revising, and editing)<br>**Mon/Wed**: *Group 2*<br>**Tues/Thurs:** *Group 1*<br>**Friday:** Publishing conferences | Small groups of children with similar strengths and needs |
| 15 minutes | Assisted writing (interactive, writing aloud, revising, and editing)<br>**Mon/Wed:** *Group 4*<br>**Tues/Thurs:** *Group 3*<br>**Friday:** Publishing Conferences | Small groups of children with similar strengths and needs |
| 15 minutes | Journal writing | Whole class writes; the teacher monitors a different small group each day |
| 20 minutes | Phonics and spelling | Whole class or small group, depending on the activity |

manipulatives for the activities. If the teacher needs to pull out a small group at this time, the other children move back into literacy corners.

On Fridays, the teacher still meets with small groups. However, she is not meeting with homogeneous groups for guided reading or assisted writing. Her Friday focus is on book talks and literature extensions. Therefore, she pulls children together for small-group discussions based on the type of stories they have been reading during guided reading. For example, groups 1 and 3 may both be reading about caterpillars and butterflies. Even though group 1 is reading an early guided reading text and group 3 is reading at a fluent level, they can all participate in a discussion and semantic mapping activity about the topic.

Schedules 2 and 3 contain the same elements of the literacy framework, altered slightly as to order and time allocations. (And neither schedule includes book talks.)

Schedule 2 (see Figure 8.2) has the teacher seeing four guided reading groups two times each week. However, the time allocation for each group has been reduced by five minutes. In addition, in Schedule 2 the teacher meets with only one assisted writing group each day, each group once a week.

Schedule 3 (see Figure 8.3) differs slightly in guided reading instruction. This teacher sees three groups for daily instruction. And like Schedule 2, this schedule has the teacher seeing only one group per day for assisted writing instruction and journal writing.

## Organizing Materials for Small Group Instruction

Any teacher arranging a work area for small-group instruction will want to make sure there is easy access to materials. Some teachers have a bookshelf near their guided reading table on which to store their book sets in baskets or boxes labeled according to the difficulty level (see Figure 8.4). Others place the guided reading books for each reading group in a basket labeled for that particular group (see Figure 8.5).

Some teachers take reading records on notebook paper attached to a clipboard. These

**Figure 8.2** Schedule 2 (for a two-and-a-half-hour literacy block).

| Time | Literacy Component | Group Size |
|---|---|---|
| 20 minutes | Shared reading | Whole class |
| 30 minutes | Guided reading and running record<br>**Mon/Wed:** *Blue Team*<br>**Tues/Thurs:** *Red Team*<br>Teams alternate on Friday | Small homogeneous groups on the same instructional level |
| 30 minutes | Guided reading and running record<br>**Mon/Wed:** *Green Team*<br>**Tues/Thurs:** *Yellow Team*<br>Teams alternate on Friday | Small homogeneous groups on the same instructional level |
| 20 minutes | Assisted writing<br>**Mon:** *Group 1*<br>**Tues:** *Group 2*<br>**Wed:** *Group 3*<br>**Thurs:** *Group 4*<br>**Friday:** *Group 5* | Small groups of similar abilities |
| 20 minutes | Journal writing<br>**Mon:** *Group 1*<br>**Tues:** *Group 2*<br>**Wed:** *Group 3*<br>**Thurs:** *Group 4*<br>**Friday:** *Group 5* | Whole class; the teacher assists the group that did an assisted writing activity that day |
| 30 minutes | Phonics and spelling | Whole class |

**Figure 8.3** Schedule 3 (for a two-hour-and-ten-minute literacy block).

| Time | Literacy Component | Group Size |
|------|-------------------|------------|
| 20 minutes | Shared reading | Whole class |
| 20 minutes | Phonics and spelling | Whole class |
| 60 minutes | Guided reading and running record (All groups daily)<br>*Group 1*<br>*Group 2*<br>*Group 3* | Small homogeneous groups at instructional levels |
| 30 minutes | Assisted writing and independent writing | Whole class journal writing while the teacher works with a different small group each day pulled aside for guided writing instruction and conferences |

records are later placed in individual student portfolios. Other teachers organize notebook binders with tabbed sections for each student's reading records. Running record forms and blank notebook paper are worthy tools as the teacher records and analyzes her observations.

Many teachers conduct their assisted writing sessions in the same area used for guided reading. The chart paper for writing can be taped to a chalkboard or placed on an easel. All of the materials (markers, alphabet charts, chalkboards, dictionaries, etc.) can be stored nearby in a portable cubby or tub (see Figure 8.6). Practices for storing and distributing magnetic letters and letter cards vary widely.

**Figure 8.4** This teacher organized book sets for guided reading by using small baskets.

**Figure 8.5** In this classroom, each guided reading group has its books in a separate basket.

**Figure 8.6**  This teacher keeps her assisted writing materials accessible and well organized.

Some teachers use Zip-lock bags attached to a clothesline strung underneath the chalkboard. Others use a fishing-tackle box or similar kind of segmented container. Still other teachers find it easier just to pass out small slips of scrap paper and have the children write on them the letters they will need for the day's activities (see Figure 8.7).

**Figure 8.7**  Some teachers pass out small strips of scrap paper and have the children write on them the letters they will need.

Distribution of magnetic letters or letter cards needs to be efficient. Choosing a different child to pass out each letter that is needed for the day works quickly. Some teachers schedule these activities after a break so that the classroom monitor can help distribute the letters. Once again, no one way works best for every teacher.

## Sharing Materials

Finding enough books of various difficulty levels for guided reading is a problem in many schools. Teachers who use guided reading are slowly accumulating materials, but many do not have a set of books that will last the entire year.

A schoolwide guided reading library is a good way to share materials (see Figure 8.8). Put sets of guided reading books in separate gallon Zip-lock bags, label them, and attach a

**Figure 8.8**  A schoolwide guided reading library.

pocket with a library card. Then place the bags in baskets labeled by difficulty level.

## Literacy Corners

A literacy corner is an area of the classroom where children read or write independently during the fifteen or twenty minutes the teacher is working with small groups for guided reading or assisted writing. Rotation systems and assignment boards for the literacy corners are as individual as the teachers who use them. No single rotation schedule can meet the needs of all teachers, and the assignment board can be designed in many different ways.

Figure 8.9 shows one version of an assignment board. Since it is a permanent classroom fixture, the assignment board needs to be made of heavy cardboard or some other durable material. It also needs to accommodate ever-changing groups, as the children develop their individual reading and writing skills. On the

**Figure 8.9** This teacher's assignment board is easy for children to understand.

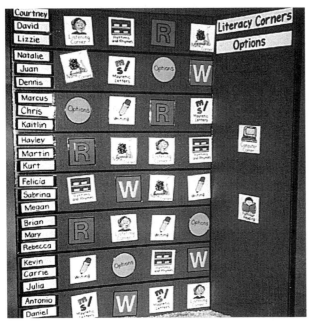

board in Figure 8.9, the children's names are attached with Velcro, so the teacher can move a name from group to group very easily. Each literacy corner is usually identified by an icon representative of the task focused on. On the board in Figure 8.9 these icons are also attached with Velcro for easy movement.

In the schedule related to the board in the photograph, the children attend three literacy corners each day, staying at each corner for fifteen or twenty minutes. For example, the first group of three children visits the listening corner, rotates to the rhythm and rhyme corner, meets with the teacher for guided reading (the *R* icon), and finally rotates to the name corner. When a small-group lesson ends, all the children rotate to their next corner, in the sequence shown on the assignment (or task) board. This teacher meets with two groups of six children for reading and two groups of six children for writing (the *W* icon) each day, as in the schedule in Figure 8.1.

Each day this teacher designates two of the seven literacy corners as options, making sure that these two corners are not included elsewhere on the board (otherwise two groups could be at the same corner at the same time).

Literacy corners work because of the way the activities are structured and organized and because the teacher has spent many hours teaching the children to be independent learners. She has modeled how to do the tasks and supervised the children in the literacy corners, gradually increasing their responsibility until they can engage in meaningful reading and writing activities without having to be fully supervised.

Activities in the literacy corners reflect the children's current abilities. Children are assigned to a corner based on the teacher's observations of things they need to practice. Some common corners are the alphabet corner, the rhythm-and-rhyme corner, the book-nook corner, the writing corner, the computer corner, and the listening corner.

Magnetic Letter Corner

**Materials**

Four sets of uppercase magnetic letters.

Eight sets of lowercase magnetic letters.

Six magnetic boards, cookie sheets, or pizza pans.

Several large ABC charts from various companies.

Two shoe pocket organizers for sorting.

Alphabet cereal or macaroni for sorting.

Letter cards of alphabet letters typed in different print styles, or fonts, in various font sizes.

Clothespins, clothesline, letter cards, and picture cards for sorting.

Task cards for letter sorts.

Picture cards for sorting letter sounds.

One pocket chart.

Pointers (chopsticks work well).

One set of large alphabet letter cards (three- or four-inch size).

Little letter books highlighting objects that begin with a certain letter.

Alphabet books of all types.

Spiral notebooks with blank paper for creating individual alphabet books.

Chart paper to create an alphabet writing wall.

Sponge-tip paint roller.

Chalkboard.

Stamp sponge for writing letters on chalkboard.

Paintbrush and water for writing letters on chalkboard.

Large chalk for writing letters on chalkboard.

Alphabet stencils.

Wikki stick for forming letter shapes.

Tactile letters: sandpaper, sponge, plastic, foam, and letter tiles.

Alphabet puzzles.

Alphabet sound games such as Sound Concentration.

Blackline masters of alphabet pictures for pasting in individual alphabet books.

Paper, crayons, and scissors for Name/Sound activity.

Picture cards with corresponding words written on the back for making words.

Word cards.

**Design Consideration**

1. You will need an area that has metal surfaces for sorting magnetic letters—for example, sides of a filing cabinet or other storage cabinets, the front of a metal desk, or a magnetic board. If metal surfaces are hard to find, you can purchase and use metal cookie or pizza sheets.

2. Baskets or plastic tubs are excellent for storing magnetic letters. However, for some activities, you may want a set of magnetic letters that are already sorted. In that case, a plastic fishing-tackle box

**Figure 8.10** Magnetic surfaces such as desks, magnetic boards, cookie sheets, and filing cabinets are needed for the magnetic letter corner. In addition, baskets and tubs for magnetic letters, alphabet stencils, and books are excellent materials storage.

works well. It is also handy for the small letter cards that are used in sorting.

3. Use four-by-six-index cards and write the sorting and word-building tasks on them. You can place a magnetic strip (available in craft departments) on the back. This will make them ready to place on the metal surface. Another idea is to attach the magnetic strip to the back of a clothespin and place the clothespin on the metal surface; the task cards can then be clipped into the clothespins.

4. A four-by-six inch plastic index-card box is a good tool for storing task cards written on that size card.

5. Use baskets to store all the alphabet books together and all the letter books together. Baskets can also be used to store the alphabet books written by the children.

## Attribute Sort

- Attribute sorts can be done using only uppercase letters, only lowercase letters, or both together.
- Begin with an easy sort, such as, by color. Display the task cards: red, blue, green, yellow, etc. Use various letters in many different colors. Instruct the children to sort the

**Figure 8.11** Attribute sorting activities.

magnetic letters according to similar color. Another way to sort by color would be to use one letter form in many different colors.

- Display the following task cards: circle; circle and stick; stick. Instruct the children to sort the magnetic letters according to similar features. For example, b, d = circle and stick; o, c = circle; l, I = stick.

- Have them attend to more specific features. For example, open circle (u, n, c), closed circle (o, D, Q), straight stick (l, t), slanted stick (v, w), straight and slanted stick (Y, k).

- Finally, put away the magnetic letters and replace them with other letter forms to sort: a bowl of alphabet cereal, for example, which can be eaten after sorting.

- Letter cards with letters in a variety of print styles can also be sorted. Use one letter typed in a variety of fonts. Clip a model of each letter font on the sorting surface. Don't use too many different styles at any one time!

## Writing Wall

- Children need ample opportunities to practice the formation of the letter movements that make each letter distinctive. A large piece of butcher paper provides incentive for novice learners to practice their developing knowledge of the alphabet. They can use markers and write BIG! Or tiny.

- Provide a model for the children to copy by clipping a large alphabet card to the wall.

- A chalkboard also makes a good writing wall. Children love to use oversized chalk, without the confines of lines on the board, to practice letter formation.

- Another fun way to practice is to dust the chalkboard with eraser dust by patting an eraser against the board. Then the children can use their index finger to write letters in the chalkdust.

- Stamp sponges can be filled with water and used to write disappearing letters on the chalkboard. A cup of water and a large paintbrush may also be used.
- Paint sponges are fun to use on the writing wall. They dry quickly!

### Word Building

- Provide picture cards and magnetic letters to make the words. Scaffold the task by placing the exact letters needed for each word directly underneath the picture. Make the activity self-checking by writing the word on the back of the picture.
- Provide word cards and a mixture of magnetic letters. The children construct the word directly underneath the word card.
- String a clothesline with word cards representing several rime patterns. For example: *cat, read, pig.* Instruct the child to read the word card in the basket and clip it to the word that has the same pattern. When they have finished, they can make the first word

**Figure 8.13** An onset-rime activity.

out of magnetic letters and practice manipulating the onset to make other words.

- Provide a word card with two words written on it; one written directly underneath the second. Instruct the child to make a new word by using the first part of the top word and the ending chunk of the second word. For example: *he* and *cat* are written on the card. The child chooses the magnetic letters needed to build the word *hat*. Finally the child can write the new words on a sheet of paper and draw pictures to go with them.
- Choose three rime patterns, such as *at, ed, ig.* Make five or six cards of each rime pattern. Fill a muffin tin with all of the *at* cards in one cup, the *ed* cards in a second cup, and the *ig* cards in a third cup. Instruct the children to take the patterns out of the cups and add a magnetic letter or letters to the beginning of each card to make words. Have them record their lists of words on a separate sheet of paper.
- Provide a word card. Instruct the children to build the word out of magnetic letters and use more magnetic letters to add the

**Figure 8.12** Word-building activities must be structured to support the level of the learner.

**Figure 8.14** Practicing word endings.

*ing* ending to the word. Finally, they are to take a separate sheet of paper and use the new word in a sentence. Example: Word card—*go*; New word—*going*. This can be done with other word endings as they are learned in assisted instruction with the teacher.

## Rhythm and Rhyme Corner

### Materials
Enlarged copies of poems, songs, and chants written on chart paper.

Two sets of sentence strips written in two different colors to match each poem.

Large notebook rings for storing the sentence strips.

One set of word cards written on different colored construction or index paper for each poem.

Gallon-size Zip-lock bags for storing the word cards.

Enlarged copies of chants and stories written

using rebus pictures and environmental print to create interactive charts.

Clothesline, clothes rack, or other place to store the rhymes on hangers with clothespins.

Overhead transparency projector.

Copies of poems, songs, and chants on transparencies and stored in clear sleeves.

One or more pocket charts.

Copies of rhymes glued on eight-by-eleven-inch brown envelopes.

Eight-by-eleven-inch colored copies of the poems cut into sentence strips and placed in the envelopes.

Eight-by-eleven-inch colored copies of the poems cut into word cards, placed into a Zip-lock bag, and put into the envelopes.

Enlarged copy of the alphabet chart.

Large pointer and small chopstick pointers.

Colored transparency windows.

Several different sizes of focus frames.

Highlighter tape.

Skinny sticky notes.

**Figure 8.15** A child reads an enlarged copy of a song using a pointer.

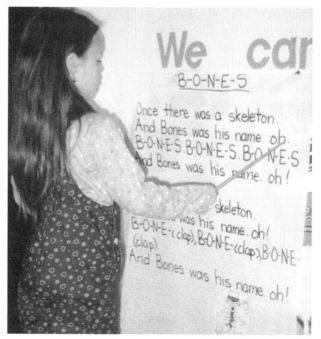

**Figure 8.16** An interactive rebus.

Fire Fighters

Fire fighters wear big red ___

Climb up ___ to rescue ___

Use big ___ to spray on ___

Ride big ___ with big black ___

Race when they hear a ___ alarm,

To help keep ___ safe from harm.

**Figure 8.17** Enlarged copies of poems and sentence strips stored on hangers and hooks.

## Design Considerations

1. You will need a place to store the copies of the enlarged poems. Hanging them on clothes hangers using clothespins and then hanging them on a clothes rack works well. You may also use a clothesline if you have the space.

2. Use a hook or a nail in the wall to create a place to display individual poems as the children pull them off the rack for rereading.

3. If you have the space and an overhead projector, place it on the floor and shine it on a wall. The children can then use the transparency poems and literacy tools for rereading, predicting, or highlighting certain elements.

4. Store the overhead transparency poems and word cards in clear, protective sleeves. Select five or six familiar rhymes to place in a container beside the overhead projector. Rotate these each week.

5. Hang the pocket chart(s) on the wall at an appropriate height for the children to use the text and word cards.

**Figure 8.18** Text- and word-matching activities using the pocket chart and a cut-up poem.

6. Make individual text-matching activities by duplicating three copies of a rhyme on three different colors of paper (for example, white, yellow, and pink). Paste one copy on the outside of an eight-by-eleven-inch brown envelope (white). Cut one copy into sentence strips (yellow). Cut the last copy into word cards (pink) and store in a Zip-lock bag. Place all of the sentence strips and the bag of word cards into the eight-by-eleven-inch brown envelope.

7. Store the brown envelopes of poems in an appropriate container. The children can select a poem and take it to their desk for text and word matching.

## Activities
- Have children reread enlarged poems, songs, or chants using a large pointer.
- Have children reread transparency poems using chopstick pointers.
- Have children use sticky notes to cover up certain words and then ask their buddies to make predictions.
- Have children locate rhyming words and mark them with highlighter tape.

- Have children use the focus frames to locate the words that they know and record them on a piece of paper.
- Have children reassemble a poem in the pocket chart using sentence strips. (One set of sentence strips can be placed in the pocket chart as a model if you like.)
- Have children match word cards on top of the sentence strips.
- Have children reread interactive rebus charts with a pointer and match word cards to the pictures using clothespins.

## Book Nook Corner

### Materials
Bookshelves.

Individualized book boxes for each child with familiar guided reading books at each child's instructional level.

Book sets organized into different levels if there are not enough guided reading books to create individualized sets.

A system for allowing children to check out books for home.

Library books organized by topic.

**Figure 8.19** Guided reading materials organized into individual book boxes or baskets.

Big Books.

Laundry basket for storing Big Books.

Chopstick pointers for reading Big Books.

Metal can for storing the pointers.

Class published stories and Big Books.

Individual poetry notebooks.

Comfortable area with carpet or beanbag
   chairs.

An assortment of stuffed animals to read to.

Clipboards with story maps or blank paper
   for story retelling.

Can full of pencils.

### Design Considerations

1. Use small baskets to store library books,
   or create individual book boxes out of
   detergent boxes painted or covered with
   contact paper.
2. Each guided reading book can have a
   library card and pocket pasted inside the
   front cover.
3. Assign each child a library pocket pasted
   on a poster. Guided reading library cards

can be removed from the book and placed
in that child's pocket.

4. Arrange a comfortable area, preferably on
   the carpet. Include soft pillows or furniture.

**Figure 8.20** Library books organized by topic and
author.

**Figure 8.21** A good system for checking out books for home reading.

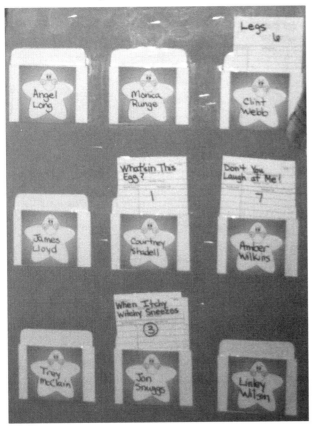

**Figure 8.22** Children reading a variety of texts in the book nook.

5. A laundry basket of Big Books can be stored underneath the Big Book stand. Pointers can be stored in a metal can.

6. Clipboards with story retelling activities can be stored in a large basket or other suitable containers.

## Activities

- Read, read, read—familiar guided reading texts, library books, class texts, poems, and Big Books.
- Read to a friend or a stuffed animal.
- Use pointers to track text in Big Books.
- Use story maps to plot narrative text.
- Use blank paper to record written story retellings or facts from expository text.

## Writing Corner

### Materials

An abundance of assorted paper.

Old calendars, checkbooks, receipt books, and greeting cards.

Miscellaneous paperwork from a post office or bank.

Various writing instruments: pencils, pens, markers.

A collection of interesting pictures to use as story starter.

Date stamp.

Individual student journals.

Small alphabet charts.

Picture dictionaries.

Books of words.

Children's personal dictionaries or spelling books.

Stapler.

Scissors.

Tape.

Single-hole punch.

Notebook rings.

Samples from a wallpaper book for book covers.

A shoe bag or other type of sorting container to serve as mailboxes.

Clipboards for writing around the room.

Revising and editing checklist.

### Design Considerations

1. This corner can be stationed near the teacher because the children usually work quietly.
2. You will need to arrange a small table and some chairs with the supplies nearby.
3. Continually collect the writing supplies.
4. Hang a shoe bag and label it with the children's names and/or addresses. This will become the post office.
5. Label everything.
6. Display children's writing.

### Activities

- Glue a picture onto a sheet of paper and write a story about it.
- Use a greeting card to write a note to a friend.
- Fill out a check and send it in a letter to a friend.
- Fill in a monthly calendar with activities you would like to do. Write a letter to your mother and tell her about them.
- Fill out a change-of-address form and write a note to a friend telling her how much you'll miss her.
- Make a book!
- Use the revision and editing checklist to edit a journal story.

### Name Corner

**Materials**

A chart with the children's names and pictures.

A pocket chart.

A basket with the children's first names written on sentence strips.

Magnetic tape.

A basket containing a picture of each child.

Magnetic letters.

Two hanging shoe bags.

Paper and crayons.

A large sheet of butcher paper.

**Figure 8.23** A child sorting children's names according to the beginning letter.

**Figure 8.24** Children can match the name with the picture at the name center.

**Design Considerations**

1. Use a small index card to label the pockets of the shoe bags with the letters of the alphabet.
2. Hang the name/picture chart on the wall beside the file cabinet that will be used for making names with magnetic letters.
3. Hang a pocket chart down low.
4. Create a basket of the children's names written on sentence strips with a small piece of magnetic tape placed on the back.
5. Arrange a small table with a sheet of butcher paper and a large marker.
6. Have other paper and markers nearby.

**Activities**

- Have children use the shoe bag to sort the sentence strip names by beginning letter.

- Relabel the shoe bag and have children sort the names by number of syllables.
- Create other labels to focus on specific letters. For example, names beginning with s, names with s as the last letter, names that have more than one s, names that have no ss, names that begin with sh, and names that begin with st.
- Create picture labels so that the children can sort names by the sound that they begin with (for example, dog, sun, and fish, or none of these sounds).
- Provide magnetic letters for name making. Have the children place a name card on the file cabinet and make their name under the model. This task can be made more supportive by placing the letters needed for a name under the name rather than having the children select from an abundance of letters.
- Label the pocket chart girls and boys. Place the children's pictures under the correct

**Figure 8.25** A sign-in sheet.

columns. Have children match the names with the pictures.

- Allow the children to use the name chart to draw pictures of their friends and label the pictures with the names.
- Use the butcher paper to create a sign-in chart. The children can sign in every day by responding yes or no to a question such as:
  - Have you ever given a dog a bath?
  - Do you have buttons on today?
  - Would you let a piglet suck your fingers?
  - Have you ever been to a farm?

By signing under the appropriate number:
  - How many letters are in your first name?
  - How many people live in your house?
  - How old are you?

By signing under the appropriate picture:
  - My eyes are (blue, green, hazel, brown, black).
  - My favorite color is…
  - My costume is scary.
  - My costume is friendly.

## Closing Thoughts

An apprenticeship classroom should be structured so that children can work in their assisted and unassisted learning zones. In a well-organized classroom, children learn self-management techniques for guiding their own learning. When established routines are in place, the children's attention can focus on the literacy task at hand. Through carefully planned literacy corner activities, the teacher enables children to practice independence. The teacher is then free to work in small groups with children who need guided instruction. A constructive learning environment is dependent on the teacher's ability to design productive learning opportunities based on careful observation of the children's reading and writing behavior. Apprenticeship literacy implies that children will become more competent learners through guided participation (as in small-group instruction) with a knowledgeable person (the teacher). The learner then applies this knowledge to independent work.

# A Day with Angela and Her First Graders

How are the principles of guided apprenticeship put into daily practice? The classroom described in this chapter is in a school that has been using literacy teams for the past three years. Classroom teachers and reading specialists work closely together to ensure that all the children achieve their greatest potential. The children are given carefully structured tasks that help them read and write effectively. They are held accountable for known information, and the teachers help them with clear and focused demonstrations.

Literacy teams meet to study how language is used to model, coach, scaffold, articulate, and reflect. The principles of apprenticeship are emphasized in daily teaching and learning interactions: observation and responsive teaching are at the core. The teachers recognize the importance of structured routines that promote the children's independence. Typical classroom interactions include opportunities for both assisted and independent work.

In this school reading is a priority. Before the morning bell rings, one hears a gentle murmur in the hallways as children read in soft whispers. Teachers stop to listen to favorite stories or to respond to children's questions about a story. Many of the children walk into their classrooms still reading.

## Whole-Group Shared Reading

Angela calls her class of emergent to early readers together and begins the morning with shared reading. Instead of following a prescribed scope and sequence for teaching concepts about print and letter-sound relationships, Angela plans each day's lesson to respond to the strengths and needs of the children. She realizes the importance of designing instruction aimed at their learning zones. The activities she chooses validate old knowledge and activate new learning.

Today, as soon as the children are gathered on the carpet in the shared reading corner, Angela introduces a familiar nursery rhyme: "I have a rhyme today about a little boy named Jack." The children guess "Little Jack Horner" and "Jack and Jill," but Angela has selected "Jack Be Nimble." After reciting the rhyme aloud, she shows the children a large colorful copy of the poem. Using a chopstick for a pointer, Angela points to each word as the children read with her. As they reread the poem, Angela's voice pauses and drops off at certain points so the children can make predictions based on the pattern.

Next Angela invites Marty to come up and use the pointer as she asks important questions that direct the children's attention to concepts about print:

- Where do I begin reading?
- Which way do I go?
- Where do I go after that?

After Marty successfully demonstrates his knowledge of these print conventions, Angela places a transparency of the poem on the overhead projector and displays it on the wall. On this copy, she has left out Jack's name. Some of the children immediately comment on this. "That's right," says Angela, "I wonder whose name I could put in Jack's place?" The children perk up as Angela writes Landon's name in the blank space in the poem. Angela guides the children in a shared reading of the poem with Landon's name; then she calls on Landon to demonstrate some more print concepts. She gives him a "magic highlighter paddle" (a small white wooden paddle that Angela uses to focus the children's attention on specific visual aspects of the text; Angela has several paddles of various sizes to accommodate letters, chunks, words, and phrases). She tells Landon, "Find your name in the poem and pull it out with the magic paddle." Landon places the paddle against the poem on the wall, and as he slowly pulls it away, he pulls his name out of the text. The children lean forward, fascinated, as Landon moves the paddle back toward the wall and replaces his name in the poem. Then Angela hands Landon a chop-

stick to use as a pointer and asks him to point to the words as the children read the rhyme together.

"I've got a rhyme about a star," Angela says next. Some children squeal with delight as their guesses of "Star Light, Star Bright" are confirmed. Angela goes through the same steps, reciting the poem orally before introducing the print, pointer, and print-concepts questions. However, this time Angela has the children locate several words in the poem that they can use to monitor their reading. Angela uses a focus frame (a colored transparency with a "window" cut out of it) to direct the children's attention to particular words in the text. The frame colors over the entire poem, and only the word or letter shows through the window in black print. Today Angela has one child locate the known word *I* in several places.

Next Angela has the children apply their knowledge of rhyme and searching strategies by prompting them to locate two words that rhyme—*light* and *bright*. Angela takes the learning to a new level of visual analysis by asking the children to tell her how the two words are alike.

Next Angela points to the picture of a monkey on the alphabet chart and writes the word *day* on her dry-erase board. She says, "Can you find a word in our poem that starts like *monkey* and rhymes with *day*?" The children exclaim, "*May!*" Angela asks Alissa to use the focus frame to locate the word *may* in the poem. After Alissa successfully frames the word, Angela writes it on the dry-erase board underneath the word *day.* She prompts the children to articulate their analysis: "How did you know that this word was *may*?" Chaddrick and Taylor respond, "Because it starts with an *m* and rhymes with *day.*" Angela uses precise language to confirm how using what they know about two words can help them learn a new word. A second, fluent rereading of the poem follows these quick, focused activities.

The children respond eagerly as Angela pulls out a chart with a poem printed on it in large black letters with large spaces. As Angela points to each word, the children join in the reading. It is clear they have read the poem before.

When the poem has been read and enjoyed several times, Angela passes out sentence strips on which she has printed the lines of the poem. She assembles a second set of sentence strips in the pocket chart and has the children search their sentence strips for each line of the poem. Several children need the model of the poem for support in order to match the lines of the text visually. They eagerly place their sentence strips on top of the model in the pocket chart to rebuild the poem. As each child adds a sentence, he or she uses the pointer and rereads the sentence. Some children need Angela to guide their hands in order to match the print to their spoken words.

Now Angela increases the difficulty of the task by passing out individual word cards to each child. The children eagerly compare their cards with the text displayed in the pocket chart. They reread the text before adding each word so that they can predict the next word needed.

Finally Angela announces, "It's rhythm-and-rhyme time. Who can tell me two words in our poem that rhyme?" The children respond with *day* and *play.* Angela directs the children to reread the poem and find the two words. When they locate *day* and *play,* Angela pulls these word cards out of the poem and inserts them in a second pocket chart. She asks the children to tell her how the words are alike. The children respond that both words have the letters *ay.* She praises them for their careful observation and highlights the *ay* pat-

tern as she explains that this chunk can help them think about some other words that they want to read and write.

To demonstrate how to use a knowledge of beginning sounds and ending patterns to read new words, Angela quickly writes the words *day* and *play* on the dry-erase board and underlines the *ay* chunk. Then she says, "If you know *day* and *play,* that can help you figure out my new word." Angela writes the word *may* on the board. The children shout out the word. Angela prompts the children to articulate their knowledge: "How did you know that my new word was *may?*" The children point out the ending pattern. Angela then guides them through one more example of the *ay* pattern, reminding them that using words that they know can help them when they get to a new word that they want to read and write. The poem is reread fluently one more time.

After a little stretching exercise, the children move on to a final shared reading activity. Today Angela introduces a new Big Book, *Where Do Monsters Live?* (Williams 1994). She has chosen the book because it has a very predictable, repetitive sentence pattern; pictures that support the sentence pattern; and an excellent text layout (consistent print placement, large type, and adequate spaces). In addition, its subject appeals to the children.

Angela guides the children to make predictions from the pictures and story line: "The title of our book is *Where Do Monsters Live?* I wonder where they might live?" Several voices chime in with a common prediction, "Under the bed!" Angela validates their response, then invites the children to look at and discuss the pictures in the story. The children laugh with enjoyment at one they say is "a polka-dotted monster!" Although the text identifies the monster as "spotted," Angela chooses to ignore the children's substitution because (a) it is meaningful and (b) it presents an opportunity to direct the children's attention to first-letter cues. After the prediscussion, Angela turns to the page with the monster and comments, "On this page, you called the monster polka-dotted. Could we also call him a spotted monster?" The children say yes. Then Angela lets the children hear the beginning sound in the word spotted, stressing the *s*: "What can you hear at the beginning of *spotted*?" The children exclaim, "*S!*" "Yes," says Angela, "Who can find the word *spotted* in our story?" Sarah comes to the chart and locates the word. As she frames it with the framing card, she comments, "That's like in my name."

Angela then asks whether anyone can find the word *a* on the first page. She invites Kimberly to locate it in the text. Next Angela prompts the children to search the page to find it in another place. Brittany locates a capital *A*. Angela praises the children and reminds them, "Words you know can help you keep your place when you are reading."

Angela points to each word as she reads the book aloud, thus modeling the relationship between spoken and written language. The children quickly pick up the structural pattern and join in the reading. Angela pauses at appropriate points to allow the children to predict a word from the rhyming patterns of the language and from the picture cues. A second reading of the text follows the first, with even greater participation by the children. Through repeated readings of the text, the

**Figure 9.1**  Angela introduces a Big Book to the whole class during shared reading.

children are able to make faster predictions and apply reading strategies.

At the end of the shared reading session, Angela tells the children to check the assignment board and go to the designated literacy corners (see Chapter 8). Before she calls her first guided reading group, she glances quickly around the room to ensure that all children are on task.

## Small-Group Guided Reading

Walking to the guided reading corner of the room, Angela is happy to see that the children are reading familiar books from their individual book boxes, texts they have previously read during their guided reading lessons. Angela has carefully selected these books to build on the children's current knowledge and to promote the acquisition of successful reading strategies. The seven children in this group of early readers are at the same instructional level, as determined by Angela's observations of their reading and writing behavior during shared reading, familiar reading, interactive writing, and independent writing.

As the children read, Angela observes their behavior, asks questions that promote problem-solving, and takes running records on one or two children. She carries a spiral-bound notebook with the children's names written on plastic tabs that extend beyond the sides of the pages—a simple record-keeping tool that lets her maintain ongoing documentation on which to base her assessment of the children's progress over time.

After checking that the other children are working productively in the learning corners, Angela tells the guided reading group she is going to introduce a new book. The book she has selected, *The Cake that Mack Ate* (Robart 1986), includes opportunities for the children

to practice old learning (in the zone of actual level) and to work with new learning (in the zone of proximal development). It is a cumulative, repetitive book about all the ingredients that went into the cake that Mack ate.

Angela begins by talking about the main idea of the story and guiding the children to discuss the pictures. She skillfully uses some of the vocabulary and phrases the children will encounter in the story—*who, this is the,* and *that went into the cake that Mack ate.* Next Angela prompts the children to predict the letters they would see in the words *ate* and *that.* The children successfully locate and frame each word. Finally Angela guides the children to reflect on the strategies that good readers use when they come to an unknown word. The children suggest a variety of things to do—rereading, making the sound for the first letter, looking at the picture, thinking about what would happen in the story, and sounding the word. Angela confirms these suggestions and restates the behavior she wants to see them using when they read.

The children begin reading the story in whispers while Angela moves around the circle listening in. She guides and prompts the children to use particular strategies to help them figure out unknown words. She notices that Brittany is having trouble with the word *planted:*

**Brittany:** (*Reading*) "This is the farmer who..." (*hesitating*)
**Angela:** Why did you stop?
**Brittany:** (*Monitoring by rereading up to the unknown word*) "This is the farmer who..." (*stopping*)
**Angela:** Is there a part of the word that you know?
**Brittany:** (*Sounding the letters*) Pl—pl—
**Angela:** Think about what the farmer is going to do with the seeds. Go back and reread

and think of what would make sense and start with those letters.

**Brittany:** "This is the farmer who planted the seed that grew into the corn that went into the cake that Mack ate."

After this first reading, Angela gives the children an opportunity to reread. Rather than focus on specific words, she chooses a teaching point that will help the children apply the checking and confirming strategies that are part of an effective processing system. Several children, Brittany among them, are not initiating effective responses to unknown words without prompting. They need repeated practice with successful strategies in order to develop a conceptual understanding of the significance of problem-solving. Angela therefore decides to direct the children's attention explicitly to the importance of predicting and

confirming textual information based on accumulating visual cues. She uses the cloze procedure on a sentence from the text to guide the children through the process of using first letters to initiate a fast response, looking at the rest of the word to collect more information, and confirming these sources with the meaning of the text. (See Chapter 3 for more on how to do the cloze procedure.)

After the guided reading lesson, *The Cake that Mack Ate* goes into the children's book boxes. During the next guided reading lesson, Angela will take a running record on one or two children's reading of this book. Now she signals that it is time to change literacy corners and guided reading groups. Angela's schedule allows her to see two guided reading groups each day for approximately twenty minutes each. (Chapter 8 discusses daily schedules in detail.) After the children in the second guided

**Figure 9.2** Angela listens as her students read.

reading group have completed their lesson, Angela announces that it is time to rotate literacy corners once again.

## Small-Group Assisted Writing

Angela's first assisted writing group is made up of children whose writing abilities have moved beyond very basic interactive writing. The children are fairly adept at hearing sounds in words and at applying the basic print concepts. They are now ready to:

- Hear sounds in sequence.
- Use words they know to write other words by simple analogy.

Angela therefore provides opportunities to apply these new problem-solving processes. She is also aware that the children are able to compose longer texts with more details and logical sequences. Today Angela and the children co-construct a story based on a personal experience that has happened to Angela. The result is a clear, well-formed story that activates the children's imagination and communicates Angela's distress: "I got mad when I had to take out the trash in the rain. I tripped over the curb and spilled the trash can in the street. I was soaking wet and muddy after I picked it all up."

Next Angela helps the children learn about simple analogies:

**Angela:** Let's go back and reread our story so far.

**Children:** "I got...(*rereading and predicting the word* mad) mad."

**Angela:** *Mad.* Do you know another word that can help you think about the word *mad*?

**Children:** *Dad!*

**Angela:** Write *dad* on your boards. (*They write the word on their dry-erase boards.*) Now erase the *d*. What is the chunk you have left?

**Rose:** *Ad!*

**Angela:** Now put an *m* in front of the *ad* chunk and what new word did you make?

**Children:** *Mad!*

**Angela:** Let's try it with one more word. What letter do you need to change *mad* into *sad*? (*The children quickly erase the* m

**Figure 9.3** Angela works with a small group of children on interactive writing.

*and add an* s.) Say and check it with your finger to be sure you are right.

**Children:** (*Confirming the word*) *Sad.*

**Angela:** Now what is the word in our story?

**All:** (*Rereading*) I got…mad.

**Angela:** Rose, come write the word in the story. I want everyone else to erase your board and then write the word *mad* quickly and check it.

Angela continues to guide the children to record the story. Throughout the process, she models important behavior, such as saying words slowly, making multiple attempts on the practice board, using word analogies, and rereading the text after each problem-solving attempt. She uses two additional examples in keeping with her focus of teaching the children a strategy for word analysis: *will, bill, spill,* and *get, bet, wet.* At the end of this interactive writing lesson, the children fluently reread the story.

## Small-Group Writing Aloud

Before sitting down to work with her next group, Angela checks that the literacy-corner rotation went smoothly and that the other children are working appropriately. This group of children is in a transitional stage of spelling development. Angela needs to coach them to think about the visual spelling patterns in the words they want to write.

During the lesson, Angela will also guide the children to compose longer and more descriptive texts. She began this yesterday by composing her own story in front of the group and modeling revising and editing skills using a transparency. The children helped her, and at the end of yesterday's lesson Angela asked them each to select one piece of his or her own writing to be revised and edited.

Today Ariana's work is displayed on an overhead transparency. It is a piece of nonfiction about animals.

First Ariana reads her piece, and Angela praises her for writing a good story about penguins. Then Angels points out a list of questions designed to prompt Ariana to clarify meaning and add descriptive details:

1. Did I tell the name of the animal?
2. Did I tell where the animal lives?
3. Did I describe what the animal looks like?
4. Did I tell what the animal eats?
5. Did I tell one or two other important or interesting facts about the animal?

She includes all the children in the group in the process: "Let's look at the checklist and see if Ariana has included all the information that we need when we write about animals." Angela then invites Ariana to reread the story once again. Ariana immediately exclaims, "I forgot to tell what kind of animal a penguin is." Angela shows the group how to make additions to a story (see Figure 9.4):

**Angela:** Where should you add that in your story?

**Ariana:** It needs to be at the beginning.

**Angela:** Let me show you what we can do when we want to add a sentence. We use this little mark called a caret. (*Drawing a caret.*) Now you can write the sentence right here. (*Ariana adds the sentence to the beginning of her story by writing on the transparency.*)

Angela asks Ariana to reread the first two sentences of her story. Then she continues guiding the revising process, asking the group to read the story and check for any other sentences that tell how the penguins look. They find two such sentences at the end of Ariana's story, and Angela tells Ariana to circle them.

**Figure 9.4** Ariana's piece in the process of being revised.

**Angela:** Would it make sense to move those two sentences to the beginning of the story with the other sentence that tells how the penguins look?

**Children:** Yes!

**Angela:** (*Drawing an arrow on the transparency*) We can do that by drawing an arrow from those sentences to where we want them to be moved.

Ariana next decides she wants to add some other interesting facts about penguins. Since there isn't enough room on the page, Angela shows her how to draw a star on the story at the place where she wants to insert the new sentence, draw the same star on another, blank

transparency, and add the new information (see Figure 9.5).

Angela concludes the lesson by having the children reread the entire story together. She praises Ariana for including so many fascinating facts about penguins. The children are now ready to revise their own stories about animals.

Tomorrow Angela will use Ariana's story again, this time to edit for mechanics (spelling and punctuation). The final draft (see Figure 9.6) is bound into a large book entitled *Animal Facts*, which is placed in the reading corner.

**Figure 9.5** Ariana's added details.

Ariana

Penguins from Antartica
Penguins are birds.
They are black and
white.
There are dirffrent
kinds of penguins.
They live in a crowded
rookery. It is crooded.
They eat fish. pounds
They weigh 10 pounds
They live on the ice
and snow.

When they
are born they stand
on their mother's
feet for two months.

**Figure 9.6** Ariana's piece as included in *Animal Facts.*

Penguins From Antarctica

By: Ariana

Penguins are birds. There are different kinds of penguins. They are black and white. They weigh 10 pounds. They live on the ice and snow. They live in a rookery. It is crowded. When they are born, they stand on their mother's feet for two months. They eat fish.

King Penguin

Lunch time

## Independent Journal Writing and Conferencing

After Angela finishes the writing aloud, she pulls the children together as a whole group and they begin journal writing. During this writing block, Angela supports the children in three ways:

1. She circulates among them and observes how they are doing. She makes sure that everyone is on task and is prepared to begin a new text or continue working on a piece already in progress. If anyone appears to need extra support, she coaches in appropriate ways.

2. She selects two or three children each day for focused conferences. This allows her to meet individually with all the children within a two-week period. These personal conferences are in addition to daily observations of and drop-in support for all the children.

3. She circulates among the children one last time and observes where they are in their writing. She occasionally stops by a child's desk and makes a relevant comment about his or her work.

Today Angela calls Chaddrick to the conference table. Chaddrick is an early writer at the phonetic spelling stage. He has control over a few frequently encountered words, can articulate words slowly, and can hear most consonant sounds in sequence. Angela is working to help Chaddrick make an important transition in his writing: to use visual information from a word he knows to write other words. She is also helping him acquire important strategies for remembering how words look.

The ultimate goal of every conference is that the child will value writing as an important means of communication. Thus, every conference begins with a sincere response to the message. Then, during the conference, Angela adjusts her support to accommodate Chaddrick's understanding of the task at hand. She uses instructional language to validate old knowledge and activate new learning.

Today Chaddrick is eager to compose a new story, which he immediately does. With excitement he tells Angela, "Me and my friend are going to play football." After Angela reacts to the message, she supports Chaddrick as he records his story in his journal. "How are you going to start it?" she asks. Chaddrick says the word *me* and fluently writes it down. When he hesitates on the word *and*, Angela prompts,

"Try it out on the practice page." Chaddrick writes it quickly, says "Oh, yeah," and then adds the word to his story. After he finishes writing his story, Angela praises him for his correct letter-sound associations by placing a light checkmark above them on his paper. Then she prompts him to reread his story and draw a picture to support the text (see Figure 9.7). As Angela walks away, she comments, "Tomorrow, you might like to write about the football game. Then you can make it into a longer story and put it into the class book."

Circulating among the other writers, Angela observes them and makes appropriate responses according to the children's strengths and needs. Then she returns to the conference table and calls for Nick to bring his story over for revising and editing. Nick's story is about his friend's bicycle wreck and the trip to the hospital. Angela's goal in this conference is to prepare the story for publication. First she prompts Nick to reread the story for clarity of message. Then she asks him to circle the spellings of words that he will need to check. As Nick reads his story, he corrects the spelling for *went*, inserts the word *and* to connect two thoughts, and tries out spellings for the words *broken* and *friend* (see Figure 9.8). Angela

**Figure 9.7**  Chaddrick's story.

**Figure 9.8** Nick's revisions. ("I got a new bike. Me and my friend had a race. We went down a hill. I saw a car. And I stopped. Tommy was gone. I saw him fall. Tommy fell down on the ground. I stopped and helped him up. He had a broken leg. We went to the hospital. He had to stay for 3 weeks. I made a letter and gave it to him and I put a stamp on the letter. He got out of the hospital and I did not know it. My mom told me.")

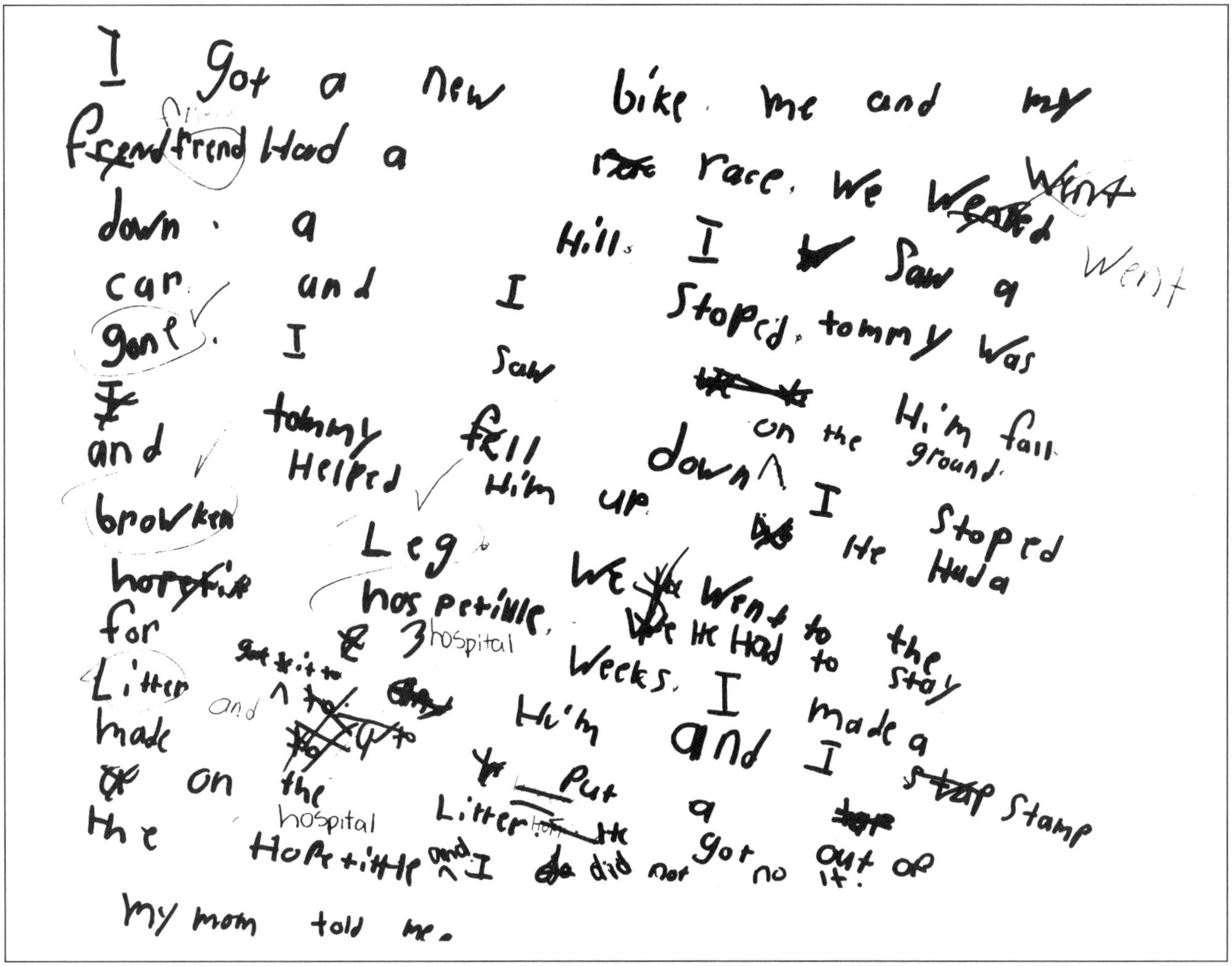

coaches Nick to think about how words look and then to use the dictionary to check his work. At the end of the conference, Angela suggests that Nick rewrite his story and put it in the class publication box.

Now Angela calls Tranisha to the conference table. Tranisha brings a story she began yesterday, which was based on her sister's trip to the nurse to get a shot. Thus far, Tranisha has written the first three sentences of her story: "One day my sister was sick. My mom took her to the nurse. The nurse got her a shot and she got a sore."

As she does in all her conferences, Angela invites Tranisha to read her story, then reacts to it: "Ohhh, that must have hurt!" In conversation, Angela coaches Tranisha to add details to her story: "What happened after your sister got the shot?" As Tranisha begins to expand on the event, Angela encourages her to record her thoughts on paper so that other people can read her story. As she talks, Tranisha adds two new details to her text, which now has a humorous ending: "And we went home and my sister said, You need a shot. No, I don't you need another." (See Figure 9.9.)

This concludes the individual conferences, and Angela now conducts a few drop-in conferences with several other children. There are twenty children in the class, and Angela recognizes their diverse needs. They are working at different points in their writing. They are using a variety of resources: ABC charts, picture dictionaries, "word strips" of frequently encountered words taped to their desks. They are also using a variety of writing materials: unlined and lined paper, pencils and magic markers, spiral-bound notebooks, bound journals. Angela instructs her emergent and early writers to use unlined paper, so that the lines do not restrict their writing forms. As the children become more accomplished writers, Angela gives them lined tablets. Ariana's first draft was written on lined paper; other children, like Nick, choose to write their "sloppy copies" on unlined paper. However, when a text is ready for publication, Angela encourages the children to rewrite it neatly on lined paper. Some children type the stories on the class computer. Although Angela believes it is important for the children to use a variety of writing materials, she insists that any published texts are presented in a format that frees the reader's attention to focus on meaning and enjoyment.

**Figure 9.9** Tranisha's story.

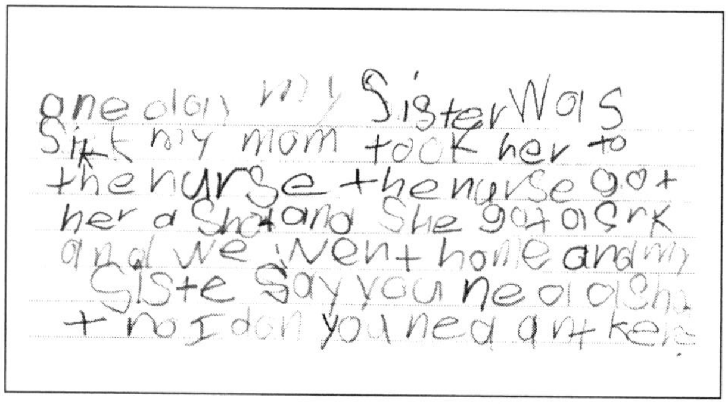
one day my Sister Was
Sik my mom took her to
the nurse the nurse got
her a Shot and She got a S rk
and we Went home and my
Siste Say you ned a sh
t no I don you ned anteker

## Phonics and Spelling

Again, Angela signals that it is time for the children to put away their writing and prepare for the next literacy block—phonics and spelling. During this time, Angela leads the whole class in instructional word-building activities designed to help learners identify words.

With the children seated at their desks, table monitors quickly pass out small letter cards for the consonants *b, c, d, m, r, s,* and *t* and the vowels *e* and *a.* Angela tells the children they will be making some words today that end in the chunk of letters *eam.* On the large magnetic board at the front of the room, Angela pulls three magnetic letters together to make the *eam* pattern. Then she prompts, "Look at the letters and say the chunk." Next she coaches, "Find the letters on your desk to make the *eam* chunk." After the children accomplish this task, she asks, "What letters did you use? What sound did you make?" Angela now guides the children to apply this knowledge at a new level: "Find the letter that starts like *bike* and make the word *beam.*" Quickly, the children pull down the *b* and place it in front of the chunk. When Angela is sure that all the children understand the significance of using first-letter cues to make a word, she goes to her magnetic board and pulls the *b* letter in front of the *eam* chunk. Then she asks the children to confirm their word with the one on the board.

Angela goes on to prompt the children to new constructive activity: "Change *beam* into the word *seam* by changing just one letter."

Walking around the room, Angela notices that Christy has spelled it *c-e-a-m*. Angela increases her support:

**Angela:** That was a good try, Christy. The letter *c* does sometimes sound like the beginning of the word *seam*. But there is another letter that makes that sound. Look on the alphabet chart and find another letter that sounds like *seam*.

**Christy:** (*Locating the letter* s *on the alphabet chart*) S—sailboat.

**Angela:** Are you right? Say *seam—sailboat*.

**Christy:** *Seam—sailboat*. Yes, it's an *s*.

**Angela:** See if you can fix it.

Christy corrects the word. Angela calls Brittany to the magnetic board to build the word *seam* under the word *beam*. Then she instructs the children to make the word *team* before moving on to some words that have blends at the beginning. She coaches and scaffolds based on her observations of individual students. Some children need specific letter-cue prompts and closer supervision.

At the end of the lesson, Angela has the children articulate how all the words are alike by examining the letter pattern at the end of each word. Next she links the task to writing by directing the children's attention to the word *dream* on the board. She models how to add the *ing* chunk on the end of the word to make the word *dreaming*. She coaches, "Now, let's think of other words that have the *ing* chunk on the end of the word." The children raise their hands in enthusiasm and begin to call out words: *jumping, climbing, reading, laughing*. As the children dictate the words, Angela lists them on the board. Then she asks, "What is the same in each word?" The children exclaim, "The *ing* on the end!" Finally Angela writes on the board, "I can hear you screaming." She says, "Find something about the last

word that you know." Some children point out the *eam* chunk and others point out the *ing* chunk. Angela then guides the children to read the sentence and use what they know about the word to help them. When they come to the new word, Angela articulates the *scr* pattern and the children fluently complete the word.

## Closing Thoughts

The morning lessons are over. The children have had numerous opportunities to read and write in their learning zones. In this typical day, Angela has observed the children and provided scaffolds commensurate with their needs. During small-group reading and writing activities, she has provided instruction aimed at her students' potential levels of development. During independent activities in the literacy corners, she has provided flexible opportunities for students to use their knowledge and practice their strategies on easy and familiar tasks.

In her classroom, Angela creates an organized and predictable environment that builds on instructional routines for promoting children's independence. In line with literacy apprenticeship, Angela uses language for various purposes, including modeling, coaching, and scaffolding the children's learning. She promotes the children's conscious awareness of their problem-solving actions as she encourages them to articulate and reflect on their literate behavior. Through guided participation, Angela enables her children to accomplish tasks with her help that they would be unable to accomplish alone. And as the children become more competent learners, Angela will create new transitional moves that reflect their increasing control.

# 10

# Supplementary Literacy
# Lessons with Carla

Some children need supplementary literacy instruction. This chapter take you
inside Carla's supplemental first-grade
literacy program, which supports the first
graders in Angela's room, both at the beginning of the school year and ten weeks later.

## Early Lessons

Carla works with four children for forty-five
minutes a day, devoting fifteen minutes each
to three primary segments: familiar and
shared reading; mini-lessons, journal and
assisted writing; and guided reading. Group
activities are structured in a predictable format
that promotes the children's independence.
The wide range of components in any given
lesson provides a natural context for helping
young children learn how to transfer their
knowledge across varied circumstances.

### Familiar Reading and Shared Reading

During the first two weeks, Carla has helped
the children acquire a collection of very easy

and familiar books. She is aided in this by the
fact that she and the other literacy-team teachers have produced a series of supportive little
books for emergent readers that emphasize
early print concepts: one-to-one matching,
directional movement, locating known letters
and words. These inexpensive little books
(they've been duplicated and stapled together)
are often first introduced during emergent
guided reading groups. Carla also selects
appropriate commercially published books
that meet the needs of emergent readers. When
the books are familiar, Carla places them in the
children's independent reading boxes.

Today, when the children enter the room,
they are familiar with the routine. Without
hesitation, Karrisa, Nick, Laterica, and Billy
immediately go to their book boxes and carry
them to a comfortable spot for reading. Billy
and Nick climb the ladder to the reading loft
and begin buddy reading, Karrisa curls up on
large floor pillows underneath the loft, and
Laterica sits in an oversized green-checkered
chair. Before the children begin reading, Carla
reminds them to use their finger and make
their words match what they are saying.

The soft murmur of voices is heard as the children read aloud. Carla observes their reading behavior. She carries a clipboard on which she records significant observations. She is particularly interested in how the children use visual information to monitor language and meaning cues in the text. Each day she takes one or more running records. Today Carla sits beside Karrisa and listens to her as she reads her book.

Like the other children in this group, Karrisa is just beginning to notice the visual cues in the text. Carla notes that Karrisa is using clear, crisp pointing behavior and that she monitors her reading with some known letters. (During shared reading and writing, Karrisa often uses special cues from the ABC chart to help with letter-sound relationships.) During her reading, Karrisa substitutes the word *chair* for *table* and immediately corrects herself. Although Karrisa can control the *t* sound in shared reading and writing, Carla is not sure whether the visual information or the strong picture cue (there is a table in the picture) is responsible for the correction. However, Karrisa's reading behavior gives Carla the chance to help her articulate and reflect on the importance of using her knowledge across changing situations:

**Carla:** (*Promoting self-reflection*)Karrisa, can you find the part on page 4 where you did some really good work? (*Karrisa points to the word* table.) (*Promoting articulation*) How did you help yourself?

**Karrisa:** First, I said *chair,* but then I saw the *t.* So, I went back and said *table.*

**Carla:** That's exactly what good readers do! You looked at your picture, and you looked at the first letter to help you with that word.

To signal the end of familiar reading, Carla begins chanting a familiar poem. She uses poetry as a transitional signal because she believes it is a wonderful tool for sharpening children's attention to the sounds of language and because she wants the children to acquire a large storehouse of visual and auditory word patterns. She also believes poetry gives children a natural context for hearing new vocabulary, linguistic phrases, and expressive reading. Her goal is that by the end of her time with these children, they will have learned over fifty poems by heart. As Carla chants the poem, the children join in, moving quickly to put their book boxes away and meet Carla in the shared reading corner.

The shared reading corner contains an easel, a flipchart, several large laminated poems, a large alphabet chart, ABC books, a large class dictionary, and three or four pocket charts for manipulating rhyming words and matching sentence strips. In addition to these group materials, each child has a special place on the rug with a small basket of personal materials: a small ABC chart, a small magnetic dry-erase board, one dry-erase marker, one magic marker, a small container with magnetic letters, and a personal dictionary for recording frequently encountered words.

When all the children are seated, Carla directs their attention to a large ABC chart. The familiar pictures on the chart are special cues they use to associate letter and sound relationships while reading and writing. As Carla leads the group in a shared reading of the ABC chart, she uses a large pointer to direct the children's attention to each letter (upper- and lowercase) and each picture cue. The children read the letters fluently, and Carla pauses at appropriate points to let the children say the name of a letter or identify a picture.

The lively pace continues as Carla turns to a pocket chart displaying a familiar poem, written on sentence strips, about a little turtle who lives in a box and catches different creatures. Carla chooses this particular poem, which is a favorite of the group's, because she knows the children enjoy its rhythm, rhyme, and opportunities for movement and because the text contains some supportive features that will build on their reading strengths. For example, the distinct placement of the word *he* at the beginning of most lines provides a nice visual anchor. The text also contains rhyming word patterns, which will help the children hear the language patterns before paying attention to the visual chunks.

Carla and the children begin reading this familiar poem expressively and fluently. The children's eyes follow the pointer as Carla explicitly demonstrates early behavior such as starting position, one-to-one matching, and return sweep. As the children read along, Carla observes their emotional response to the story as they engage in the movements being described and predict upcoming words based on the natural rhythm of the language.

After the reading, Carla calls Billy to the chart and asks him to point to the top starting position and the first return sweep. (Billy is inconsistent in his control of directional movement when writing his stories, but has no difficulty with correct movement when he reads.) Billy's successful performance gives Carla a chance to highlight his actions: "Billy, you pointed to the beginning of the story and followed the first line. Then you went to the beginning of the second line. Always going in this direction can also help you when you write."

Next Carla pulls out a framing window to focus the children's attention on a known word. She asks Laterica to come to the chart and locate the word *he*. (Laterica has written the word *he* several times in her journal, so Carla expects her to be able to locate the word with ease.) After Laterica frames the word, Carla validates her action: "You found that

word really fast, didn't you?" Carla then passes out to each member of the group a word card with *he* written on it. She instructs the children to match the word card to the same word in the pocket chart. After the children position their word on the appropriate spot, Carla says, "Now I want you to write the word *he* on your boards. Be sure to say the word as you write it." Quickly the children write the word *he* three times.

Now Carla prompts Nick to come to the chart and locate an unknown word based on his knowledge of a known letter, *r*. She scaffolds the process with a language cue: "Now where in the poem did the little turtle climb?" "On the rocks," the children exclaim. Then she says to Nick, "What can you hear at the beginning of the word *rocks*?" Nick responds, "*R*." Carla then prompts, "Find a word in the poem that starts like *rocks*."

After Nick locates the new word, Carla guides the children to think of other words that begin like *rocks*. She pulls out a simple letter book that contains several words, all starting with *r*. She says to the children, "Listen to the words as I read them. Can you hear how they all start the same?" Then Carla and the children read the letter book together, paying special attention to the beginning sound.

## Mini-Lesson and Assisted Writing

Carla has planned a mini-lesson that will help the children acquire fluent and flexible control of letters, sounds, and words. She tells the children to take a group of preselected magnetic letters (*h, m, w, e*) from their basket and place them at the top of their board. In order to promote fluency with known letters, she says, "Pull each letter down fast and say the name of the letter as you pull it down." Afterward Carla asks the children to push the letters back to the top of the board. Then she focuses the children's attention on letter-sound associations by asking them to pull down the letter that makes the beginning sound of the word *hot*. The children quickly pull down the letter *h*. Next Carla asks, "Do you know any other words that start like *hot*?" The children call out several words: *happy, Halloween,* and *house.* Carla writes the responses on the board. Then she does the same thing with the words *mouse* and *wet.*

Next Carla prompts the children to use a known word to form an unknown word. She says, "Make the word *he* from your letters. Check it after you make it to be sure you are right." The children quickly construct the word; then they run their finger under it as they say the word slowly. Nick exclaims with delight that this word was in the poem they had just read. Carla then directs the children's attention to the large magnetic board on the easel, where she quickly constructs the word *he* with magnetic letters. With the other two letters over to the side of the board, Carla demonstrates how to remove the beginning letter *h* and to insert the letter *m* in front of the *e* to make the new word *me*. She uses clear and explicit language to describe the process. As the children construct the word *me,* Carla watches them carefully to ensure that they are confirming their actions by saying the word and checking it with their finger. Since this is a new word, Carla provides them with several opportunities to learn it. First, she asks the children to write the word *me* underneath the magnetic model. Her next prompts are designed to help the children acquire a strategy for memorizing the visual pattern: "Now I want you to shut your eyes and look at the word in your head. What is the word you are looking at?" "*Me!*" the children exclaim. "Tell me how it looks," Carla prompts. In unison, the children repeat the names of the letters *m-e.* Then Carla says, "Now keep your eyes shut

and write the word *me* in the air three times." After this she tells them to look at the pocket chart with the poem of "Little Turtle": "Can anyone locate the new word *me*?" Continuing to model the analogy process, Carla returns to the first word *he* (since this is a more secure word for the children), removes the onset letter, and replaces it with a *w* to make the new word *we*.

Again returning to the base word *he,* Carla prompts the children to make *me* one last time. Now that the children are somewhat familiar with the word, Carla asks them to open their personal dictionaries to the *m* page with its special picture cue, *mailbox.* As the children start flipping through the book, Carla increases her support: "Would you find the letter *m* at the beginning, middle, or end of your dictionary?" Nick exclaims, "In the middle!" The children quickly find the *m* page and record the word *me.* Carla's final question highlights the relationship between the new word and the page it's entered on: "Why did we put the word *me* on the mailbox page?" In unison, the children exclaim, "Because they both start with *m*!"

## Interactive Writing

Carla moves on to an interactive writing lesson. Each child has a dry-erase board, an individual alphabet chart, and a different-colored marker for making contributions on the writing chart. The different-colored markers allow Carla to document each child's progress over time. And since Carla always uses a black marker, she can also see how the children begin to take over more of the writing task when black appears less often.

During interactive writing, Carla uses her knowledge of the children's strengths to help them focus on print concepts, sounds in words, letter knowledge, and fluency.

Through these experiences, the children will gain control of emergent reading and writing behavior, and be able to move on to more complex learning.

To begin the lesson, Carla tells the children about her meal at McDonald's the night before. She holds up a brown paper bag bearing the McDonald's logo and asks the children, "Guess where I went to eat last night?" All the children exclaim, "McDonald's!!" Nick asks, "What did you eat?" Carla answers, "I ate a hamburger, french fries, coke, and ice cream! I ate so much that I got a tummyache!" The children contribute similar experiences of their own.

Then Carla guides the children to help her compose a story: "Now I want you to help me write the story. Let's think about the most important thing and write about it. What can we say?" During guided participation, the children and Carla articulate the story: "I ate at McDonald's and I ate too much. I got a tummyache!" Carla takes the children through this brief rehearsal because their control of the oral composition will help them write it down. (She also realizes that oral rehearsals will not be necessary for very long, because the children are quickly learning how to plan, hold, and organize their thoughts into written creations. As they become more competent writers, Carla expects them to revise and correct their messages as they transcribe their thoughts to paper. But for now, the children in this emergent group require guided participation and scaffolding to teach them the process of moving from spoken ideas to written messages.)

Next Carla asks, "What is the first word in our story?" Without hesitation, the children respond, "I." All the children know this word, so Carla instructs Billy to write it on the chart while everyone else writes it on their lapboard. As Billy approaches the chart, Carla asks, "Where should we begin writing?" prompting him to notice the starting position (since he sometimes deviates from it during journal writing). As Billy locates the starting position and correctly writes the word *I* on the page, Carla instructs the children to reread and predict the next word, so that their thoughts don't get ahead of the words actually written—as often happens with young writers. As the children reread and anticipate the upcoming word, they begin to articulate it slowly and respond with the letters and sounds they can hear within the word. They all hear the beginning sound of the word *ate*. Carla tells them to locate the letter *a* on their individual ABC charts, and she asks Karrisa to write the known letter on the chart. Then Carla guides the children to slowly articulate the word again and listen to the next sound. They quickly notice the *t* sound. As each letter and sound is analyzed, a child comes up to the chart and writes the known letter with his or her colored marker. Laterica remarks that the word *ate* needs an *e* on the end of it. Carla reinforces the importance of visual attention to words: "Yes, it needs the *e* to make the word look right." After the word is recorded in the story, Carla prompts the children to reread to see what comes next. The next word in the story is *at*. Since this is a known word, the children do not need to articulate it slowly. Instead, Carla encourages the children to write the word "real fast" on their boards, and she calls Nick to the chart to record the word in the story. Rereading the story, the children realize that the next word is *McDonald's*. Several of them exclaim, "*M*," and Carla writes the entire word into the story with no further analysis.

The lesson continues like this, the children continually being prompted to go back and reread to predict the next word. Carla uses the lesson as an opportunity for the children to practice slow articulation of sounds within words and to promote fluency with known words. Throughout, Carla prompts them to locate and practice letter forms, spacing between words, and punctuation at the end of the sentences. She encourages them to rehearse their attempts on the practice board before recording them on the chart.

After the story is completed, Carla tells the children to consult the editing chart they have constructed together. This chart lists important behavior relevant to where the children are in their actual and potential learning zones. There are currently eight checkpoints to remind them to become better writers:

1. Did you start in the right place?
2. Did you leave spaces between the words to make it easier to read?
3. Did you say the words slowly and write the letters that made those sounds?
4. Did you use the alphabet chart to help you with letters and sounds?
5. Did you reread to help you know the next word to write?
6. Did you use your practice page to help you work on the hard parts?
7. Did your story make sense?
8. Did you use an ? or ! or . at the end of each sentence?

Carla and the children review the points one by one to check on their group composition. The editing chart is a temporary scaffold to help children learn how to evaluate their own work in terms of appropriate benchmarks. A reduced copy of the chart is placed in the writing center for independent work.

Although the written text is short, the interaction between Carla and the children is very powerful. Carla's language is specific to the learning task. She observes the children closely and monitors her support to accommodate their understanding. When the children

are writing the word *and* on the dry-erase boards, Billy writes *ad;* Carla coaches him to say the word slowly and listen to the letter after the *a.* She also encourages him to "feel the letter in your mouth." With this gentle reminder, Billy is able to supply the missing letter and confirm the correct spelling. Nick notices the word *my* inside the larger word *tummy.* He is beginning to notice visual patterns within words. Karrisa comments, "If you take off the *y* and put in an *e,* you would have the word *me.*" Her strategies for analyzing words are becoming stronger. As the children gain competence in phonemic awareness, letter identification, directionality, spacing, and control over some frequently encountered words, Carla creates transitions that move the children to a higher level of cognitive activity.

## Journal Writing

Carla now tells the children that it is time for them to write their own stories: "Talk with your neighbor about a story you would like to write about today." Laterica turns to Karrisa and says, "I saw a black cat when I came to school this morning." Karrisa giggles and says, "Last night I saw a lion." Then she laughs. "I really didn't, but I want to write it anyway." After sharing their stories, the girls get up and walk to the writing center, where they gather their journals and begin to write.

Carla glances at Nick, who appears to be deep in thought. She asks him, "What would you like to write about today?" Nick immediately responds, "Rosie walked over the table." Carla smiles. "Oh, you want to write about *Rosie's Walk.*" She knows that *Rosie's Walk* does not include this particular detail, but she is pleased that Nick is embellishing the story. Billy also rehearses a message based on a familiar story: "Ten little cows are rolling in the mud." Karrisa's, Billy's, and Nick's stories reflect their previous experiences with book structures, patterns, or vocabulary phrases.

As the children begin to write, Carla circulates among them and talks with them about their stories and their problem-solving. Each child has an ABC chart, a personal dictionary, and an editing chart to use as resources. Carla observes the children's ability to articulate words slowly, write frequently encountered words fluently, attempt words on the practice page, use spaces between words, follow directional movement across the line and return sweep, reread to predict the next word, and use the ABC chart, editing chart, and dictionary to help solve problems. She notes that the children are applying the teacher-modeled behavior from interactive writing to their independent work. (The children's stories are shown in Figures 10.1 through 10.4.)

As Carla holds conference with the children, she focuses on these points:

- She responds to the message with interest and enjoyment.
- She records the story correctly underneath the children's writing.
- She praises the children for concepts of print that are relevant to the children's learning zones.
- She channels the children's attention to letter-sound associations by placing a light checkmark over the children's responses.
- She points to the story copy and asks the children to read it with their finger.

## Guided Reading

It's time for a new instructional move. Carla begins to chant a familiar poem, and the children join in. They close their writing journals, gather their resource materials, and move to the guided reading table.

Based on her observations of the children's

**Figure 10.1** Laterica's independent writing. ("I see a black cat on a fence.")

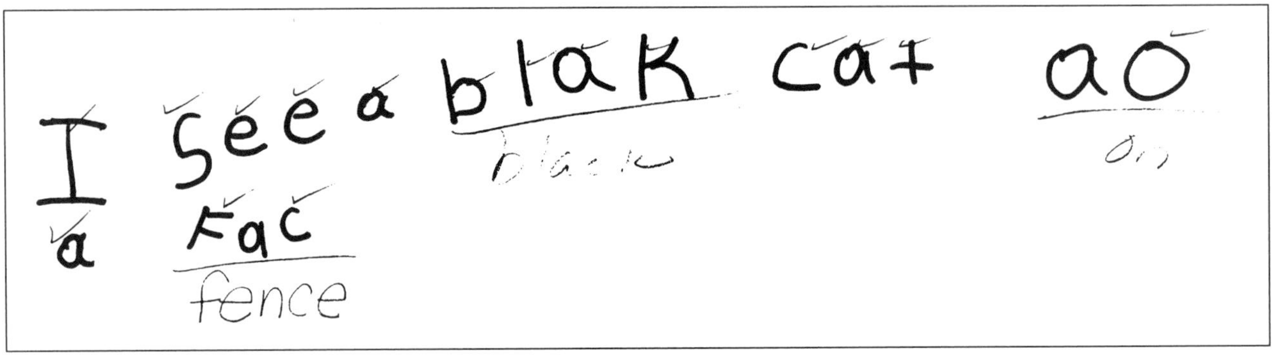

**Figure 10.2** Karrisa's independent writing. ("Last night I saw a lion. The lion said, "roar!")

**Figure 10.3**  Billy's independent writing. ("Ten little cows are rolling in the mud.")

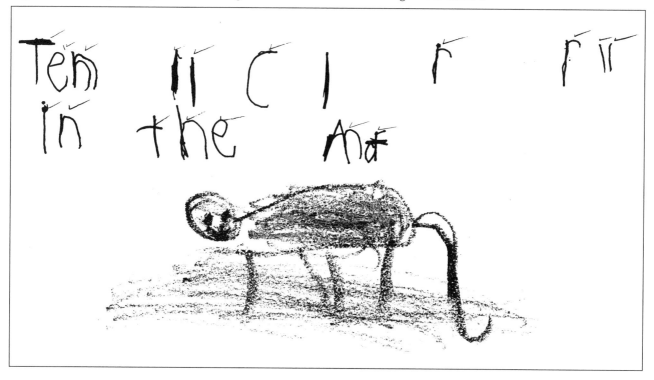

**Figure 10.4**  Nick's independent writing. ("Rosie walked over the table.")

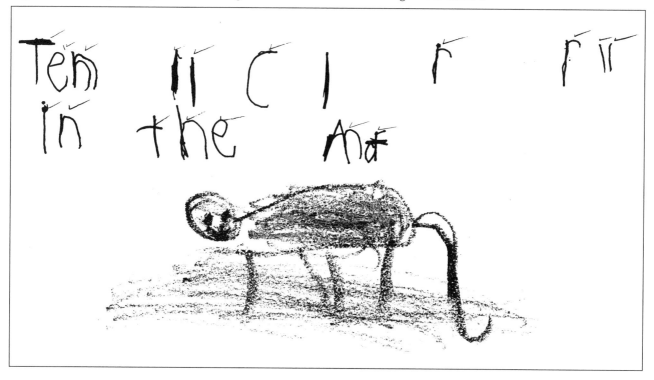

strengths, Carla has selected the book *At the Beach* (Parkes 1997) for this session:

- The print is positioned consistently.
- There is enough space between the words so that the children can point and read.
- The words *I* and *a* are used frequently and serve as solid visual anchors for monitoring one-to-one matching.
- There is strong picture support to help the children with unknown words.
- The text consists of simple, complete sentences that are compatible with the children's oral language.
- There is a high correlation between picture and text.
- The text contains more supportive features than challenging features.

Carla begins by handing each child a seashell. The children's excitement is obvious; they ask Carla questions about where she got the shell. Carla tells them a brief personal story about her trip to the beach. She listens attentively as the children share similar experiences. Then Carla introduces the new book, which is about a little boy who goes to the beach. Carla encourages the children to think about some things the boy might see at the beach. The children exclaim, "A seashell!" Carla acknowledges their response and invites them to look at the pictures to expand their predictions. When the children turn to the page with the picture of the shell, they cry with excitement, "A seashell!" Although the text contains only the word *shell*, Carla makes no mention of this, for she wants to see if the children will monitor their one-to-one matching on this page. On the final page, Carla directs the children's attention to the visual features of print, asking them to predict the letter at the beginning of the word *picked*. Although this is an unknown word, Carla

expects the children to locate the word quickly based on their knowledge of letter and sound associations for *p*. Last, Carla constructs the word *saw*, which occurs frequently throughout the text, with magnetic letters on the overhead projector: "This is an important word in your story. Look on the first page and see if you can find the word *saw*." The children locate the word and frame it with their fingers. Then Carla instructs them to read the first page so that they can hear the word *saw* in the context of the story pattern (see Figure 10.5).

"Now," Carla says, "turn your book back to the title page and let's read the title and author together." The children begin reading the story in whispers. Carla circulates and observes their behavior. She intervenes only if she believes a child is in danger of losing meaning.

When the children finish reading, Carla initiates a brief discussion geared to help them understand the importance of first-letter cues for checking on their reading:

**Figure 10.5** Using magnetic letters to point out frequently occurring words.

**Carla:** Billy, on page 3 you really did some good checking work. First you said *lobster,* but then you changed it to *crab.* Why did you change it?

**Billy:** Because it didn't start with *l.*

At the end of the guided reading session, Carla and the children reread the story together fluently. Carla regulates her participation according to the children's control of the task. As the children prepare to leave, they select two or three books from their familiar-reading boxes to read at home. After the children are gone, Carla quickly records some important observations that she will use to plan her instruction tomorrow.

## Later Lessons

The next literacy lesson we're going to sit in on takes place ten weeks later. In the interim Carla and the first-grade teachers have communicated frequently about the children's progress. Several transitions in reading and writing have taken place:

| Early Lessons | Later Lessons |
| --- | --- |
| Familiar reading of easy books and charts, "reading around the room," etc. | Familiar reading of books from personal baskets. |
| Shared reading of ABC chart. | May not be needed. |
| Shared reading of Big Books, poems, student-made books. | Poems may occasionally be used for word analysis and fluent reading. |
| Letter knowledge, frequently encountered words, simple analogies (in isolation and during assisted reading and writing activities). | Word analysis during text reading and independent writing lessons; planned mini-lessons if needed. |

| | |
| --- | --- |
| Interactive writing. | Revising and editing during and after independent writing. |
| Journal writing in simple sentences. | Long, complex stories that may span several days; writing for a variety of purposes. |

Karrisa, Nick, Laterica, and Billy now spend more time at the beginning of the lesson reading familiar books, since Carla has eliminated the ABC chart and shared reading.

The children's spelling abilities fluctuate between phonetic, transitional, and conventional levels. Since they have learned strategies for analyzing words, most of their word work is done while writing independently. Occasionally, Carla designs a mini-lesson focusing on irregular spelling patterns, suffixes, affixes, or other areas she decides need attention based on the children's writing samples.

As the children have become more strategic readers, they have simultaneously achieved greater competence in their writing. They are now writing complete stories for a variety of purposes and audiences. Also, the children have become more self-regulated in revising and editing their independent writing:

| Early Lessons | Later Lessons |
| --- | --- |
| Story generation with teacher guidance. | Not needed, ongoing stories across days. |
| Sentence level with emphasis on early concepts. | Complete stories with revisions and editing. |
| Teacher conferencing with explicit attention to early concepts. | Child uses personal knowledge and resources to problem-solve with minimal teacher support. |

The children are now reading with early fluency and are beginning to read increasingly longer texts with less assistance from the teacher. After silent reading, Carla guides the children in some type of literature extension: a discussion group, retelling a story, preparing language charts that compare textual features. The three major sections in Carla's literacy lesson are now guided reading, writing aloud, and independent writing.

## Guided Reading

As the children in the group have become more strategic readers, Carla's focus has shifted from problem-solving to developing an increasing range of comprehension strategies. She now gives the children opportunities to develop knowledge, skills, and strategies through silent reading. Afterward the children participate in oral and written retellings, discuss the texts in terms of story elements, and compare and contrast them with other stories they have read. The discussion-group format presents many opportunities for the children to interact with various types of texts.

Today the children are going to extend their range of experiences by reading and discussing *Little Bear and Owl* (Holmelund 1959). Carla begins by building on the children's background knowledge, talking about make-believe, and asking whether they have ever pretended to be somewhere else when they were playing. The children offer some personal make-believe experiences.

Next Carla gives the children a brief synopsis of the story: "Father Bear is far away at the ocean on a fishing trip, but Mother Bear needs some fish right away. So she sends Little Bear down to the river to catch some fish. As Little Bear and his friend Owl are fishing, Little Bear makes believe he is on a big boat." Carla encourages the children to make predictions about why Little Bear pretends to be on a big boat. Billy says, "Because he has never been on a boat and he thought it would be fun." Karrisa responds, "He would be catching lots of fish." Nick comments, "So he can be at the ocean like his father." Carla accepts the children's predictions and then sets the purpose for reading: the children are to read the story silently to find out what happened in Little Bear's imagination as he pretended to be on a big boat.

Carla tells the children to place a sticky note on the page if they are unable to solve a word. As a brief reminder, she then asks them to articulate some strategic ways to problem-solve at point of difficulty. The children quickly respond with flexible solutions: "Look for something I know about the word." "Look all the way through the word and make sure it makes sense and looks right." Carla praises their understanding of problem-solving actions and then directs them to read the story silently.

After the children finish the story, Carla talks with them about Little Bear's experience: "Why did Little Bear make believe he was fishing on a big boat?" Laterica responds, "Because he wanted to be a real fisherman just like Father Bear." Nick adds quickly, "He also wanted to catch something really big, like an octopus." Karrisa chimes in, "This story is a little bit like the one we read a while back, *Just Like Daddy*." Carla responds enthusiastically, "That's right Karrisa. How are they alike?" Karrisa explains that both little bears wanted to be like their daddies and they both went fishing. Carla draws a Venn diagram on the board summarizing the children's discussion of the similarities and differences between the two stories.

At the end of the guided reading, Carla and the children examine any difficult words they have marked with sticky notes. Carka uses the chalkboard or her magnetic letters to illustrate analysis strategies for solving a *few* selected words.

## Writing Aloud and Independent Writing Over a Three-Day Period

During the past few weeks, Carla has guided the children to write narratives based on their own personal experiences. To model the process, she has shared stories from her own life. Her oral rehearsal is a meaningful framework for actively participating in the writing. Furthermore, her expressive use of oral language prepares the children to expect the same expressive elements in the written account. Within the context of this model, the children are guided to apply problem-solving strategies and editing and revising techniques. Carla's instructional goal is achieved when the children can transfer these skills and strategies to their own work.

### Day 1

The writing aloud begins as Carla gathers the children around her chair and sets the stage: "Today I have a story to tell you about when I was a little girl. I want you to listen carefully because after I have finished, you can help me write it."

The children lean forward with interest.

Karrisa says, "I like your stories."

"Me too," says Nick.

Carla begins, "When I was a little girl, I lived in this little white house on Crestwood Street and I had a brother," she leans forward slightly and raises her voice, "a *pesty* brother."

Laterica nods her head as though she can relate to this type of brother.

Realizing the importance of connecting text to life (Cochran-Smith 1989), Carla says, "You know when we read about that pesty fly who was always making us mad and getting in our way…well, that is how my brother was. He was a pesty brother!"

Carla watches the children carefully to monitor their understanding. She is prepared to rephrase or repeat information if needed.

She knows that the children must understand the story in order to reconstruct it successfully.

Satisfied that the children understand, Carla expands her message with natural, descriptive language: "He always did things to scare me. He would go out in the yard and get these *creepy, crawly* bugs and things, and he would throw them on me!"

"Yuk!" Laterica says.

Carla acknowledges Laterica's comment with a slight nod of her head. "I would scream. I would go, 'Aaaa-ahhh!' Do you know what my brother would say? 'Fraidy cat, fraidy cat, fraidy cat!'"

Several voices softly echo, "Fraidy cat, fraidy cat!"

Now Carla changes her voice slightly, signaling that something important is about to happen: "One day it was kind of rainy. It had been raining a lot…like it has been here lately. I went into my room and heard the rain *pittering* and *pattering* on the roof; it felt so good to get into my bed and snuggle up."

Carla has set the scene extremely well, sprinkling her story with clues about the antics of her pesty brother (he liked to scare her; he would get creepy, crawly things and throw them on her). She hopes the image of a "rainy day" will trigger some expectations of what the brother might do. She continues, "Then my brother came into my room and said, 'Look at this new pair of shoes Mom brought you!' And I thought, 'Oh, great! I got a new pair of shoes!' And I opened up the box and what do you think jumped out!" Her statement is not a question; she goes right on, her voice rising in excitement, the words tumbling out of her mouth. "A frog! It was a bullfrog! And it was going 'Croak, croak!' It jumped up…it was really big, because bullfrogs are big. It jumped on me and it scared me to death. I was screaming and Mom came running into my room."

By this time, the children are totally involved in the story. Nick asks, "What did your mom do?"

Carla brings the story to a close: "Well, my brother got sent to his room and he was grounded for a little while. He really didn't think he did anything wrong, because he just kind of had fun doing it."

With her well-told story as background, Carla engages the children in helping her compose a written version of it. "So how am I going to start my story?"

Laterica suggests, "Once upon a time."

Carla accepts Laterica's suggestion and begins to record the phrase. When she comes to the word *upon*, she repeats it two times and says, "Is that one word or two words?"

Billy answers, "I think it's one."

Carla confirms Billy's response as she writes down the word. She quickly rereads the phrase "Once upon a time" as a language unit and continues writing. As she writes, she thinks out loud, prompting the children to refine their knowledge of spelling patterns, something she has noticed in their journal writing. "I lived in a white house," Carla says. She writes the *h* for *house* and comments, "Now I've got to think about it, because I know two chunks that make that *ou* sound." She writes two spellings (*howse* and *house*) on the practice board and asks the children, "Which one looks right?"

The children answer, "The bottom one."

Carla records the correct spelling and continues writing. When she finishes the sentence, she and the children reread the story so far. Some details that were part of the original story have been omitted. Carla prompts the children to recall this information; "I lived in a white house. Where was my white house? Do you think I need to tell you that? Do you think I need to tell you what street I lived on?" As she says this, she rereads the line and inserts a caret. "I lived in a white house on Crestwood Street with my dad, my mom, my sister, and my brother." She hesitates when she comes to the word *brother*. "What did I tell you about my brother that I need to put in my story? What kind of brother was he?"

Laterica and Karrisa exclaim, "Pest!"

"He was a pest brother? Does that sound…?"

"Pesty!" Laterica interjects.

Carla confirms, "Pesty! Okay! That describes my brother, doesn't it!" Next she engages the children in a brief discussion about word patterns. "I've got to come down here to my practice board and try that word out. There's *pest*. What am I going to put on the end of it to make it *pesty*? Think about what we add to the end of *Nick* to get *Nicky*."

"*Y*," the children respond.

Carla adds the *y* to the end of the word and asks, "Does that look like *pesty*? Yes, because if we took Nick's name and put a *y* at the end of it, it would be *Nicky*. Let me try that." She writes the two words under each other and invites the children to compare the endings.

"Now where am I going to add this word in the story? Would I say 'my sister and my brother pesty'?"

"No!! Put it before *brother*. My pesty brother," says Billy.

The writing continues, Carla guiding the children through the process of composing, editing, and revising another sentence. Details are added ("When I was a little girl"), and words are worked on within the context of the story. As the session comes to an end, Carla directs the children's attention to the writing checklist (see Chapter 5). She says, "Okay, that is as far as I am going to get with my story today. Remember, I am right here." She points to steps 1 and 2 of the checklist. "I'm writing my story. I'm making sure it makes sense, and

I'm adding to my story and crossing out what I don't want."

After the children reread the story, Nick reminds Carla that in the original version she had described the house as a "little white house." Carla asks, "Do you think I should add that?" Then she inserts a caret before *house* and adds the new information.

**Day 2**

"Raise your hand and tell me where I am in the writing of my story."

Nick looks at the writing checklist and responds, "Writing our story and seeing if it makes sense. And crossing out the things that we don't want."

"Yes," says Carla. "So what do we need to do before we finish writing our story today?"

The children respond in unison, "Go back and reread it."

Carla and the children reread the story together. "Once upon a time, I lived in a little white house on Crestwood Street with my dad, my mom, my sister, and my pesty brother. He always picked up creepy, crawly things and threw them on me."

Now Carla picks up her marker and fluently adds new information: "Then I would scream, 'Stop, Joey!' And he would call me…" she pauses to invite the children to contribute.

"Fraidy!" Nick answers.

Carla rereads the previous phrase and adds "fraidy cat" to the story. She continues thinking out loud as she records the message: "One dark rainy night, I crawled into my warm bed and went to sleep. I was sleeping so good. The rain was going drip, drip, drip on the roof." As she writes the words into the story, she says, "Doesn't that make you sleep good when you hear the rain dripping?" Interestingly, the story is being clarified. For the first time, we learn that Carla was asleep when her pesty brother came into the room.

Carla writes the following sentence: "My pesty brother crawled into my room and flipped on the light." When she hesitates momentarily at the word *light*, Billy comments, "It's like *night.*"

"Wake up, Carla! Look at what Mom bought…bought." Again, the hesitation in her voice signals that Carla is thinking about the word. She decides on the correct spelling for the word and records it in her story. She adds the phrase "I popped up," quickly marks through the word *I*, changes it to *My head*, and continues writing. "My head popped up fast and I saw a big shoebox. I opened the box and…"

The children exclaim, "Out jumped…"

"Out jumped a huge bullfrog," Carla writes as she speaks. "He said, 'Croak, croak.' I screamed, 'Oh, Mom, come here!!'" Carla reflects, "What do you think Mom did?" In response, she quickly adds the new information, "Mom came running. She saw what Joey had done. She said, 'Joey! Go to your room now!'"

"AND DON'T COME OUT!" Nick exclaims boldly.

Carla repeats Nick's statement and quickly records it in the story. She continues writing aloud, "The next morning Joey apologized and said, 'I'm sorry, I thought that is what big pesty brothers were supposed to do to little…'"

When she hesitates, the children respond, "Sisters!" and the story comes to an end.

"Now what do I need to do?" Carla asks.

"Go back and reread it."

"Cross out what you don't like."

"Add some more things."

Carla and children reread the story and conclude that it is ready to be edited for punctuation tomorrow.

**Day 3**

"Look at our steps in writing. What do I need to do now?" Carla asks the children. "Okay, first I need to go back and reread it. So everybody read it with me."

After the reading, Carla prompts again, "What do I need to do now?"

"Read the story and put in the punctuation," says Laterica.

"Right, I need punctuation so my story will make sense and sound interesting to other people," Carla says. "So where my voice stops, what am I going to put?"

"Punctuation!" Billy and Karrisa exclaim.

"Some kind of punctuation mark. It could be a period, or talking marks, or an exclamation mark," Carla explains.

Nick adds, "Or it could be a question mark!"

"What am I going to put if my voice just slows down a little?" Carla asks.

"Put a comma," Karrisa answers.

**Figure 10.6** Karrisa's story. ("One day when me and my brother was playing in the living room my brother hit the table He knocked my mom's favorite glass down He broke it He got me in trouble but I told mom what happened and then my mom said not to play in the living room again So then my mom said go to your room My brother did not watch tv again Mom apologized to me I said That is ok The next morning I woke up My mom said Good morning I had to wake up my brother I did not like to wake up my brother Then I went to school.")

The children still need guidance in this area. They are able to talk about punctuation in an assisted situation, but their writing does not reflect their control of this behavior yet. They need lots of practice listening to how sentences with varied punctuation sound to their ears. Using this rich story as a model, Carla provides the children with opportunities to apply punctuation to enhance meaning. They reread it together with fluency and expression, and appropriate punctuation is added.

## Closing Thoughts

From an apprenticeship point of view, the purpose of assisted writing is to provide children with clear models and guided practice that will carry over to their independent work. So how are these children doing in their journal writing (see Figures 10.6 through 10.9)?

Well, there is evidence that they are applying editing and revising strategies when they compose their texts. Karrisa writes the phrase

**Figure 10.7** Billy's story. ("March the 5th was my brother's birthday and on my brother's birthday my mommy gave me a present to. And my brother gave (me one) to. What I got was a punching balloon and some cars to. At night I played with my punching balloon and my cars, and the night before last it went pop.")

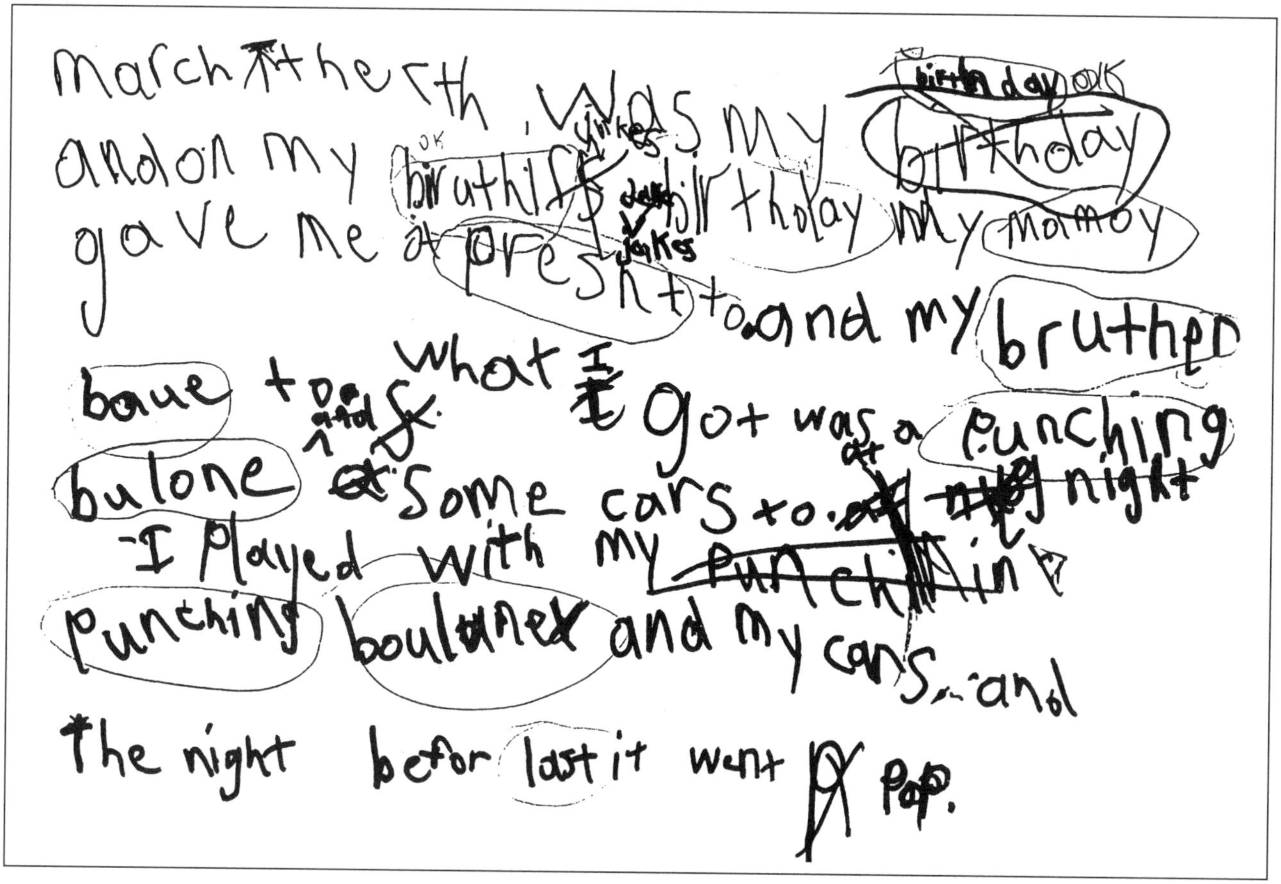

**Figure 10.8** Nick's story. ("When I was a little boy I caught a bullfrog and I gave him a lot of flys. But my baby brother gives him more flys But I don't care because he will not be hungry. One day me and my mom went to see Turbo Rangers. I got home but I did not see my frog. My mom spotted him. He jumped on my baby sister and she cried. I jumped off some steps. I was so mad I would jump off 7 steps. My baby brother caught him. I gave him a hug. I was happy because I got my frog back.")

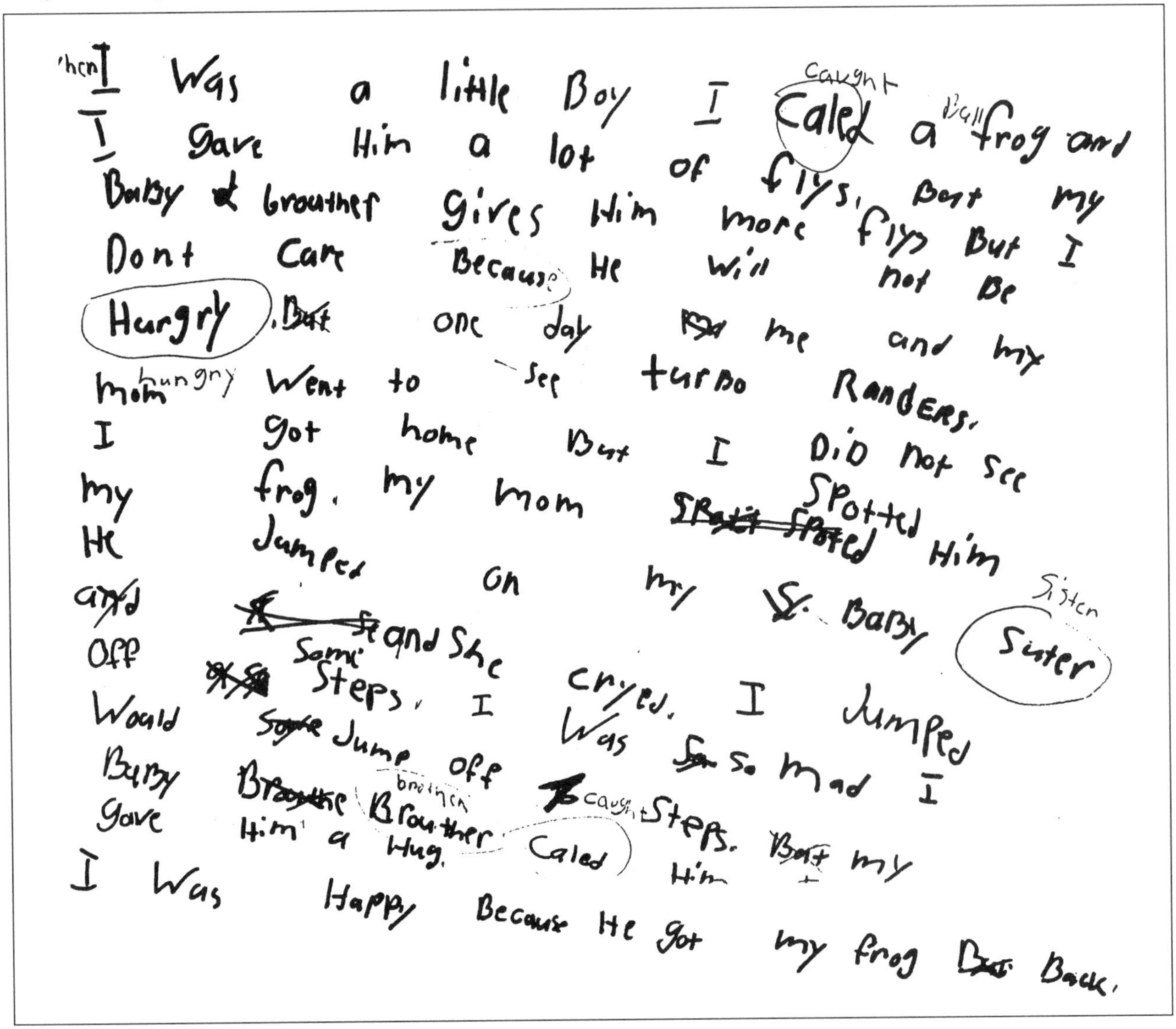

"Then I went to," rapidly draws a line through it, and revises it to reflect a new beginning ("The next morning"). Nick edits the unnecessary word *but* from his story and continues to write quickly and fluently. All the children monitor their spellings by circling words and making new attempts.

Not surprisingly, all four children write stories that involve a brother. Karrisa, Nick, and Laterica write about incidents in which their brother caused a problem for them. Karrisa uses the word *apologized* in her story, probably because she was exposed to it during the writing aloud experience. Laterica uses the

**Figure 10.9** Laterica's story. ("Friday my mom cooked some spaghetti and my brother took mine and I said Quit Scott. I am going to tell mom I called mom mom Scott is taking my food. She said "no desert he said I'm sorry Laterica do you forgive me I said Yes I forgive you.")

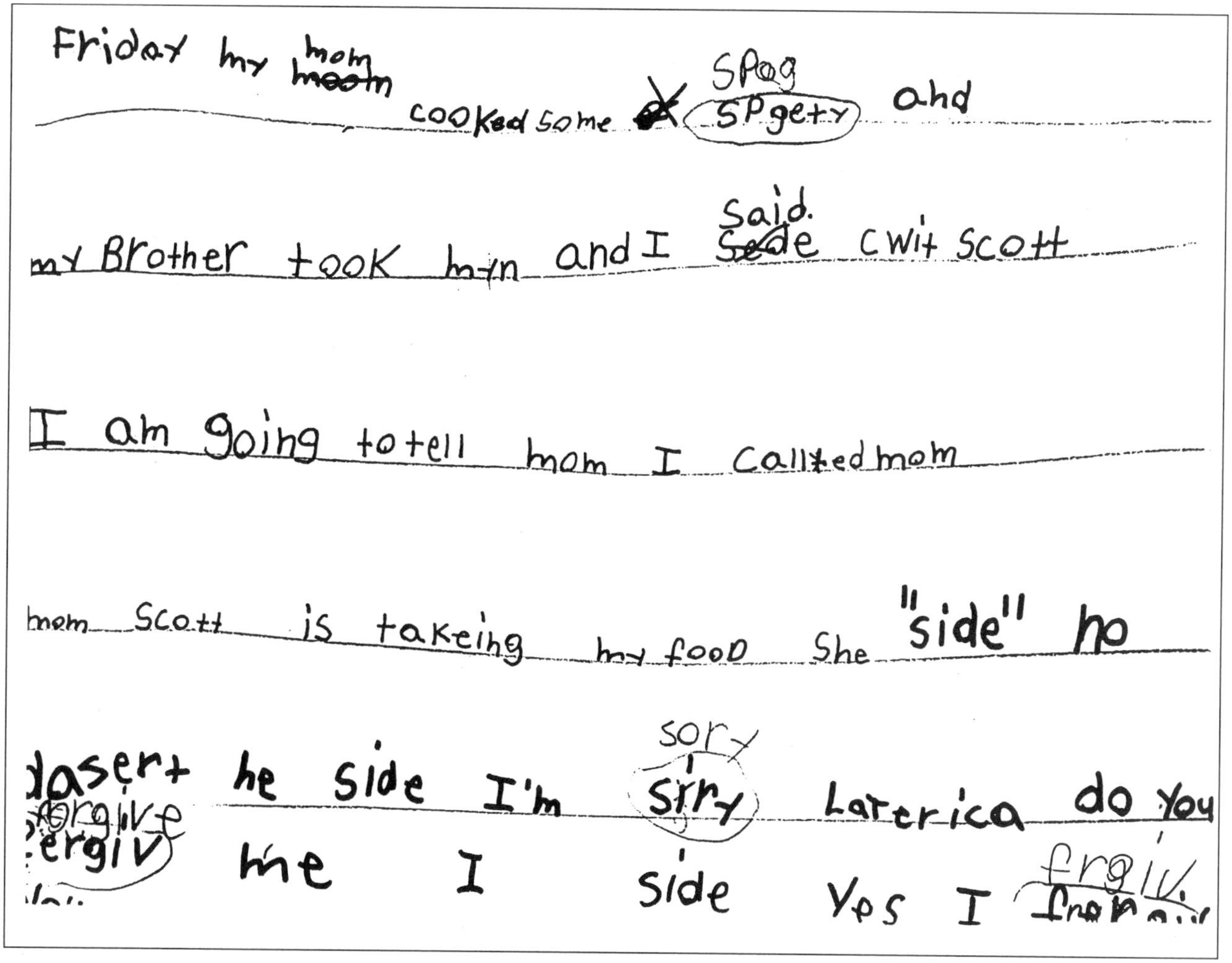

phrase "I'm sorry" and carries the concept further by describing her brother's punishment and his appeal to be forgiven. Nick includes a frog in his story, also a part of Carla's story. All four children's stories are based on real events in their lives, and they are all reminiscent of Carla's story, even though there was no pre-discussion of journal writing topics.

The children use descriptive language and complex sentence patterns to communicate their messages. Nick expresses his feelings with his comment, "I was so mad I could jump off 7 steps." The children use transitional words (*then, so, and, but, when*) to connect meaningful units and identify time elements (*one day, March the 5th, when I was a little boy, Friday*). Laterica uses dialogue that requires three types of punctuation to express the appropriate meaning (exclamation mark, period, question mark). Although she is unable to apply correct punctuation, Laterica reads the story to the teacher with appropriate phrasing and intonation.

Based on Carla's writing aloud lesson and the children's journal samples, we can assume that the children applied knowledge gained from the assisted writing activity, including concepts, vocabulary, transitional words, composing strategies, and revising and editing techniques.

At the beginning of the year, the children in Carla's literacy program needed supplemental literacy support. Their instructional program included a high degree of teacher-regulated activities, with special emphasis on modeling, coaching, and scaffolding. Ten weeks later, as they became more competent learners, their literacy lessons reflected an obvious movement toward more child-regulated activities.

# Working Together

Literacy must be viewed through a wide-angle lens. It takes many dedicated people working together to ensure every child's right to literacy. A single program or a single teacher cannot bring about comprehensive changes within the school.

The importance of teachers working together as a team of educators whose goal is to support the total child cannot be understated. Teams of teachers with a common goal can do much more than an individual teacher working alone. Teachers must be knowledgeable about learning theory and effective literacy practices for working with young children. Literacy teams guide their members to improve their teaching abilities in order to promote literacy for all their students. This is the best vehicle for restructuring classrooms to best educate our children.

Each of us has recently worked with school districts to help build a strong networking system in which teachers actively support one another through team meetings and colleague visits. These teams are usually made up of classroom teachers, special education teachers, Reading Recovery teachers, and principals.

Teams are usually formed to meet the teachers' needs in dealing with the flourishing population of low-achieving children. Literacy teams bring teachers together to problem-solve and to share responsibility for ensuring that all children receive the support they need for ongoing success.

Literacy teams meet to explore issues related to early intervention and student achievement. They identify long- and short-term goals for personal change. They focus on student learning to guide assessment. They support one another through active demonstrations and follow-up discussions of teaching and learning interactions, and they seek help in specific areas of professional development. They problem-solve together, monitor children's progress, and share the nuts and bolts of what really works in their classrooms. They build a support system for implementing change in theory and in practice.

In Chris Dayer's school, the teachers formed a literacy team to actively support one another and the children they each work with. In the beginning, the teachers met and discussed their curriculum and the number of children they felt were falling through the cracks. They discovered that although they were each using the adopted basal program as their primary method of reading instruction, there were many differences in their two-hour language-arts block. Some teachers were doing whole-class reading; some used fixed-ability groups. One grade level used a structured phonics program; one grade level taught phonics within context. When the teachers looked at how they were incorporating writing into the curriculum, they also found many inconsistencies. Many teachers had their students write every day, others only sporadically.

The team set out to revise their teaching practices into a cohesive curriculum across the primary grades. They looked to Lynn Raney, the reading specialist, to guide and support them in targeted areas of assessment and instruction. At team meetings, the teachers examined portfolios of children's reading and writing progress and used this information for planning reading and writing groups. The teachers noted that the children who were receiving help from Lynn during Reading Recovery and supplementary group instruction were making significant gains. They felt that all of the children could benefit from a balanced literacy approach in the classroom. The teachers began working together and building a real team.

One of the first goals of the team was to examine the materials they had available for teaching reading. All the teachers were somewhat frustrated with the basal program. The levels of difficulty did not appear to be consistent and supportive of the children. One teacher said, "Some of the stories are too easy for the children; and other stories are so hard that the children just fall apart when they try to read them." Several of the first-grade teachers felt that the basal was too difficult for their lowest readers, so they didn't use the book until later in the school year. Lynn showed the teachers how to look at features of text and how to determine appropriate levels of difficulty.

At the next team meeting, the teachers brought in their basals and began to organize the stories according to emergent, early, and fluent levels. Everyone was shocked and dismayed at the vast range of levels in the basal. After the teachers had identified the stories by level of difficulty, they looked at which ones could be used in a guided reading group and which ones could be used for shared reading or a read-aloud. Recognizing the need for more guided reading materials at the children's instructional reading levels, and with the support of Chris, their principal, they purchased guided reading sets for all the teachers to use.

In Georgeanne Peel's school, the teachers also recognized the need for more guided reading materials. Supplemental books that could be used as appropriate texts for guided reading had originally been packaged in sets of six, but one copy of each title had been distributed to each teacher. At a team meeting, the teachers initiated a schoolwide "book search" in an effort to locate all six copies of each title. As teachers began bringing in the books, Georgeanne, the principal, formed a committee to organize the books according to text difficulty. This committee cleaned out a storage area and created a guided reading library for everyone in the school to use. Another committee devised a checkout system for the book sets. The teachers put each set of little books into a Zip-lock bag with the name and level of the book on a library card. When a teacher wanted to check out a set of books, she simply pulled out the library card and placed it into her pocket on the "checkout" wall chart. The teachers were able to keep track of the books they needed for a particular group of children and had access to more appropriate materials for supporting their young readers.

Patsy Fleniken, director for curriculum and instruction in a large school district, implemented a districtwide team approach. The teachers were given time during the school day to meet with their grade-level colleagues from the other schools. There were inservice sessions on how to implement a balanced literacy approach in the classroom. An on-site staff developer gave the teachers personal support in transferring their learning back into the classroom. Their team meetings involved clear demonstrations, using explicit language, of how to introduce the components of balanced literacy. After the sessions, the teachers implemented what they had learned in their classrooms. Follow-up meetings allowed the teachers to review the new topic and to discuss the successes or failures they had encountered.

At each literacy team meeting the teachers brought in teacher-made books, literacy-corner ideas, picture and word dictionaries, writing samples, running records, books they had selected for guided reading, the literacy portfolios of their hardest-to-teach children. These meetings enabled the teachers to make important changes in their theories and practice.

The district administration provided ongoing support and assistance:

- Regularly scheduled meetings throughout the year during the school day.
- Current professional materials and books for each teacher to stimulate interactive discussions on theoretical and practical aspects of high-quality classroom instruction.
- Developmentally appropriate classroom materials and resources to support children as they advance to higher levels of cognitive development.

**Figure 11.1** Making books for guided reading groups.

- Opportunities to observe other classrooms and to network with other teachers.
- Professional consultants to provide literacy support in targeted areas of assessment and instruction.

Esther Crawford, assistant superintendent of a large urban district, recognized the importance of literacy teams in promoting schoolwide change. Four years ago, Esther encouraged her Reading Recovery teachers to observe one another teach. This proved so successful that Esther expanded the concept to include first-grade literacy teams and, more recently, districtwide literacy teams. Two types of team meetings were conducted in collaboration with the local university. First, fifteen school-based meetings were held to provide training to all first-grade teachers in assessment and guided reading. Harriet Pool and Esther Watson, the school's Reading Recovery teachers, were important members of the team. Second, the university provided training to districtwide teams comprising of reading teachers, kindergarten through second-grade teachers, and several principals. During these team meetings, new understanding occurred as teachers applied theories of learning to the everyday practices of the classroom. For example, the teachers learned how to:

- Observe and analyze children's reading and writing behavior.
- Use this information to assign children to guided reading and assisted writing groups.
- Select appropriate materials to support children's strengths and needs.

At each meeting, team members brought in portfolios of children's progress that included running records and writing samples. Often the teachers would make transparencies of par-

ticular documentation and present it to the team for discussion and feedback. During the team meetings, the teachers learned how to use materials appropriately for instruction and testing purposes. They categorized their basal texts and other reading materials by level of difficulty; they developed word tests; and they identified benchmark books and wrote standard book introductions that were used for testing and placement purposes.

The team meetings focused on creating a literacy-rich environment for the children. When new topics and approaches were introduced, the teachers implemented them in their classrooms. They brought in videotapes or other documentation of their teaching and learning interactions for discussion and feedback from their colleagues.

Nancy McGrew, a Reading Recovery teacher leader, worked closely with one of the school-based literacy teams. As part of a research study (McGrew 1998), Nancy transcribed videotapes of classroom reading instruction at three different points in the year. Nancy found that teacher reprimands and student speech unrelated to learning diminished significantly as teachers and students began to construct knowledge jointly during reading instruction. Her study suggested that the change in the teachers' language was influenced by the topics of discussion at the literacy team meetings.

The literacy team meetings provided the teachers in Esther's district with an internal support system for implementing changes in their assessment and classroom practices. During team meetings, the teachers planned personal areas of growth, sought out professional guidance, and worked together to address the needs of their children.

Sandy Bryant, a reading teacher in a small rural school, began a literacy team made up of herself and the first- and second-grade teachers. The five teachers observed each other and collaborated on effective literacy practices. They began viewing commercial videotapes of guided reading and shared reading in order to learn how to teach using a balanced approach. After they learned the mechanics, they began observing and coaching one another during their own guided reading groups. They viewed video clips of themselves and their children to study the children's behavior and to refine their teaching interactions.

Sandy was also a member of another type of literacy team. As the Reading Recovery teacher for the school, she worked closely with each classroom teacher in planning supplemental reading instruction for their lowest-achieving children. The teachers collaborated individually with Sandy on how they could best support their children's literacy development. The teachers shared running records, writing samples, book selections, and word-building activities to ensure their methodologies and analysis of children's reading behavior were congruent.

Carla Soffos's school has been using literacy teams for three years. The K–1 school is committed to ensuring that all first graders are successful readers by the end of first grade. This commitment to literacy is supported in the following ways:

- Reading Recovery is available for all first graders who need intensive tutorials.
- Small-group supplemental services are provided to first graders who need extra support in the classroom.
- Small-group emergent literacy services are provided to kindergarten children who need extra support in the classroom.
- Enriched classrooms with appropriate materials for high-quality small-group and large-group instruction is available in all kindergarten and first-grade classrooms.
- Literacy team meetings are held at least twice a month.
- There is solid backing from the administration.
- The university provides strong professional development opportunities.

Over the past three years, the teachers have conducted bimonthly team meetings to discuss categorizing books according to text characteristics; analyzing spelling patterns; using running records; designing assisted writing activities; making transitions across reading and writing events; holding produc-

**Figure 11.2** A teacher analyzes the spelling development and writing style of a first grader during a literacy team meeting.

tive writing conferences; setting up literacy corners; and working with guided reading groups. These professional development sessions have enabled them to grow as learners.

During the three-year period, Carla studied the process of change at the school as part of her advanced studies at the university. Her classroom observations and teacher interviews revealed dramatic changes in assessment and classroom practices. One classroom teacher wrote, "The literacy team meetings have caused me to challenge my theories of how children learn and to seek more effective ways of helping my children." This sentiment was echoed by other teachers in the school, who commented on how the team meetings supported their professional growth. As the literacy team worked together, the teachers formulated new theories concerning the learning processes of their students and talked with their colleagues about these new insights. The changes across time are illustrated here:

| Category | Year 1 | Year 2 | Year 3 |
|---|---|---|---|
| running records | 0% | 40% | 90% |
| guided reading | 0% | 40% | 90% |
| familiar reading | 0% | 20% | 98% |
| assisted writing | 0% | 30% | 100% |
| journal writing | 50% | 97% | 100% |
| writing conferences | 0% | 20% | 86% |

These vignettes are only a small glimpse into the powerful interactions of literacy teams. As university teachers who work very closely with school districts, the three of us have had the opportunity to watch these literacy teams develop. In many instances, we have played a role in facilitating collegial involvement through study/share sessions and university-related courses. Our goal from the beginning has been to help teachers become self-regulated learners who design their own questions and seek their own answers through problem-solving discussions with other professionals.

As teachers observe and analyze children's reading behavior, they acquire an important tool for testing and refining their theories of how children learn. When teachers apply theory to practice, they understand the significance of important concepts associated with apprenticeship learning: they learn the relevance of scaffolded instruction aimed at children's potential levels of development; they learn the importance of modeling and coaching as instructional tools that enable children to accomplish new learning tasks; they learn the value of establishing routines, assisted versus independent activities, explicit feedback, and problem-solving solutions to common issues.

Literacy learning is complex—not only for our children, but for us as well. As teachers, we are constantly learning and experiencing transitions that reflect our new understanding. The children in our classrooms need us to work together as a team to support them on their pathway to literacy. *Systemic change lies in our understanding how our children learn and in our ability to problem-solve with colleagues who work with our children, who share our common experiences, and who speak our language of literacy.*

# Appendix

# Selected Lessons from a Ten-Week Program of Independent and Assisted Writing Activities

## Lesson 1

Journal Analysis (semiphonetic stage of spelling)

- Writes name.
- Hears *l* in beginning and ending positions.
- Adds letters to a word to make a word look longer (*oatmeal*).
- Returns to second line and makes new attempt for *likes*.

- Experiments with periods.
- Shows directional movement.
- Does not use spacing between words.

Focus of Group Assisted Writing (interactive writing at the emergent level)

* Focus on spacing and hearing sounds in words.
* Demonstrate early strategies (rereading, letter formation, linking to ABC chart, etc.).

LAterICA IOMIOIN.

IEKS.

Laterica   likes   Oatmeal .

## Lesson 3

Journal Analysis (semiphonetic stage of spelling)

- Shows risk-taking behavior through early editing attempts.
- Hears consonant sounds (*c, k, l, t*) in beginning and ending positions.
- Writes familiar word from shared reading (*pig*).
- Uses exclamation point.
- Does not use spacing.

Focus of Group Assisted Writing (interactive writing at the emergent level)

* Focus on spacing, hearing sounds in words, and rereading.
* Introduce dictionary for recording known and partially known words.

CAKLEO pi6 !

Come    back    little    pig .

## Lesson 8

Journal Analysis (phonetic stage of spelling)

- Shows good control of spacing.
- Writes known words.
- Hears consonant sounds in beginning, middle, and ending positions.
- Shows awareness of visual features in common words.
- Writes more complex sentence.
- Ignores ending punctuation.

Focus of Group Assisted Writing (interactive writing at the emergent level for one or two more lessons)

- Focus on hearing sounds in sequence.
- Attend to visual features of frequently encountered words.

I LC the COW

Be COS

it hav

mioK

I   like   the   cow   because   it   have   milk.

- Introduce role of punctuation (quotation marks) in expressive reading.

## Lesson 11

Journal Analysis (phonetic stage of spelling)

- Good control of spacing.
- Uses known word (*the*).
- Uses punctuation (exclamation mark) for emphasis (also underlines text to show excitement).
- Experiments with dialogue in text and bubble.
- Hears beginning and ending consonant sounds.
- Shows awareness that words contain vowels and experiments with these as visual markers (with no letter/sound correspondence).
- Edits attempt for *now* (crosses out *a* and revises with *o*).

Focus of Assisted Writing (interactive writing at early level with two or three sentences)

- Introduce how to use key words (*where, when, why, how*) to build on meaning.
- Continue to use varied punctuation (exclamation points, quotation marks, periods) to support meaning.
- Continue to work on hearing sounds in sequence and attending to visual information in frequently encountered words.

# Lesson 15

Journal Analysis (phonetic stage of spelling)

- Hears consonant sounds in beginning, middle, and ending positions.
- Hears some vowels.
- Uses known words.
- Uses two sentences to communicate message.
- Uses lead sentence to include "when" element.
- Experiments with commas.
- Uses quotation marks and exclamation point to express meaning.

Focus of Assisted Writing (early revisions with overhead transparency)

- Use overhead transparency of children's writing samples to illustrate how to add details for writing longer stories.
- Use overhead transparency of page copied from guided reading book to illustrate writer's techniques (descriptive language, lead sentences, etc.)
- Invite peer prompting using key words (*where, when, why, how,* etc.).
- Begin writing aloud demonstrations.
- Introduce editing and revising techniques (carets, insertions, crossing out, etc.).
- Emphasize use of punctuation for expressive reading.
- Demonstrate simple analogies with visual patterns from known words.

One. Hattw, nt I. SoN ɑ
Wiso She Set, "Boo!".

One Halloween night I saw a witch, She said, "Boo"!

# Lesson 20

Journal Analysis (transitional stage of spelling)

- Uses lead-in sentence (when).
- Expands message to three sentences.
- Edits on the spot to include descriptive information (starts to write *day* and changes it to *Thanksgiving day*).
- Uses varied punctuation (period, comma, quotation marks, and exclamation point).
- Uses known words.

Focus of Assisted Writing (writing aloud with revising and editing)

- Continue to emphasize editing and revising techniques while writing aloud.
- Illustrate importance of writing for different purposes and audiences.
- Demonstrate problem-solving analogies visually.
- Use personal resources, such as the dictionary and word wall.

("One Thanksgiving day I saw a turkey and it went gobble, gobble, gobble. My mom said, "Oh, a turkey!")

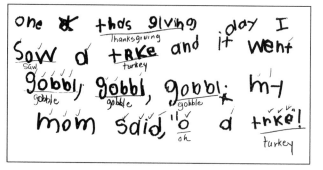

## Lesson 30

Journal Analysis (transitional stage of spelling)

- Uses a balance of problem-solving techniques for editing spelling (corrects the spelling at the time of error, circles the spelling after the story is completed, and uses other resources to confirm spelling).
- Understands how to write a letter.
- Uses commas and periods to communicate meanings.
- Attends to visual patterns in words.

Focus of Assisted Writing (writing aloud with revising and editing)

- Continue to demonstrate flexible ways to problem-solve on the spot.
- Continue to demonstrate editing and revising techniques.
- Continue to demonstrate composing process with various topics.

("Dear Mrs. Soffos, I went out to play in the snow and my brother threw a snowball at me. Love Laterica.")

## Lesson 48

### Journal Analysis (transitional stage of spelling)

- Composes well-organized and coherent texts.
- Uses punctuation to support meaning.
- Uses editing and revising techniques.
- Applies problem-solving strategies on the spot.

### Focus of Assisted Writing (writing aloud with revising and editing)

- Continue to focus on composing various texts for different purposes.
- Continue to emphasize editing and revising techniques.

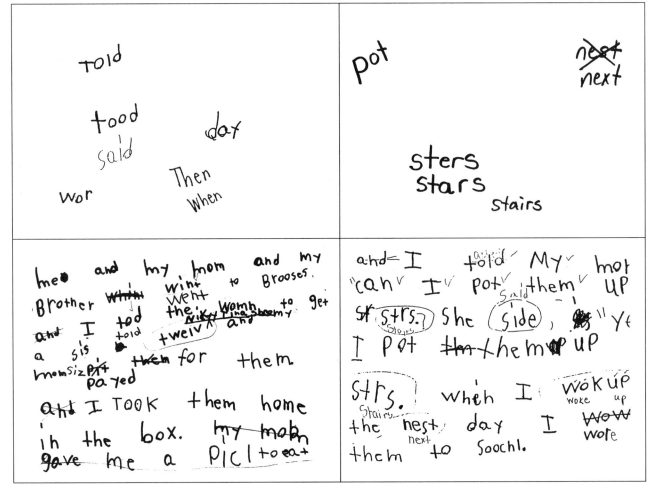

("Me and my mom and my brother went to Bruces and I told the woman to get a size twelve Nike tennis shoe and my mom paid for them and I took them home in the box. My mom gave me a pickle to eat and I told my mom "Can I put them upstairs?" She said "Yes." I put them upstairs. When I woke up the next day I wore them to school.")

## Lesson 50

Journal Analysis (transitional and conventional stages of spelling)

- Retells a detailed and chronologically organized version of a story.
- Includes various punctuation to express meaning.
- Identifies first draft as "sloppy copy."
* Using editing and revising techniques (lines drawn through phrases, crossing out, carets and insertions, circling).

Focus of Assisted Writing (writing aloud with revising and editing)

* Phase out the assisted writing activities.
* Devote extended periods to independent writing.
* Be ready to model the writing process and provide assisted writing activities as needed.

("Sloppy copy. One day mother fox "said" I am hungry but I have to take care of my babies. I will get some food for you said father fox. Father fox went to look for some food. He went down to the farmer's hen house and opened the door. The hen said kkkkkkk and the farmer hit the fox. Oh! Is he dead. No. Hen is foxing the farmer. Then the farmer went out. He went out the door and went in the house and the fox got a hen and took the white hen.")

# References

Adams, M. 1996. *Beginning to Read: Thinking and Learning About Print*. 9th ed. Cambridge, MA: MIT Press.

Barr, R., and W. Parrett. 1995. *Hope at Last for At-Risk Youth*. Needham Heights, MA: Allyn & Bacon.

Bodrova, E., and D. Leong. 1996. *Tools of the Mind: The Vygotskian Approach to Early Childhood Education*. Englewood Cliffs, NJ: Merrill.

Bruner, J. 1967. *Studies in Cognitive Growth: A Collaboration at the Center for Cognitive Growth*. New York: Wiley.

———. 1986. *Actual Minds, Possible Worlds*. Cambridge: Harvard University Press.

Button, K., M. Johnson, and P. Furgerson. 1996. Interactive Writing in a Primary Classroom. *The Reading Teacher* 49, 6: 446–454.

Campione, J., A. Shapiro, and A. Brown. 1995. Forms of Transfer in a Community of Learners: Flexible Learning and Understanding. In A. McKeough, J. Lupart, and A. Marini, eds., *Teaching for Transfer: Fostering Generalization in Learning*. Hillsdale, NJ: Lawrence Erlbaum.

Carle, E. 1990. *The Very Quiet Cricket*. New York: Philomel.

Clay, M. 1991. *Becoming Literate: The Construction of Inner Control*. Portsmouth, NH: Heinemann.

———. 1993. *An Observation Survey of Early Literacy Achievement*. Portsmouth, NH: Heinemann.

Clay, M., and C. Cazden. 1990. A Vygotskian Interpretation of Reading Recovery. In L. Moll, ed., *Vygotsky and Education: Instructional Implications and Applications of Sociohistorical Psychology*. Cambridge, UK: Cambridge University Press.

Cochran-Smith, M. 1989. *The Making of a Reader*. Norfork, NJ: Ablex.

Collins, A., J. Brown, and S. Newman. 1989. Cognitive Apprenticeship: Teaching the Crafts of Reading, Writing, and Mathematics. In L. Resnick, ed., *Knowing, Learning, and Instruction: Essays in Honor of Robert Glaser*. Hillsdale, NJ: Lawrence Erlbaum.

Cowley, J. 1990. *Nighttime*. Bothell, WA: Wright Group.

———. 1992. *The Music Machine*. Bothell, WA: Wright Group.

———. 1996. *The Seed*. Bothell, WA: Wright Group.

Cunningham, P. 1996. *Phonics They Use*. New York: HarperCollins.

Cutting, J. 1988. *I Like…*. Bothell, WA: Wright Group.

Dewey, J. 1935. *Liberalism and Social Action*. New York: Putman.

Diaz, R., C. Neal, and M. Amaya-Williams. 1990. The Social Origins of Self-Regulation. In L.

Moll, ed., *Vygotsky and Education: Instructional Implications and Applications of Sociohistorical Psychology,* pp. 127–172. Cambridge, UK: Cambridge University Press.

Donaldson, M. 1978. *Children's Minds.* New York: W. W. Norton.

Dorn, L. 1996. A Vygotskian Perspective on Literacy Acquisition: Talk and Action in the Child's Construction of Literate Awareness. *Literacy, Teaching, and Learning: An International Journal of Early Literacy* 2, 2: 15–40.

Fisher, B. 1991. *Joyful Learning.* Portsmouth, NH: Heinemann.

Fountas, I., and G. S. Pinnell. 1996. *Guided Reading: Good First Teaching for All Children.* Portsmouth, NH: Heinemann.

Gentry, R., and J. W. Gillet. 1993. *Teaching Kids to Spell.* Portsmouth, NH: Heinemann.

Goswami, U., and P. Bryant. 1990. *Phonological Skills and Learning to Read.* Hillsdale, NJ: Lawrence Erlbaum.

Healy, J. M. 1990. *Endangered Minds: Why Children Don't Think and What We Can Do About It.* New York: Touchstone.

Heenman, J. 1985. *Product and Process.* Auckland, New Zealand: Longman Paul.

Hill, M. 1989. *Home: Where Reading and Writing Begin.* Portsmouth, NH: Heinemann.

Holdaway, D. 1979. *Foundations of Literacy.* Sydney: Ashton Scholastic.

Holmelund, E. 1959. Little Bear and Owl. In *Father Bear Comes Home.* New York: HarperCollins.

Humphrey, A. 1997. Effects of an early literacy group on the writing development of at-risk first graders. Unpublished thesis. University of Arkansas at Little Rock.

Hutchins, P. 1986. *The Doorbell Rang.* New York: Scholastic.

Johnston, P. 1992. *Constructive Evaluation of Literate Activity.* White Plains, NY: Longman.

Juel, C. 1988. Learning to Read and Write: A Longitudinal Study of Fifty-Four Children from First Through Fourth Grade. *Journal of Educational Psychology* 80: 437–447.

Lobel, A. 1970. *Frog and Toad Are Friends.* New York: Harper & Row.

Lupart, J. 1996. Exceptional Learners and Teaching for Transfer. In A. McKeough, J. Lupart, and A. Marini, eds., *Teaching for Transfer: Fostering Generalization in Learning.* Hillsdale, NJ: Lawrence Erlbaum.

Luria, A. R. 1973. *The Working Brain: An Introduction to Neuropsychology.* New York: HarperCollins.

———. 1982. *Language and Cognition.* New York: Wiley.

Lyons, C. A., G. S. Pinnell, and D. E. DeFord. 1993. *Partners in Learning: Teachers and Children in Reading Recovery.* New York: Teachers College Press.

McCormick, S. 1977. Should You Read Aloud to Your Children? *Language Arts* 54: 139–143.

McGrew, N. 1998. A journey through the change process: Team building and its impact on classroom reading instruction. Unpublished thesis. University of Arkansas at Little Rock.

Melser, J. 1990. *The Chocolate Cake.* Bothell, WA: Wright Group.

Moustafa, M. 1997. *Beyond Traditional Phonics: Research Discoveries and Reading Instruction.* Portsmouth, NH: Heinemann.

Parkes, B. 1986. *The Great Enormous Watermelon.* Crystal Lake, IL: Rigby.

———. 1989. *Goodnight, Goodnight.* Crystal Lake, IL: Rigby.

———. 1997. *At the Beach.* New York: Newbridge Discovery Links.

Pinnell, G. S., and A. McCarrier. 1994. Interactive Writing: A Transition Tool for Assisting Children in Learning to Read and Write. In B. E. Hiebert and B. Taylor, eds., *Getting Reading Right from the Start: Effective Early Literacy Interventions.* Needham Heights, MA: Allyn & Bacon.

Phillips, G., and P. Smith. 1997. *A Third Chance to Learn.* Wellington: New Zealand Council for Educational Research.

Potter, B. 1993. *Tale of Peter Rabbit.* Ottenheimer.

Randell, B. 1996a. *Me.* Crystal Lake, IL: Rigby.

———. 1996b. *Late for Soccer.* Crystal Lake, IL: Rigby.

Robart, R. 1986. *The Cake that Mack Ate.* Boston: Little, Brown.

Rogoff, B. 1990. *Apprenticeship in Thinking: Cognitive Development in Social Contexts.* New York: Oxford University Press.

Routman, R. 1991. *Invitations: Changing as Teachers and Learners.* Portsmouth, NH: Heinemann.

Sylwester, R. 1995. *A Celebration of Neurons: An Educator's Guide to the Human Brain.* Alexandria, VA: Association for Supervision and Curriculum Development.

Smith, F. 1994. *Understanding Reading.* Hillsdale, NJ: Lawrence Erlbaum.

Snow, C., W. Barnes, J. Chandler, I. Goodman, and L. Hemphill. 1991. *Unfilled Expectations: Home and School Influences on Literacy.* Cambridge, MA: Harvard University Press.

Sousa, D. 1995. *How the Brain Learns.* Reston, VA: National Association of Secondary Principals.

Teale, W. H. 1984. Reading to Young Children: Its Significance for Literacy Development. In H. Goelman, A. Oberg, and F. Smith, eds., *Awakening to Literacy,* pp. 110–121. Portsmouth, NH: Heinemann.

Titherington, J. 1986. *Pumpkin, Pumpkin.* New York: Greenwillow.

Tharp, R., and R. Gallimore. 1988. *Rousing Minds to Life: Teaching, Learning, and School in Social Context.* Cambridge, UK: Cambridge University Press.

Vygotsky, L. 1978. *Mind in Society.* Cambridge, MA: Harvard University Press.

Waterland, L. 1985. *Read with Me: An Apprenticeship Approach to Reading.* Stroud, UK: Thimble Press.

Wells, G., and G. Chang-Wells. 1992. *Constructing Knowledge Together.* Portsmouth, NH: Heinemann.

Wertsch, J. V. 1984. The Zone of Proximal Development: Some Conceptual Issues. In B. Rogoff and J. V. Wertsch, eds., *Children's Learning in the Zone of Proximal Develoment,* pp. 7–18. New Directions for Child Development, No. 23. San Francisco: Jossey-Bass.

———. 1985. *Culture, Communication, and Cognition: Vygotskian Perspectives.* Cambridge, UK: Cambridge University Press.

Williams, R. L. 1994. *Where Do Monsters Live?* Cypress, CA: Celebration Teaching Press.

Williams, S. 1989. *I Went Walking.* New York: Harcourt Brace.

Wood, D. 1980. Teaching the Young Child: Some Relationships Between Social Interaction, Language, and Thought. In D. Olson, ed., *The Social Foundations of Language and Thought,* pp. 280–296. New York: W. W. Norton.

———. 1988. *How Children Think and Learn.* Cambridge, UK: Basil Blackwell.

Wood, D., J. Bruner, and G. Ross. 1976. The Role of Tutoring in Problem Solving. *Journal of Child Psychology and Psychiatry* 17, 2: 89–100.

# Index

# Organizing for Literacy
## Four Inservice Videotapes

**Linda J. Dorn**

*Produced by Ron Blome Productions*

Four 1/2" vhs • ISBN 1-57110-312-0

These four programs are designed to support classroom teachers as they implement a balanced literacy program that applies the principles of apprenticeship theory. The videotapes illustrate the reciprocal nature of teaching and learning across a range of reading and writing events. The study guide included in the set provides focus questions for viewing teacher-student interactions and for analyzing the children's reading and writing behavior over the four tapes.

### Organizing the Classroom

*Includes:*
Scheduling for a balanced literacy program
Managing literacy corners for independence

### Learning About Reading

*Includes:*
Familiar reading
Shared reading
Reading aloud
Emergent guided reading group
Early guided reading group
Fluent guided reading group

### Learning About Writing

*Includes:*
Interactive writing in a small group
Writing aloud in a small group
Editing and revising at the overhead
The writing workshop

### Learning About Words

*Includes:*
Poetry for analyzing patterns
Reading aloud and shared reading for studying expressive language
Letter sorting and classification activities in a small group
Teaching for analogy during spelling lessons
Using the dictionary and thesaurus
Literacy corner activities for learning about words